Date Due

GETTING
PARTNERING
RIGHT

GETTING PARTNERING RIGHT

How Market Leaders
Are Creating
Long-Term Competitive
Advantage

NEIL RACKHAM

LAWRENCE FRIEDMAN

RICHARD RUFF
Huthwaite, Inc.

McGraw-Hill
New York   San Francisco   Washington, D.C.   Auckland   Bogotá
Caracas   Lisbon   London   Madrid   Mexico City   Milan
Montreal   New Delhi   San Juan   Singapore
Sydney   Tokyo   Toronto

Library of Congress Cataloging-in-Publication Data

Rackham, Neil.
    Getting partnering right : how market leaders are creating long-
term competitive advantage / Neil Rackham, Lawrence Friedman, and
Richard Ruff.
       p.   cm.
    Includes index.
    ISBN 0-07-051782-7
    1. Strategic alliances (Business)   2. Partnership.
3. Interorganizational relations.   4. Competition.   I. Friedman,
Lawrence (Lawrence G.)   II. Ruff, Richard.   III. Title.
HD69.S8R33   1996
658'.044—dc20   95-20680
                                                     CIP

McGraw-Hill

A Division of The McGraw-Hill Companies

1 2 3 4 5 6 7 8 9 0 QBP/QBP 9 0 9 8 7 6 5 4

ISBN 0-07-051782-7

*The sponsoring editor for this book was Betsy N. Brown, the editing
supervisor was Caroline Levine, and the production supervisor was
Donald F. Schmidt. It was set in Fairfield by Ron Painter of
McGraw-Hill's Professional Book Group composition unit.*

Printed and bound by Quebecor-Book Press

Contents

Acknowledgments

Organizations are learning to cooperate in ways that would have been unimaginable a few years ago. Through partnering, they are "locking in" profitable business relationships and permanently raising the bar of competitiveness in their industries. Writing a book on this fundamental shift has been an exciting journey for us. As we discovered during our two-year research effort, an increasing number of companies are radically redefining how they work with other businesses to create value. In doing so, they are building long-term, high-impact business and gaining a durable competitive edge. We were fortunate, through writing this book, to get a first-hand look at how and why partnering is changing the business landscape.

We owe a debt of gratitude to the people at Huthwaite who worked with us on this book. Elaine Lasky, Scott Pierce, and Gene McCluskey headed up our research team. They contacted hundreds of organizations, interviewed executives and line personnel around the world, and painstakingly analyzed thousands of pages of interview transcripts and partnering cases across industries. To a large extent, their skills at finding the right people and getting information of real value made this book possible. Stephanie Woods, Beth Jacobsohn, Nancy Dunnels, and Nell Lennon took time away from their account management responsibilities to visit partnering organizations and interview decision leaders. John Wilson and Ken Webb reviewed the manuscript and provided the always-necessary second opinion; their merciless editing has given us—and our readers—a better book.

Our largest debt of gratitude must go to the hundreds of people who generously gave us their time to talk about their companies' experiences with partnering. Many flew in to our offices in Purcellville, Virginia—a little off the beaten path—to meet with us in discussion groups and to trade ideas. Others invited us to visit them and to see partnerships in action, on location. We were continually impressed by how willing and enthusiastic so many people were to participate in this effort. Special mention must go to Lance Dixon, developer of JIT II, who provided us with ongoing access to his suppliers and his own team at Bose Corporation—as well as his insightful opinions on partnering. John DeVincentis of McKinsey and Company met with us several times to work through our conceptual frameworks and discuss the applicability of partnering principles in different industries. Oracle Corporation provided us with research access to dozens of their busy people, ranging from senior vice presidents to sales representatives, over many months. United Parcel Service brought their sales leadership team *en masse* to Huthwaite for partnering discussions and let our researchers sit in on a number of high-profile partnering meetings with their clients. John Pelligrino of Mead Packaging and Patrick Hore of McGregor Cory provided us with documentation and tools that have helped us understand how partnering actually gets accomplished between successful organizations. To others who'd be far too numerous to mention here, we hope the book itself, with its stories and observations from many of these participants, does justice to the time and effort they gave us.

Neil Rackham
Lawrence Friedman
Richard Ruff

GETTING PARTNERING RIGHT

CHAPTER ONE

THE PARTNERING REVOLUTION

Open almost any recent business book. What does it say? Most likely it begins by telling you that there's a revolution taking place. Whether the book is on marketing or manufacturing, on computers or competition, the central message is the same. The old rules don't work anymore. Unprecedented changes are in progress. The future will belong to the privileged few. The unprepared will be swept away. It's enough to make a reader cynical, as each new-and-improved business revolution is overtaken by yet another.

But if ever the word *revolution* deserved an honest place in business, it's to describe the major changes under way in how corporations are working with each other to create value. Companies are inventing new ways of doing business together that are bringing unprecedented gains in profit and competitiveness. For many companies, the bottom-line results from these new relationships—even at this early stage—have already outweighed years of savings from internal cost-cutting efforts such as downsizing or restructuring. The emerging term for these new relationships is *partnering*. In the United States alone, partnering is delivering billions of dollars of value annually in terms of greater productivity, reduced costs, and new marketplace value. Globally, it is literally transforming the way multinational corporations operate. Although partnering is still in its infancy, it has already brought about fundamental changes in how most big corporations transact business with each other. These changes are redefining purchasing and completely transforming large-account selling. Partnering is growing in magnitude and influence—and it's here to stay.

1

Because partnering is evolving so rapidly, it doesn't have a neat and tidy definition. But everyone actively involved in it agrees on one thing: Partnering is about a fundamentally different kind of relationship between organizations. It is a relationship where many of the old rules and definitions don't apply. Labels such as "supplier" and "customer," or "vendor" and "purchaser," lose their meaning. Watch partnerships in action and you'll see the partners transacting huge volumes of business. Yet as you sit there it's hard to figure out who comes from which company and who has which role. You'll barely be able to tell who is "selling" and who is "buying."

But partnering is much more than a business relationship in which roles become blurred. After all, in the fast-paced and changing environments that most of us work in nowadays, people have learned to live with increased ambiguity. Blurring of roles has become commonplace. What makes partnering remarkable is not so much the nontraditional roles of the players but the scope of the bottom-line impact that the new roles have allowed the partnering organizations to achieve. Take some examples from the dozens of partnerships you'll meet in this book:

- Bose Corporation, a recognized leader in partnering, has chosen a handful of top suppliers and, in a radical rethinking of organizational boundaries, given them the roles of salesperson, purchasing agent, and production planner. In so doing, Bose has sharply reduced purchasing overhead, streamlined production buying, and "designed in" its top suppliers into new products. Bose has saved millions and is developing higher-quality products as a result. And Bose's top suppliers have seen their revenues double or triple through the partnership. Four suppliers now handle a third of Bose's total production-purchasing volume.

- Baxter Healthcare shows the variety of partnerships that can exist within a single company. On the one hand, Baxter is involved in cutting-edge biotechnology partnerships, like one with Weizmann Institute to develop cells that can recognize and kill tumors. But Baxter also has less exotic partnerships that have grown out of traditional vendor relationships, like one with their supplier Stone Container. During the course of this partnership, Baxter and Stone have undertaken more than 200 projects together aimed at reducing costs and improving mutual profitability. Individually, many of these projects involve only small changes in the way Stone and Baxter work together. But collectively, these changes add up. The savings on each side run into the millions.

- Partnerships can transform and revitalize difficult supplier-customer relationships. When Pillsbury began partnering discussions with their packaging supplier Mead, Pillsbury was actively looking for ways to end the relationship. But within a year of starting to partner, Mead had won Pillsbury's "comeback supplier" award, major improvements had been made in machinery design and performance, Mead's sales were up, and so were Pillsbury's satisfaction ratings.

- Even businesses often thought of as commodities can add value through partnering. Cable manufacturer Okonite is one of several suppliers who have partnered with Public Service Electric and Gas. In the process, both Okonite and PSE&G have made value-added changes in the types of cable used, how it is ordered, and how its production is scheduled, leading to savings and competitive advantages for each partner. Okonite's sales to PSE&G have grown substantially and, through partnering and other new strategies, the utility company has been able to reduce inventory costs by more than $100 million.

In this book, we'll go behind the scenes in dozens of partnerships like these, letting the partners speak in their own words about what it takes to partner effectively. We'll see what the most successful partnerships have in common and how they achieve such impressive results. We'll show how partnering affects the bottom line and what makes partnering succeed. But first let's take a brief look at some of the underlying forces that have brought about this partnering revolution.

DOWNSIZING THE SUPPLIER BASE

In the last few years, customers have been rejecting traditional transaction-based vendor relationships at a dizzying pace. They've been downsizing their supplier base, and replacing their myriad vendors with a very small number of long-term relationships offered only to a select few. There's a widely quoted figure that customers are working today with a third fewer suppliers than they did 10 years ago. Some industry giants have gone much further than that. Ford Motor

Company is at this moment reducing its supplier base from 52,000 to 5000—a reduction of over 90 percent. Public Service Electric and Gas (PSE&G), who we'll meet in the next chapter, has let 1500 suppliers go. The president of Scott Aviation, Glen Lindeman, told us that he's cut back his supplier base from 800 to less than 250 "and we're looking to go further." We mention a few disparate examples just to help focus on how broad the trend really is. A *majority* of suppliers are losing their customers; where are these suppliers and all the salespeople representing them supposed to go? There's no safe haven; it's happening in every industry and with almost every customer. Customers are discarding hordes of suppliers in favor of a well-chosen few. Many salespeople and their companies have been left outside the door wondering what ever happened.

What happened is straightforward enough. Customers are under the same pressure as everyone else. Cheap technology, easily available information, and the explosion of global markets have commoditized their businesses and driven down their margins. Their products have converged with their competitors', and they're acutely aware of the need to find new sources of competitive advantage. With less and less competitive advantage available in the products themselves, they've turned to other areas where there is potential to find new productivity and competitiveness. For a few years it looked as though focusing on improvement in internal processes was the answer. But that too is a well which has begun to run dry.

THE SHIFTING FOCUS OF PRODUCTIVITY

Go back a few years and look at what a typical company was doing to improve its productivity. You'd find it was cutting its overhead, reducing management levels, redesigning its processes, improving information systems, and automating routine functions. What did actions like these have in common? They were all about changes *within* a company and its functions. Until recently, that was the only way most organizations thought about productivity. Productivity—whether through cost reduction or performance improvement—was strictly an internal issue. Few organizations looked outside their own borders for productivity improvement. The notion that you might find huge untapped reservoirs of productivity lying outside of the company—at the border *between* organizations—wasn't the subject of urgent conversation in many corporate boardrooms. Corporate managers, intent on overhead reduction or cutting labor costs, had their attention firmly rooted inside their own corporations.

Yet for all their accomplishments in improving internal efficiency, many organizations have come to realize that it is not enough. For one thing, the ruthless search for internal efficiency has left many organizations at "parity" with their competitors who have gone through the same struggle. For another, years of productivity improvement inside the average large corporation has meant that the internal productivity well is beginning to run dry. As a recent article by Shawn Tully in *Fortune* pointed out, overhead today usually doesn't exceed 3 percent of an average manufacturing company's costs, and it's unusual for labor costs to be above 6 percent. The most efficient overhead reduction or the most productive automating of labor-intensive processes would be hard-pressed to cut overall costs by more than a few percentage points. Significant productivity improvements *within* organizations are getting harder and harder to find. There simply is not much fat left to cut.

In contrast, the average company pays out 55 percent of its revenues for goods and services. In other words, more than half of a company's revenues are spent on purchases outside the company—while less than half goes into the internal costs that traditionally have been the focus of productivity improvement efforts. Increasingly, organizations have thought hungrily about this 55 percent and wondered how they could get a bigger slice of it for themselves. Some corporations took a get-tough approach. Instead of the old "safety in numbers" practice of putting small amounts of work out to hundreds of suppliers, they ruthlessly consolidated their supplier base. Then, armed with the powerful weapon of very large volumes, they bullied their suppliers into setting drastically lower costs. General Motors, for example, became infamous in the automotive industry for pressuring its suppliers in this way. They demanded huge price reductions, with high volume as the incentive.

At first, these bully tactics seemed to work. GM was reputed to have cut purchasing costs by $4 billion through these methods. On the face of it, using purchasing muscle to get a bigger share of the suppliers' pie made good sense. But over time, as GM and others who adopted similar strategies found out, it wasn't that simple. For one thing, by grabbing a disproportionately large share of the pie, some customers lost supplier loyalty and trust. This loss might not be damaging in a buyers' market. But what happened during periods of short supply? As GM discovered, when the shoe was on the other foot, some suppliers had long memories. Scarce capacity went to support GM competitors like Honda, who had earned supplier loyalty.

Not everyone was in agreement that squeezing suppliers to get the largest possible piece of the 55 percent was the answer. While companies like GM were aggressively pursuing grab-a-bigger-share-of-the-pie strategies, others were having doubts. There were many hidden costs from changing suppliers, in terms of ramp-up time and quality. Equitable treatment of long-term suppliers seemed to be a more cost-effective option in the long run. And among a new generation of purchasing and procurement managers, some creative thinkers were beginning to ask interesting questions: "Why are we fighting with suppliers about how to divide the pie? Is the pie really a fixed size? What if we joined forces and looked for new ways to make a *bigger* pie together? Wouldn't we both benefit?"

Questions like these weren't idle speculations. They were driven by deep dissatisfaction about the unproductive way suppliers and customers characteristically worked together in traditional vendor relationships. There was a growing realization among a new generation of thoughtful managers that the old transaction-based purchasing processes were no longer working productively. And what began with dissatisfaction over unproductive supplier relationships has, over the past few years, evolved into a widespread revolution in the way customers work with their top suppliers. At the heart of this revolution is a focus on getting beyond transactional, short-term business and into more profitable, more durable relationships. We'll see many forms of it in this book, such as:

- Customers and suppliers who have moved beyond traditional notions of organizational boundaries to integrate processes, and sometimes whole functions, between companies

- Customers who watch out for their suppliers' profitability, and suppliers who turn over business to competitors to make sure the overall solution is right for the customer

- Salespeople who have changed all the rules of information sharing and opened their accounting books to customers. And customers who, in turn, have given suppliers access to financial data that a couple of years ago wouldn't even have been available to most of the customer's own internal departments

- Suppliers and customers who have created millions of dollars in new value by forming joint teams that represent only the "partnership," and that exploit every ounce of potential productivity between the two organizations

Partnering is rewarding companies who can get beyond traditional notions of organizational boundaries—and it is punishing companies who cannot get outside the transactional mindset. Partnering is giving suppliers and customers a long-term competitive advantage in their respective marketplaces. They are getting "locked in" to more productive and profitable business relationships, and their competitors are getting locked out. Customers are getting better products to market faster and cheaper. Suppliers are getting "evergreen" contracts (perpetual business) and insider status and access that provide long-term competitive advantage within accounts. As partnering organizations continue to achieve lower costs and higher value, they are creating sustainable advantage that's virtually impossible to compete against with a transactional approach.

Just how pervasive is the shift toward partnering? In industries such as high technology, logistics, distribution, professional services, and even some commodity businesses such as utilities and packaging, partnering is well established and continues to grow in influence. In some industries the shift toward partnering is just now emerging. But overall, partnering is not something that many people can afford to ignore. Its bottom-line impact and the competitive advantages it provides are enabling leading organizations to trounce their less sophisticated competitors. Learning to partner effectively is imperative for companies looking to compete into the future.

LOOKING AT IT FROM A SUPPLIER'S PERSPECTIVE

Take a look through the business section in your average bookstore. What do you find? Books on certifying your suppliers, partnering with your suppliers to control costs, or perhaps segmenting your suppliers to achieve different levels of partnership. There's a lot of interest in partnering, and for good reason. But what do all of these books have in common? They all assume that *you* are the customer. Maybe you're not the customer. Maybe you are a supplier. After all, suppliers make up half of every business transaction. If you're a supplier, what help is available to assist you in building partnering relationships? Not much. It's unfortunate, but the fact is that compared with the careful thought that's gone into partnering from a customer perspective, suppliers are facing a dearth of information. You'd have to look awfully hard to find practical, clear-cut, serious advice on partnering from the *supplier's* perspective.

This is the challenge we took on when we started this book two years ago. As sales effectiveness consultants for over 20 years, we saw an enormous shift taking place for suppliers and, specifically, people who are involved in selling. At one time all you needed for success were good products and a sales force who could sell them skillfully. Today, it's a different game. Customers continue to reduce their supplier base at an ever-faster pace, and they're locking in long-term relationships with a handful of carefully chosen suppliers.

Most suppliers are not making the cut. These suppliers have adequate products, good sales capability, and a strong customer focus, but they're not bringing the productivity or the competitiveness to their customers to justify selection as one of the chosen few. They are being permanently replaced by partnering suppliers, organizations who've learned how to tap into every available source of productivity with their customers—and with other suppliers—and who've learned to forge long-term partnering relationships. In more and more industries, competitive differentiation is no longer about products, selling skills, or internal efficiency. Increasingly it's about how you work with other organizations to leverage capabilities and create durable, productive business relationships over time. It is about *partnering*.

GETTING IT RIGHT

So what does it take to partner effectively as a supplier? What exactly do you have to do to build durable, productive partnering relationships with your customers—and with other suppliers? How do you get beyond a competitive shootout over every sale and into the long-term competitive advantages of partnering? These are the questions we have researched for the past two years at over 100 leading organizations. We analyzed successful partnerships from both the supplier and customer perspective, across industries, geographies, and markets. We met with senior executives and sales reps, individuals who were getting it right, and partnering teams that have moved way beyond transactional business. Our research team met with people all over the world who are partnering—and not just partnering, but doing it successfully. After all, this book isn't just about partnering. It's about *getting it right*. To help you get it right, this book sticks to three key principles:

✔ *A practitioner focus.*   We've tried to avoid elaborate theory. Most of us already have more theoretical frameworks than we know what to do with. This book is about partnering as it's really being done today at actual organizations. We've used real cases, not abstract models. We've let practitioners describe their own experiences in their own words.

✔ *A how-to focus.*   We assume that if you're reading this book, you probably already see the shift toward partnering and know it's a reality in your industry. We're not going to spend a lot of time trying to sell the idea of partnering. This is a book for people who already know they need to partner and want to know *how to partner* based on the successful experiences, insights, and lessons learned from market-leading organizations. This is a book for supplier executives, managers, and frontline personnel who know they need something radically different from traditional selling if they want to survive, and who want to find out exactly what it takes to build more profitable, more durable business relationships.

✔ *A supplier focus.*   As we've suggested, almost all of the established wisdom on partnering has come from a customer perspective. Most existing partnerships have been set up at customers' initiatives, and inevitably the majority of best practices have been created from a customer point of view. This book, where appropriate, *does* present customers' points of view and, in keeping with the spirit of partnering, presents everything in as bilateral a fashion as possible. Customers as well as suppliers will benefit from the best practices and practical lessons in this book. But the bottom line is that the book exists to help suppliers—people at all levels who are involved in marketing and selling products—to play the coequal role that effective partnering demands.

We'll look at how leading suppliers maximize impact and create durable relationships with their customer partners over time. We'll look in depth at the critical issue of selecting the right customers for partnering relationships. And we'll examine the best practices of how to partner with other suppliers to bring maximum value to the marketplace and become more competitive. This book will provide you with a picture of what the best-in-class are already doing to create strong partnerships. It will, we hope, help you in creating long-term competitive advantage for your organization.

THE INGREDIENTS OF SUCCESSFUL PARTNERSHIPS

"What does it take to make partnering successful?" During our research we posed this question to hundreds of people who were actively involved in setting up and running partnerships. It wasn't an easy question for many to answer. One vice president of sales told us, "Some of our people have a good gut feel for partnership, but they'd be hard-pressed to describe what works and what doesn't. We've never really figured out what makes some partnerships stronger, or more lasting, than others." After long pauses, most people gave us the partnering equivalent of Justice Potter Stuart's definition of pornography: *impossible to define, but you know it when you see it.* "All over the world people are trying partnering," Motorola's Thomas Beaver told us, "and they are really struggling with it." Partnering, it turns out, is not an exact science. There is no simple answer to the question, "What makes a partnership successful?"

On the other hand there *are* the real experiences of the many partnering companies who provided us with a wealth of information about what made their experiences successful. Some partnerships, we found, were successful because there was a good fit between the people from the partnering organizations. Sometimes partnership worked because of product synergy; the partners' products were natural candidates for tight integration. Some partners seemed to thrive because they had achieved a high degree of trust as partners—higher than the individuals involved had achieved with people from their own organizations. Some partnering teams had achieved remarkable productivity by establishing aggressive but attainable goals and aligning both organizations behind them

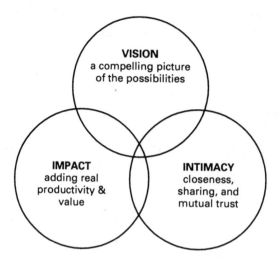

Figure 2-1   *Impact, intimacy, and vision are the critical success factors of partnering.*

with strong metrics. Some organizations had built lasting, profitable relationships out of a strong sense of shared values with their partners.

In all, the people we interviewed provided us with well over 100 answers to the question "What makes partnering work?" One conclusion we reached is that every partnership has its unique success factors that arise from the specific circumstances of the partnering organizations. But as we went deeper into the success stories of companies in different industries, countries, and markets, the fundamental drivers of success turned out not to be so different from partnership to partnership. In successful partnerships, three common elements repeatedly and consistently emerged. We called them *impact, intimacy,* and *vision.* (See Fig. 2-1.) Their presence tended to make partnering successful; without them, partnerships rarely got off the ground or soon failed.

Impact.   We use the term *impact* to describe a partnership's capacity to deliver tangible results. Successful partnerships increase productivity, add value, and ultimately, improve profitability. Every successful partnership has impact as its raison d'être.

Intimacy.   Successful partnerships have moved far beyond transactional relationships and have achieved a level of closeness that would be unrecognizable within the old buyer-seller model. *Intimacy* is a challenging word; it conjures up images of people relating on an intensely close level. That's exactly what successful partners are doing, in a business context.

Vision.   It is not enough to increase productivity and achieve closeness. Some organizations have both of those elements and yet are not able to make partnership a reality. Successful partnerships also have vision—a compelling picture of what the partnership can achieve and, specifically, how it is going to get there.

Impact, intimacy, and vision are the *critical success factors* of partnering. Let's take a look at each of them in more detail.

IMPACT

Above all else, partnering is about achieving impact. When organizations move beyond traditional working relationships, they can attain markedly higher levels of productivity and competitiveness that are not easily reachable through more traditional vendor relationships. A few examples:

- Cable manufacturer Okonite is one of several key suppliers who have partnered with Public Service Electric and Gas, allowing the utility company to reduce inventory from $276 to $160 million.
- McDonnell Douglas cut almost $300 million from the development cost of its new MD-95 by partnering with a number of suppliers including Dalfort Aviation—who will actually assemble the new plane.
- Fedex has partnered with Intel to take over part of Intel's logistics. As a result, guaranteed delivery time has improved from four business days to three—and delivery errors have been substantially reduced.
- Eaton, a supplier of gas valves and regulators, has an innovative partnership with Whirlpool Corporation. Whirlpool has used Eaton's design expertise to get their new gas range to the market several months faster than they could have done by relying on their own internal design capability.

What do these cases, and others like them, have in common? They each show *impact*—a significant and measurable gain in productivity that could not have been achieved within the constraints of a traditional vendor relationship. Whether this gain takes the form of cost savings, or increased effectiveness, or better quality, the hallmark of successful partnering is that it creates new impact.

The source of this impact is the huge and untapped reservoir of productivity that lies at the boundary between organizations. By rethinking the way in which organizations work together—by redesigning organizational boundaries to make business relationships more productive—partnering taps into a vast reservoir of productivity that traditional vendor relationships usually are unable to reach. As a supplier, for example, Eaton could provide some degree of impact through the gas valves it sells to Whirlpool. However, because of the design partnership, Eaton has been able to play a much higher-impact role in getting Whirlpool's new product to market months ahead of the best schedule achievable under the old design process. Put simply, partnering is a means of maximizing impact.

Impact isn't unique to partnering. It is more accessible, and you can achieve more of it through partnering, but traditional vendor relationships do have impact. Within a traditional relationship, for example, you can introduce unilateral changes that add incremental impact. You can redesign, customize, and improve your products to provide greater value and productivity for customers. Indeed, few companies survive today on a take-it-or-leave-it, fixed-product offering; the days of you-can-have-any-color-so-long-as-it's-black are long gone. Most organizations, even when working within routine vendor relationships, offer customized or unique product options.

However, adding value within a classic vendor relationship means that it's the *suppliers* who make the changes and improvements to increase the value of their products. And *because the changes are unilateral, that puts constraints on the amount of value they can add.* In partnering, on the other hand, the changes are not one-sided. As Eric Marcus, a Vice President at CSC Vanguard, describes it: "In a vendor-customer relationship, no one wants to make any deep-seated changes in what they are doing. But in partnering, *both* sides are willing to make changes in how they do business." This is a crucial distinction. Let's look at an example to get a sense of the difference.

Imagine that you are a carrier competing with the likes of UPS and FedEx. You do business with a very successful and rapidly expanding company called 1-800-ORCHARD. This is a telephone sales operation where customers call to order gifts of fresh fruit and berries. You've won a contract to pick up these highly perishable items literally from the orchard, and deliver them to recipients' homes. It is a growing account and you would like to keep it. So you look for ways to add value and to increase your impact as a supplier.

You find there is a lot of spoilage, particularly during the hot summer months, which leads to inevitable customer dissatisfaction. You see a way to reduce spoilage by customizing your delivery times. The present pickup time from the orchards is 10 A.M., late enough for the heat to damage highly perishable items such as berries. So you offer the customer pickup at 8 A.M., and as a result there is less spoilage. By customizing your service you have added impact as a supplier. It has cost you little and has given you some slight competitive advantage, because any potential competitor must now match your early delivery schedule. But although this cuts down on spoilage, it still does not solve the problem entirely. There may be as many as five days between picking and final delivery; some fruit sits at the orchard for up to three days waiting to be packaged for dispatch. Produce is still arriving in less-than-perfect condition.

What more can you do as a supplier to solve this problem and to increase your impact? You might take a clean sheet of paper and try to design a completely new solution. For example, you could build special refrigerated vans to carry the 1-800-ORCHARD produce. This would certainly increase your impact and act as a barrier to entry to competitors who do not have refrigerated vans. You've successfully provided more impact, although you've done so now at a considerable cost, which has probably cut into your margins.

Beyond this, what else can you do to add impact? Not much. You've added most of the unilateral value available to you as a supplier, and given the cost of refrigerated vans, you've paid a high price to do it. It still takes up to five days from picking to final delivery, even though the fruit is now arriving in better condition. *Your capacity to add worthwhile new value may now have reached a plateau.* Aside from trivial improvements there's not much more value you can add, unless there's a fundamental shift in the way that you and 1-800-ORCHARD do business. This shift can come only through a partnership, one in which both organizations are prepared to rethink how they work together for the purpose of achieving high impact. By partnering with 1-800-ORCHARD you might, for example,

- Take over the whole distribution process, so that fruit is packed and dispatched from your warehouse. This would eliminate most of the packing delays at the orchards and cut down the picking-to-delivery time from five days to two.
- Design new containers for easier packing and shipping, leading to faster, cheaper handling and lower spoilage.
- Handle phone orders and billing using your data processing and logistics capabilities, which are more sophisticated and reliable than 1-800-ORCHARD's, thus saving costs and reducing billing errors.

Changes like these could radically cut cost, speed delivery, reduce billing problems, and increase customer satisfaction. The savings and improved productivity can be distributed in all sorts of beneficial ways: more rewards to both parties, lower costs and better service to customers, and so on. But these high-impact changes can be made only if both parties are prepared to redesign the way they work together and, through partnering, to create additional impact that could not be achieved through the existing vendor relationship.

Many companies who have prospered by adding value in vendor relationships have now reached an impact plateau with their customers. They have added all the value unilaterally available to them, and there's nowhere further to go. Bob MacDowell, a Vice President at Microsoft, explains: "Added value isn't an inexhaustible well that you can keep pumping forever. Sooner or later the value well runs dry and you have to look for a new source of fuel—a brand-new way to do things." For many organizations, partnering is providing that new fuel source.

The examples of impact in the 1-800-ORCHARD case—redesigning packaging or taking over logistics—are two of the many types of impact available through partnering. In the high-technology field, impact may result from combining the technological capabilities of supplier and customer. Professional services suppliers and their clients often achieve impact by integrating consultative capacities into client organizations. In retail, impact usually comes through the integration of systems (e.g., Electronic Data Interchange—EDI) and operating procedures between organizations. Impact has a different look and feel from industry to industry. But the 1-800-ORCHARD example does highlight three key characteristics of impact that are generally present in successful partnerships, regardless of industry.

1. *Both parties change to maximize impact.*   The impact from partnering, where both parties make changes to increase impact, is much more substantial than the unilateral adding of value that a good supplier provides. In our 1-800-ORCHARD case, unilateral changes by the carrier—such as more convenient pickup times or special refrigerated vans—would certainly reduce spoilage and add worthwhile impact. But that's a minor improvement compared with the impact from the significantly cheaper, more efficient, and faster distribution that becomes possible when both organizations partner to redesign the way they work together. By tapping into the productivity potential that exists at the boundaries between organizations, partners can routinely cut design time dramatically, reduce distribution costs, slash delivery times, and significantly improve quality. This is not the everyday "value-added" story that is so common in vendor relationships ("Our product is backed by the best-trained service technicians in the industry."). This is something different. When *both* parties are willing to rethink the existing relationship and to make changes to increase productivity, they can open up new and productive sources of impact. Kevin Brownsey, Director of Sales for W. H. Smith, a U.K.-based contract stationer, has seen how mutual change can bring impact to a partnering relationship:

> When the customer is willing to change with us, we can remove whole processes out of their organizations for them. We can become the stock controllers, the distributors of their standard print items. So, effectively, what we're doing is actually removing part of the administrative burden that our customers incur within their organizations, and we take it in-house for them. We provide a lot more value when we can do this.

Mutual change is the basic source of impact in partnering. When both organizations are willing to rethink how they work together, the results can be, and often are, dramatic.

2. *The pie gets bigger and more equitably distributed.*   When a supplier makes changes to add value (like the refrigerated vans in our 1-800-ORCHARD example) somebody has to pay for the changes out of their share of the pie. More often than not, that turns out to be the supplier, who makes investments to increase impact that hopefully will bring a return in terms of customer loyalty, extended contracts, or—if the customer is prepared to dip into their share of the pie and accept some of the cost—higher prices.

Suppliers who hope for a bigger piece of a fixed pie, though, are playing a dangerous game. Customers today are increasingly resistant to paying for the value that suppliers add. They demand added value, but expect it to be on the supplier's nickel. A toll-free hot line, for example, once seen as adding value and commanding a price premium, now has become an expected part of the most basic service in many industries. Quality too has become an expectation rather than a bonus. Ten years ago it was not uncommon to pay a 20 to 30 percent price premium for a car because of its reputation for reliability and sound construction. That same added value today is a built-in expectation in even the cheapest standard models. Increasingly both the general public and industrial buyers have come to expect more from their suppliers for less. Consequently, traditional vendor relationships involve constant haggling over how the profit pie should be divided and whose share should be used to pay for the value-added elements. That's a battle that suppliers fight—and lose—every day in traditional relationships.

Partnering, on the other hand, often achieves greater all-around productivity, as well as gains that can be distributed in all sorts of creative ways to the partners. In a word, the pie gets bigger. Instead of haggling over the size of each partner's slice, partners can often collaborate to make the pie itself bigger. Howard Getson, President of Veritas Technologies, explains: "Selling is usually a zero-sum game. But in partnering, when it's done right, there is a less adversarial relationship, and there is more of a win-win that people can share." In partnering, *both* parties can get a larger piece of pie.

3. *Mutual competitive advantage.*   In traditional selling, suppliers are constantly at risk of displacement by competitors. Slight changes in a competitor's capabilities, or a customer's needs and perceptions, or just pricing alone, can cost an entire account. Suppliers often fret over the transitory nature of their customer relationships, but the fact is that vendor relationships almost always are transitory and highly vulnerable. Partnering, on the other hand, offers a real source of durable competitive advantage. Think back to our 1-800-ORCHARD example to get a taste of the difference. A competitor might easily match a simple product customization, such as early pickup. With more difficulty, the same competitor might match the idea of refrigerated vans. The limiting factor here is primarily financial—can the competitor afford to match the dollar cost of the added value? However, once you're handling the phone bank, the distribution, and the billing for 1-800-ORCHARD, it becomes far more difficult for a competitor to displace you because:

- A competitor will require more than financial investment; supplanting you will require know-how and intimate understanding of hundreds of complex operational details.

- The customer will no longer be willing to change partners at whim with the fabled promiscuity of traditional purchasing departments. What you are bringing to the partnership has measurable, significant value that can't easily be replaced.

- Disentangling the relationship, by either party, can be achieved only through significant effort and organizational redesign—not something that either supplier or customer will want to do without a compelling reason.

In short, your capacity as a supplier to deliver impact through partnering has given you a competitive lock-in. The customer too gains competitive advantage from a partnership. In the 1-800-ORCHARD case, fruit is arriving fresher, spoilage and costs are down, and customer satisfaction is up. *The partnership has resulted in mutual competitive advantage.*

We'll look more closely at impact in the next chapter, in the context of what successful partnering companies are doing with their partners. But how do you create the kind of fertile environment where impact can be fostered? What kind of business relationships do you need for high impact to be possible? That brings us to another key component of successful partnering.

INTIMACY

Successful partnering organizations have moved way beyond business transactions into a level of organizational closeness that is often exciting and dramatic. IBM, for example, has suppliers who wear IBM employee badges, maintain offices at IBM, and have access to all but the most proprietary of design engineering data. Salespeople from IBM's top suppliers sit in on key purchasing and product design meetings, and influence IBM's requirements as well as their own organization's capabilities to meet them. McGregor Cory, a U.K.-based contract distribution specialist, is engaged in far-ranging, future-oriented business discussions with customers, and in some cases has acquired such expertise on their customers' business needs that their customers have awarded them major contracts without even going to bid. Sometimes the degree of closeness can get humorous. Commerce Clearing House and Oracle Corporation have a joint development team that's agreed not to shave until their project is completed. At Bose Corporation, we were told of a supplier working on-site who mentioned, casually over dinner to a Bose employee, that he was headed back to his home office to do some paperwork. "What home office?" he was asked. During three years of daily contact with his Bose counterpart, it had just never come up in conversation that he was not an employee of Bose.

What is happening at all these companies—and many others that we'll encounter in this book—is clearly not a linear extrapolation from the world of selling, some incremental change in how organizations work together. It is something new; we call it *intimacy*. Partnering-level impact simply cannot be achieved without it. As Jeff Gaus of NEC Business Communication Systems (East),* put it: "There is no way you can bring impact to an organization without intimacy. When I am partnering, I am no longer an outsider. I am an insider. Before I achieve that, I have nothing to offer." Intimacy makes the high impact of partnering possible.

Intimacy differs dramatically from the solid relationships of supplier-customer transactional business. Think for a moment about what is really involved here. McDonnell Douglas is allowing its partner Dalfort Aviation to assemble the new MD-95, and in doing so has put a central

---

*A direct-sales subsidiary of NEC America, Inc.

part of its business into the hands of another company. IBM's top suppliers are writing purchase orders to themselves. W. H. Smith, the contract stationer, has customers who have turned over whole functions—like distribution—to them. The level of trust that's required to make all this work would be truly frightening if judged from the vantage point of a traditional vendor relationship. This is trust with a capital T. What does it take to establish and maintain this level of trust between partnering organizations? Certainly something more than the basic honesty and high ethics of most large-account salespeople and their purchasing counterparts. Organizations are learning, together, to act in the overall interests of a partnership rather than in the short-term interests of either supplier or customer. For many companies this is a radical departure from how they are accustomed to doing business.

But it isn't just trust, and a focus on the common good, that separates intimate partnering relationships from good transactional ones. Those are "soft" elements of intimacy—they're hard to quantify—but there are hard elements as well. For example, partnering requires information sharing on an entirely different level than traditional buying and selling. Partners routinely share overall business and strategic plans, confidential cost and pricing data, and proprietary industry and product expertise. The information they're sharing extends way beyond individual transactions and over time becomes increasingly business-focused. In partnering, information becomes tightly integrated with impact and vision; the depth of shared information makes a strong vision possible and provides the data necessary to bring impact to larger business problems. In partnering, information itself becomes a key source of competitive advantage.

Partnering-level intimacy also affects the "buying" and "selling" teams themselves. In traditional relationships, oftentimes a single point of contact from each organization hammers out transactional business, with an occasional assist from an engineer or technical expert. Recently, some sales organizations have moved a little beyond that by focusing on team selling. Some customers as well have formed purchasing teams that bring wider expertise into supplier selection. But the emphasis still tends to be on putting authority into a narrow point of contact between organizations; it's about depth, not breadth.

In partnering there's an entirely different logic in play. Breadth of contact between partnering organizations is the key to collaboration. Hank Dunnenberger of Siecor, a fiber-optic-cable supplier, observes:

"Here's the issue. Any partnership that does not have relationships at all levels of the organization is going to have a real problem. That's the only way you can be successful in partnering." Breadth is key to partnering, because you cannot get outside a transactional focus without broad representation of the expertise and capabilities within each organization. But it isn't just a question of bringing more people into the process. In traditional relationships both parties sometimes bring in teams, but usually for the purpose of ensuring that their individual goals are achieved in the most effective manner. In the most successful partnerships, a *partnering* team, representing nothing except the partnership itself, takes on a life of its own, with its members' company of origin being almost irrelevant.

We'll come back to the concept of intimacy in Chap. 4. Successful partners put a great deal of effort into building relationships that can accommodate the nontransactional, business orientation of partnering. They have to develop a level of trust within the partnership that does not come easily to most organizations. They have to make real choices about what kinds of information they're going to share and who is going to be on the partnering team.

Intimacy is a critical component of successful partnering, and it is not easy to achieve. Later we'll take a very close look at intimacy and exactly what it takes to make it happen.

Before we move on, though, just a few words about *who* exactly should participate in partnering—from a supplier point of view. In all the research we've done on partnering, we've seen a consistent underutilization of salespeople within the partnering process. Many organizations we met with admitted candidly that they lacked the intimacy to get partnering relationships off the ground. Worse, they sometimes did not even have enough intimacy to know where their partnering opportunities *were*. These were companies who, not coincidentally, had decided that partnering was an executive-level undertaking, one ill-suited to salespeople. George Friddle, a Business Development Manager at Bechtel, the engineering and construction firm, has commented on this:

> The idea that salespeople are not necessary in partnering is not uncommon. But it is an absolute myth. It's critically important that we never walk away from a customer. It's important for sales to be involved so they can understand any critical issues and really help in calling in resources or reinforcing requests to management that cer-

tain things need to be done in different ways. Sales has a very important, ongoing role in partnerships.

Salespeople, given their understanding of the customer base and their customers' needs, are critical resources when it comes to identifying where partnering opportunities exist and getting partnering relationships started. Where intimacy is lacking—and where as a result partnering is weak—it is often for lack of a participant who is professionally trained in creating and nurturing customer relationships—a salesperson. For many organizations, this is a useful point to keep in mind as they proceed toward partnering.

VISION

Organizations that have been able to combine impact and intimacy—not an easy task—have found themselves with a strong competitive advantage. As Ed Ossie, a Vice President at Texas Instruments, put it: "When we have added both value and closeness, we are light years ahead of the competition." If you have impact and intimacy, you could stop right there and have a viable, successful large-account strategy. But successful partnering requires something more. When partners have a real willingness to change together, a tremendous range of possibilities opens up. The number of different directions in which a partnership can proceed greatly exceeds the number of possibilities in a typical vendor relationship. This new potential generates excitement and enthusiasm, but it also creates risk and uncertainty. As David Montanero of NEC observes: "Partnering is not for the faint of heart. It is changing organizations from the top down." Partnering can and often does have a radical effect on both supplier and customer. As a result, partnerships need a clear sense of direction. Partnerships must have a vision of what they are seeking to accomplish.

By "vision," we do not mean an abstract exercise in creative thinking. That is not what successful partners are doing. We mean something much more tangible: a compelling but realistic picture of what the partnership could potentially achieve. In successful partnerships the parties always have a shared road map that helps them to set expectations, measure success, and maximize the potential value—the impact—of collaboration.

At one extreme the vision might totally transform both partners and enable new and exciting possibilities that neither could contemplate alone. When Intel's design capability was partnered with Applied Materials' manufacturing technology, the resulting chip literally changed the world. On a more modest level, many partnering "visions" are just straightforward propositions that, by working more closely together, the organizations can improve efficiency to the mutual profit of each partner. A vision does not have to be all-encompassing or radical, but it does have to exist. The vision is what gives the parties an incentive to partner. It is the enticing goal. It shows how, together, the partners can be more than the sum of their parts. It provides overall guidance for partners who, as time goes on, will spend most of their time dealing with the minutiae of day-to-day business issues.

In Chap. 5 we'll talk about how visions are created and sustained. We'll see how they provide direction and incentive to help the parties through the often difficult process of creating and managing a partnership. But whether the vision is grand and sweeping or just a simple indication of how both parties can gain by working together, vision is always present in successful partnerships. Vision can originate from the seller's organization or from the customer's. It does not matter who initiates it. What *does* matter is that it become shared. Unilateral vision cannot sustain a partnering relationship.

THE TRAP: OVERRELIANCE ON ANY ONE SUCCESS FACTOR

Partnering organizations succeed when they actually achieve results, develop a close, almost seamless, relationship, and have an articulated, shared view as to what they can accomplish together. In short, it is when impact, intimacy, and vision come together that partnering works.

What if you don't have all three, though? Can you partner if you have, say, high potential impact without an intimate relationship—or vice versa? If you're lacking in one area, can you compensate by improving or increasing performance in another?

Unfortunately, our research suggests that partnering generally does *not* work over time when either supplier or customer is focused too heavily on one dimension over another. You can certainly get started without all three, but we've never seen a partnership succeed in the longer term without strong elements of impact, intimacy, and vision. There are some real traps involved in not taking seriously the need for all three in a partnering relationship.

The Damn-the-Torpedoes, Maximum-Impact Trap

High-technology organizations have mastered the art of impact. From enterprisewide integrated systems at one extreme, to specific desktop applications at the other, technology suppliers have brought legendary productivity and change to their customers. Where would business be today without information systems? Could the private sector even *exist* without the access to information and automation that a relatively small number of high-technology organizations have developed? Probably not.

For all these successes, however, high-technology companies are experiencing some of the toughest challenges in building partnering relationships. And they know it. One of the authors made a keynote address on partnering at a conference hosted by Texas Instruments last year. After the speech a sales manager from Sybase commented: "Sounds good. But are there more than two or three high-technology organizations who are actually doing it well?" Companies in industries that are product-driven, like high technology, are having great difficulty making the transition to partnering. As one insurance industry executive commented to us on a technology leader he's worked with for years:

> For all their innovation, they've left a lot of our people alienated. They come in with whiz-bang solutions, take over a floor or two of our building for a year, and totally ignore rank-and-file managers and staff. We need their products, but a lot of our people really dislike them. Now they talk about partnering. That's a joke, given our history with them. The day someone comes up with a better solution, we'll switch in a minute. This supplier has not earned the right to partner with us.

His is a common customer view of product-driven suppliers who pursue high-impact, "hot box" strategies. Today, despite their impact, many of these suppliers are poorly positioned to tap into the competitive advantage of partnering relationships, unless they can combine product leadership with intimacy and vision.

Consulting firms, too, provide some excellent examples of overreliance on impact. In recent years, most major consulting firms have adopted a strategy of pursuing long-term advisory and change management relationships with their clients. Some have succeeded; many have not. Like their high-technology counterparts, many consulting organizations have alienated their clients by pursuing radical organization change strategies that were insufficiently communicated to, and bought into by, their clients' personnel. Top consulting firms are very cognizant of this problem. Here's what Jon Katzenbach, author of the best-seller *The Wisdom of Teams* and a Director at McKinsey and Company, told us:

> Until recently, good consulting firms measured their success in terms of the impact they delivered. Could they, for example, bring the client a return that was at least ten times the fees they received? If so, they were satisfied they had delivered value. That led to an emphasis on the quantifiable short term, at the expense of building the kind of close, trusting relationships that, in the longer term, would serve to help clients think through their aspirations and have the vision needed to radically change.

His observation is an important one. Consulting firms who once relied solely on impact are now realizing that it is not enough. In partnering relationships, you must move beyond a hot box technology strategy, a high-return consulting intervention, or whatever your industry defines as "impactful." Partnering requires impact, but it cannot be sustained in a vacuum.

The Intimacy-for-Intimacy's-Sake Trap

In our partnering research, we encountered many salespeople whose great strength was their skill at developing customer relationships. They were not necessarily practicing partnering-level intimacy in the way we've described it, but they were very close to their customers. They knew their accounts in depth and in breadth. They had created high degrees of trust, and the reputation they had built for caring about their customers kept them comfortably in business. Assuming that their products performed and their service was adequate, they were vulnerable only to competitors with significantly superior products or pricing. In a *selling* environment, these skilled sales professionals were successful, and they seemed to be well positioned for the future.

Yet for all their closeness with customers, they were not only failing to build partnerships but were increasingly losing strategically important business. They were vulnerable to competitors who were pursuing partnerships based not solely on relationships, but on impact and a vision of change as well. Intimacy is not sufficient against competitors who have learned to integrate relationship building into a more complete approach to partnering. This is a real challenge for sales forces trained (and skilled) in developing strong customer relationships, and who, at least in the past, were never asked to be particularly visionary or to take responsibility for defining the potential impact of their product offerings within customer environments.

The unfortunate fact for skilled relationship-building suppliers is that intimacy is not an end in itself. It is only an enabler. It provides the access, the information, and the trust needed to create impact. The problem we saw in suppliers who could not get partnering off the ground was that the intimacy they had so carefully nurtured with key customers was not being leveraged to achieve impact. In short, the enabler was not enabling anything; intimacy had become a goal in itself. Dick McIlhattan, a Vice President at Bechtel, drawing on his organization's learning experience with its customer Eastman, said this to us about ensuring that intimacy is not a goal in itself:

> At first we spent a lot of time talking about trust, and it did not take a long time in the meetings for me to determine that this is not an issue which you need to spend a lot of time on. You're not going to talk yourselves into trusting each other. It's going to have to be done by actions, probably over time. We were having meetings every quarter to talk about the trust issue, and I think we were wasting a little bit of time doing that. We have a great relationship with Eastman, and I think we view it that we have the trust, which allows us to provide more value to them as the customer.

Intimacy, no matter how strong, is not enough to sustain a partnering relationship. That's because it does not, in and of itself, provide value. It simply makes value possible. If you have no vision of what that value is, or no way to make it real for a customer (impact), you're at a tremendous disadvantage in the world of partnering.

Flying at 60,000 Feet: The Vision-in-a-Vacuum Trap

Vision rarely, if ever, works in a vacuum. Suppliers with real vision can achieve a substantial competitive edge—but only if the vision can be achieved. Take for example this story, from the Vice President of Sales at a specialty laminates and coatings firm:

> When we first developed the new coating, we realized the ideal application would be as a liner for paper containers that could be then used to contain high-acidity liquids, like vinegars. Our market research indicated that there was a great little niche here, worth about $100–$150 million a year. We had not worked in this industry before, but we were very excited about the opportunity. So we approached a Swedish container company with an offer to partner with them to create a new acid-resistant paper container. We flew to meet them in Stockholm with a whole bunch of figures and, so we thought, a really exciting story to tell them. But the meeting bombed. The more excited we got, the more they resisted. The whole idea never got off the ground.

What went wrong? It's hard to know for sure. But essentially their problem stemmed from not having an existing relationship with the potential partner. The stakes were too high for the customer to get involved without existing organizational intimacy. In addition, inexperience in the industry meant there was no track record of impact and, as a consequence, a very real credibility gap. Vision does not work in a vacuum. In partnering, it cannot succeed without sufficient organizational intimacy to make it viable, or without a track record of demonstrable impact to make it realistic.

WHERE TO START?

You have decided that you want to partner with another organization. Now what? Do you come in with a compelling vision of change that will, through sheer potential value, earn you the right to engage in serious business discussions? Or do you rack up some quick and tangible successes to earn a closer relationship to the potential partner? Or do you work on the relationship for a while so that you've got the right conditions to talk about partnership?

In other words, which comes first: impact, intimacy, or vision? This is a question that, whether they put it in these words or not, many suppliers struggle with. They probably struggle with it too much, in fact. When we interviewed successful partnering organizations and asked them "Do you start with impact, intimacy, or vision?", it quickly became apparent that it was like asking "Which comes first, the chicken or the egg?" Organizations who have had multiple partnering successes, we found, tend not to worry too much about whether they're starting with a tangible success, a strong relationship, or a compelling vision. *They take whatever they've got and leverage it to get the others.*

In the course of reading this book, you will encounter partnering organizations who started with a strong shared vision, organizations who launched into partnership on the basis of an intimate relationship and little else, and organizations who kicked off a partnering relationship on the basis of some high-impact products and solutions. In our research we could not identify a "typical" starting point. Partnering is not like a sales cycle; there is no formal series of steps to follow, such as "Go form a vision, and then...." What's important in partnering is not the sequence. What's important is that would-be partners take whatever they've got, whether it's a sweeping vision of change, a record of success, or a history of close ties, and leverage it to create all three conditions for successful partnering.

PSE&G AND OKONITE

In this chapter we've described, at least at a conceptual level, the core elements of successful partnering. It takes impact, intimacy, and vision to partner successfully. We've also suggested that organizations who want to partner must be willing to change how they do business with each other, and must often make internal changes as well. Let's take a quick look at one of the typical successful partnerships we researched, and see how these themes played themselves out.

Public Service Electric and Gas, based in Newark, New Jersey, is one of the largest utility companies in the country. Facing potentially tough competition from anticipated regulatory changes, PSE&G realized that the future survivors in their industry would have to find dramatic ways to reduce costs. Their inventory levels of $276 million looked reasonable in a comfortable regulated environment, but were clearly excessive in light of the lean-and-mean future industry trends. A few years back they determined that reducing the number of suppliers they work with, and entering into partnering relationships with a select group of them, could be a smart strategy.

At the same time Okonite, a wire cable company and one of PSE&G's suppliers, was looking for partnering relationships; the President of Okonite spoke about partnering at the opening of a new laboratory that PSE&G attended. PSE&G was interested in finding good partners, and, over a period of several months, the two companies brought people together across functions to hammer out a plan for radically reducing inventory, lowering lead times from six months to three, and standardizing products to cut by two-thirds the types of cable that PSE&G was purchasing. In short, these two companies created a compelling vision of change. But what else did they have going for each other as potential partners? Bill Budney, Vice President of Distribution Systems for PSE&G, explained to us how PSE&G settled on Okonite out of a large field of potential partners:

> The Okonite sales team had continuity. They had been in place for at least seven years, and we knew the players. As a customer, we judged potential partners by two factors. The first was trust—and trust had to exist at all levels. But it's a competitive game out there and trust alone does not cut it. A partnership must also make good business sense. We can meet socially, but if we cannot make money, I'll find other friends. So it's got to create value for both parties if it's going to survive. That was the starting point for partnering with Okonite: trust and value.

Bill Budney's comments, emphasizing the basic need for both intimacy (trust) and impact (value) were typical of most of the customers we interviewed in our research. These were critical factors that enabled PSE&G to overcome some potentially difficult internal issues. Tom Johnson, PSE&G's General Manager of Support, observed:

> It takes a lot of trust before someone in procurement feels happy about suppliers working directly with field people. And the psychology of field people is to want full technical control and to let the specs proliferate. We soon realized that if we partnered with Okonite it could lead to clashes between procurement people and the field. We realized we'd have to communicate with each other better if this thing was going to work out. It was a difficult internal realignment, and it would not have been viable without a lot of trust in Okonite people and the feeling that all this work would result in big inventory savings. Either way, if one of those things had been missing, the partnership would have never got off the ground. If Okonite had not built the trust, it would be too risky letting them be a sole supplier. On the other hand it was the

value added of the inventory savings that paid for all the effort, and without the savings we couldn't have justified it.

Impact and intimacy, following on the heels of a strong vision, made partnering desirable from PSE&G's perspective. But what about Okonite? Okonite saw an opportunity, through partnering, to provide better value and, as a result, attain a privileged role as a sole-source supplier. They are getting other benefits as well, benefits that are transforming their organization. Tom Reilly, Vice President of Okonite, described how the partnership is changing his organization's capabilities and the value they can bring to customers:

> In the old days, as a supplier, if we delivered 85 percent of orders on time we'd expect a gold star. But now we're expected to deliver *every* order on time. Before we started partnering with PSE&G we'd sometimes bid on a contract and then, at the last minute, a competitor would come along and cut the price and we'd lose the business. It led to an attitude at the factory of "If one of their jobs is behind schedule we'll try, but why should we go the extra mile?" You can't think that way in partnering, where you depend on each other. It meant we had to make lots of soft changes. We had to feel more responsibility. As the sole supplier, if we didn't perform or deliver we really hurt PSE&G. It is a philosophical change. That's why you can't just rely on a good relationship. From the sales point of view, you've got to deliver results to a higher standard than before. The partnership keeps pushing up the bar. It's changed us.

Okonite had to change the value they delivered, as well as their "philosophy" of working with customers. But as we suggested earlier, partnering is not about unilateral change. It's about mutual change. Ken Doyle, PSE&G's Manager of Procurement & Materials Management, described the effect of the partnership on PSE&G's organization:

> Traditionally, in a utility, you never buy everything from a single supplier. From a purchasing point of view, the idea of going to a single source was a big hurdle. You need a lot of savings to overcome the resistance. To make the partnership with Okonite work, we had to schedule and forecast differently and much more accurately. We had to take new approaches to materials management. It was harder for us on the customer side of the partnership to change from the old relationship. When you begin this kind of relationship, you expect to learn a lot about the partner. You end up learning much more about yourself.

PSE&G's partnership with Okonite illustrates nicely some of the basic dynamics of partnering. Both Okonite and PSE&G were forced to make significant shifts in their thinking and in their ways of doing business. Both organizations faced internal challenges to success. Without intimacy, they never could have succeeded in carrying out the many changes each organization has had to make. Without the impact of massive savings, the effort of partnering could never have been justified. And without a strong, shared vision of change, the organizations would never have accomplished the huge inventory reductions, reduced lead times, and standardization of parts that they have together; these would have been unattainable goals in a traditional vendor relationship.

When all is said and done, though, the whole reason for this partnership—like almost every other successful partnership we studied—is impact. For Okonite, impact means increased and more reliable business and the competitive advantage of a close relationship. For PSE&G the impact involves inventory reduction, cost savings, reliability of supply, and, ultimately, the service it can provide to its customers. In a word, the pie is bigger for everyone, and that's what makes the partnership feasible, worthwhile, and, to this day, successful. Impact is what sustains and justifies partnering relationships. In the next chapter we'll take a close look at impact and its role in partnering.

IMPACT:
THE BOTTOM LINE

It's almost impossible to live through even the first hour of a normal day without feeling the impact of partnering. The alarm that wakes you in the morning is likely to be controlled by a chip created as a result of at least one partnership; the snooze button you grope for to give a merciful extra few minutes of rest may well have been designed or improved through the manufacturer's partnership with their thermoplastics supplier—and your clock radio may have cost you a couple of cents less as a result. The soap you shower with, your toothpaste, the various toiletries scattered around your bathroom, have all reached you from the factory through a logistics process that almost certainly involved partnering to speed distribution and reduce cost. The clothes you put on have probably been cut in a particular style or color as a result of point-of-sale data made available to the manufacturer through a series of partnerships. If you're awake enough to notice, your cereal box is plastered with Disney characters and special offers, all brought to you through the good offices of promotional partnering arrangements. And don't think you can escape when you leave the house! Your car is a top-to-bottom traveling testament to the world of partnerships, all the way from the paint on its sunroof, through the design of its drive shaft and its seats, right down to its kickable Dunlop tires.

Partnering is changing our everyday lives. As consumers, we can see the impact of partnering all around us. Every day, through partnerships we aren't even aware of, we obtain products more cheaply, are offered more choices, and get better quality. By enabling organizations to work more effectively together, partnering creates productivity gains that ultimately translate into benefits for the end consumer. Everyone who reads this book has bought something at a lower cost because of savings created by partnering, whether it's a computer from Compaq, groceries from Safeway, household goods from Wal-Mart, or even this book itself, which has been produced, printed, and distributed faster and more cheaply through the publisher's partnerships. The consumer is the final beneficiary, situated at the end of the productivity value chain. When we talk of "impact," we're ultimately talking about something that affects the end customer. Impact may mean that a product was cheaper for the partners to produce, but more importantly it means that it cost the end consumer less. Impact may mean that the partners' logistics and distribution systems became more efficient, but what matters is that it got to that end user more quickly. Impact can mean that the partnership reduced error rates and defects, but its true measure is that the end customer perceived that quality was better and was more satisfied as a result.

The impact of partnering on the end consumer sets it apart from many of the organizational fads that sweep through the business world and then just as quickly fade into oblivion. Anything new that alters the expectations of the marketplace is potent and dangerously irreversible. Once consumers get used to having catalog items delivered within 48 hours, for example, no competitor will survive who offers delivery in the six to eight weeks that, until recently, was the norm for many direct-mail organizations. Once consumers have the expectation that a new car will be trouble-free, it's no longer acceptable to them to have to take it back to the shop half-a-dozen times to have assembly defects corrected. The marketplace quickly gets used to improvements, whether in quality, price, choice, or responsiveness, and comes—rightly—to take these things for granted.

The impact of partnering on the marketplace has created an irreversible expectation. There is no going back. Not only is partnering here to stay, its very impact has ensured that the marketplace bar has been forever raised by a couple of notches. If partnering were now to be declared illegal, then the resulting increased cost of goods, the stark reduction in their choice and availability, and the dramatic slowing of innovation would likely precipitate a consumer revolution. Unlike most here-today-and-gone-tomorrow organizational fads, partnering already has worked its way irreversibly into the fabric of our consumer society. We can no longer live without it. And as companies learn to partner more and better, its impact will continue to grow.

WHERE IMPACT COMES FROM

Partnering is a relatively new way of doing business. It currently accounts for less than 20 percent of all sales volume, although this percentage appears to be growing fast. How is it that something that makes up just 20 percent of business can exert as powerful an influence on the marketplace as the vendor relationships that account for the other 80 percent of all sales? Cynics might say that it's just another inexplicable case of the famous 80/20 rule, in which the 20 percent always comes out the winner. But the truth is that partnering exerts a disproportionate impact precisely because the creation of impact is what partnering relationships are all about. Unlike traditional vendor relationships, partnerships are specifically designed to maximize impact.

That isn't to say that a vendor relationship lacks impact. Far from it. However, the impact from a vendor relationship is necessarily limited because it's one-sided. It's all about what the supplier can provide in terms of product, pricing, and support. Naturally, any good supplier will constantly strive to increase impact by designing better products, offering them at lower prices or with additional support. But these changes and improvements are things that the supplier does unilaterally. The supplier changes to accommodate the customer; there's no expectation, in a vendor relationship, that the customer also needs to change.

Impact through mutual change is the defining characteristic that differentiates partnering from traditional vendor relationships. In a partnership, both parties must be prepared to make changes to maximize impact. If only one side is willing to change, then it's a vendor relationship, not a partnership. Why is this idea of mutual change so important that you can't partner without it? What's so special about the impact that results from both parties making changes? The simple answer is that when both parties are prepared to do things differently, the productivity pie gets bigger. That brings us back to the central productivity hypothesis that underpins partnering.

The hypothesis is this: Organizations have worked hard for years to make themselves more productive, both through improving the performance of individual functions and—more recently—by rethinking the ways in which their component functions work together, using methodologies such as reengineering, core process redesign, and cross-functional teams. As a result of all this hard work, much of the productivity potential inside organizations may have already been captured. The productivity wells within organizations are now beginning to run dry. But in contrast to the attention that has been given to the productivity potential *within* organizations, comparatively little attention has been given to the potential that lies *between* organizations. The manner in which supplier and customer organizations work together is characteristically haphazard, and capable of dramatic improvement. So the productivity hypothesis underpinning partnering states that:

> There is now greater productivity opportunity *between* organizations—in terms of working together more efficiently and effectively—than there is *within* organizations.

The new productivity frontier lies at the boundary between organizations—and partnering is the mechanism through which that productivity can be captured.

There's a strong analogy between what's happening today in partnering and what was happening some years ago inside most organizations. Go back a few years in the life of the average large corporation. It was dominated by functional fiefdoms, little empires that it has since become fashionable to call "silos." Often these silos were very efficiently run internally. The design silo, for example, introduced the latest in CAD/CAM technology and employed sophisticated computer-modeling tools. Meanwhile, the equally efficient engineering silo did a great job of reducing its costs and streamlining its processes. The manufacturing silo investigated and installed the latest in robotics and production automation. Each silo worked hard and apparently productively, but it still took only a fraction less than forever to bring a General Motors car from conception to the showroom.

The problem lay not within the silos but between them. The interface, or boundary, between each silo was ineffective and inefficient. The right hand of design didn't know what the left hand of engineering was doing, and horrendous redesign costs inevitably mounted up when it became clear that the elegant design concepts just weren't practicable in engineering terms. And because neither silo understood manufacturing, there were unimaginable delays, unworkable compromises, and right at the end of this unhappy chain, late deliveries of inferior products to dissatisfied customers.

By improving the way the silos worked together—by concentrating on the areas *between* functions rather than within them—it became possible to make productivity gains that would have been unimaginable inside any individual silo. The idea of breaking down the walls of the silos and redesigning the way functions worked together, released a whole productivity revolution. The underlying logic was simple: There's more productivity to be gained by looking at how the pieces fit together than by looking inside each individual piece.

The same logic underlies partnering. Instead of two silos such as engineering or manufacturing, we have two distinct companies. Each of them, like the silos of old, has worked hard internally to become productive and efficient. But just like the silos, when you put the pieces together the whole doesn't work as well as it should. The biggest productivity opportunities of the last five years resulted from rethinking the relationships between functions. The opportunities of the future are likely to result from rethinking the relationships between organizations. And to do that, silos on the organizational level have to be dismantled. As a Kodak representative on the Kodak/UPS partnering team put it: "There are functional silos on an industry level; so we're a product shipper, they're a carrier. The way to break the silos down is that we have to become more of a carrier, and they have to be more of a shipper. You can't do that by yourself. That's the reason you partner."

The impact of partnering comes from mutual change and not from the unilateral actions of one party. Just as, within an organization, you couldn't much improve the interface between two silos if you were allowed to change only one of them, so you can't build a more productive way for two organizations to work together if just one of them is prepared to change. The impact of partnering results from improving the way two organizations work together—from rethinking the boundaries between organizations and how they operate. It takes the active cooperation and coordination of both parties to change a boundary and to make it more effective.

CAN BETWEEN-ORGANIZATION CHANGE REALLY WORK?

In many organizations, management has tried hard to break down the functional barriers between silos, excited by the possibility of building better organizations by rethinking the boundaries between functions. But the promised productivity gains have sometimes proved elusive. If it has been difficult to capture the productivity that exists between functions of the same company—under one management, and supposedly working toward an identical mission—isn't it likely to be even harder to capture the productivity potential that lies between two separate companies, each pursuing disparate goals and each managed independently? Aren't there likely to be insurmountable practical barriers when it comes to getting real-world productivity gains out of partnering?

Yet, look at the facts. There are now many thousands of successful partnerships and, as we've seen, these partnerships are not only changing the way in which business is done, they are changing the whole fabric of consumer society. Their impact is real, and it's growing. Of course partnering, just like reengineering, has its casualties. But what is surprising is not that some partnerships fail. Rather we should be surprised that so many succeed—and in doing so, provide an impact that is visible all around us. It seems remarkable that two organizations with different and sometimes competing goals, with different management, with different measures of success, and sometimes with a history of mutual distrust, can nevertheless develop effective partnering relationships. After all, the evidence shows that it's a difficult enough business to get any two functional silos within the same organization to rethink their boundaries, even when the initiative to do so comes from their common boss and the whole effort is part of a single corporate policy. It seems improbable that partnerships between corporations should succeed when so many equivalent activities *within* corporations have failed to live up to their productivity potential. How do we explain this apparent paradox?

Making the Pie Bigger

The answer lies in the different nature of the impact that results from partnering. Look inside a typical embattled functional silo facing a corporate restructuring. The silo's management and staff may accept, on an intellectual level, that breaking down the walls of their silo will bring overall productivity gains for the company. They will readily admit that potentially there's a big win for the corporation. But what's the impact on them *personally?* For many the impact is a reduced empire, greater uncertainty, and a whole lot of discomfort and risk. In other words, the corporation wins but the silo's stakeholders lose. And that, like all win/lose situations, can lead to resistance or—in extreme cases—to sabotage.

In contrast, the impact of partnering between organizations is much more likely to be a true win/win. The supplier wins in terms of such things as increased sales, longer and more durable relationships, and a locking out of the competition. The customer wins in terms of responsiveness, improved quality, access to expertise, and lower prices. The reason so many partnerships thrive is that both parties correctly perceive themselves to be winners. This mutual win is made possible by a basic characteristic of partnerships: Partnering makes the pie bigger. The following are some typical examples.

A BIGGER PIE. Hillenbrand has six geographically dispersed divisions that manufacture a diverse product range, including hospital room equipment products such as infusion pumps and specialized flotation beds for burn victims. Their businesses use a lot of transportation, including their own 400-truck fleet and both domestic and international carriers. They are partnering with UPS, looking for joint opportunities to improve the cost, quality, and responsiveness of Hillenbrand's overall logistics. By leveraging such things as the UPS expertise in fleet management and UPS logistics knowledge, Hillenbrand has been able to create $1.5 million in cost improvements in the partnership's first year. During this period, UPS revenues with Hillenbrand have grown by upward of $2 million. So the pie is bigger, and both parties come out as clear winners.

A PIE DELIVERED FASTER. Eastman Chemicals partners with Bechtel, the international engineering and construction contractor. One element of the partnership has involved setting up joint teams to look for improvements in work processes and ways to reduce cycle times and costs. Eastman recently developed a product line with high growth potential, but that potential depended on getting it to market ahead of competitors. Under the old vendor relationship, the engineering and construction work needed to bring the product on-line would have taken up to 18 months. But because of the Bechtel partnership, engineering procurement was able to start within a week of notification. The Bechtel team's early work on engineering and design criteria has allowed another of Eastman's construction partners, Floor Daniels, to get a faster start on construction, so that capacity will be on-line within a year. This use of partnering will save at least four months in time-to-market, bringing significant value and competitive advantage to Eastman in a field where a faster pie is the surest way to a bigger pie.

A CLASSIC SHRINKING PIE... Sweetheart sells paper cups that hold soft drinks. Georgia-Pacific supplies Sweetheart with the paperboard used to manufacture cups. Major customers are squeezing Sweetheart on price; McDonald's, for example, has told a number of its suppliers, including Sweetheart, to reduce prices by 10 percent if they want to keep the business. Meanwhile the cost of paperboard is rising so steeply as to have almost doubled.

This is a classic shrinking pie. In a traditional vendor relationship, everyone would tighten their belts, reduce their margins, and initiate damaging win/lose negotiations over who has to give up the largest share of this much-reduced pie. However, by partnering with Georgia-Pacific, Sweetheart has been able to make the pie bigger and offset some of the rising cost of board and the falling price of cups. Shared electronic data interchange has reduced paperwork and administration and cut expensive inventory. Joint planning has optimized production runs. Sweetheart gets a more consistent product from Georgia-Pacific at a better price. And because the cups remain competitive, Sweetheart continues to satisfy their demanding high-volume customers, while Georgia-Pacific gets more business as a result.

...AND A REAL NUTS-AND-BOLTS EXAMPLE. IBM is facing turbulent times in the mainframe business—but the news isn't all bad. Reports that mainframes are dead have been greatly exaggerated. Demand, however, is unpredictable, and IBM may suddenly need to change order quantities from its suppliers, including those of one of its partners, North American Bolt and Screw. In these days where there's often no link between a company's name and what it does, it's comforting to know that North American Bolt and Screw (NABS) actually supplies IBM with nuts and bolts, albeit of a somewhat specialized kind.

In a traditional vendor relationship, with the inevitable delays due to purchase orders and paperwork, NABS—like other suppliers—just couldn't respond fast enough to fluctuations in demand. So IBM's only options were to keep expensive (and possibly wasted) inventory or to authorize costly emergency production runs. Even then, with a typical 10-day order cycle, there was the risk of an idle assembly line waiting for parts. Now, through the partnership, cycle time has been cut to two days, expensive overtime or chargeable idle time is reduced, and NABS is helping IBM to design more standard parts for cheaper future products. The pie is bigger, and both parties are benefiting.

Competitive Advantage at the Border

These examples, and many others like them, illustrate how partnering enlarges the pie and, in doing so, lets each party emerge a winner. The partners have opened up the borders between their companies, borders that traditionally have constrained information exchange, reduced creativity, slowed responsiveness, and perpetuated the old inefficient and ineffective vendor relationships. By rethinking their relationships and by making changes on both sides, these partners have each been able to tap into the productivity that lies between their organizations and have made substantial mutual gains as a result.

How could conventional suppliers compete with these partnerships in terms of impact? Imagine what it must be like to be a competitor to any of the suppliers in these cases. What can you offer, in terms of shaving your prices or increasing your support, that can begin to match savings such as those emerging from these partnering relationships? You may be a good low-cost carrier, and you may even be a cent or two cheaper than UPS, but why should Hillenbrand switch to you when their UPS partnership saved them $2 million last year? You may be a dynamite engineering and construction firm with the latest in efficient design technology, but there's no way you can bring Eastman on-line as quickly as the Bechtel partnership can. And imagine you're a competitor of Georgia-Pacific offering board that has doubled in price to Sweetheart. What extra value can you possibly offer as a traditional supplier that will let Sweetheart cut its prices to McDonald's? Put yourself in the shoes of a conventional supplier to IBM; what are the chances they will deal with you through the old and slow purchase-order framework, when an unexpected upswing in demand means that they need parts within two days and North American Bolt and Screw has a full-time person inside the IBM plant ready and waiting to expedite delivery? The impact that results from partnering creates an almost unassailable competitive advantage.

Three Sources of Impact

Impact, we've said, lies at the boundary between organizations. But in practical terms, what does that really mean? What, specifically, should you look for, to assess whether there are productivity gains waiting for you at the border between yourself and a potential partner? The partnering cases we analyzed during our research suggest that there are three main sources of impact.

1. *Reduction of duplication and waste.* Duplication happens when each party operates parallel functions that, essentially, mean they are unnecessarily doing the same thing twice. So, typically, when each company has its own independent inventory, warehousing, logistics, and distribution processes, this will involve unnecessary duplicate steps and costs. Partnering can reduce duplication, cut steps out of the processes, and in doing so, streamline them so that the between-company processes become much faster, cheaper, and more effective.

Other forms of waste typically come about because of inadequate information exchange, in that the left-hand partner doesn't know what the right-hand partner is doing. For example, in traditional vendor relationships, lack of accurate and timely customer information means that the supplier's production scheduling typically isn't well-tuned to the customer's demands. As a result production runs are not optimized and there is overproduction or panic shortages, all of which create waste and cost. Both Georgia-Pacific and NABS, in our examples, have been able to schedule more efficient production based on timely customer-demand forecasting made available to them through partnership. And as we'll see when we look at some more cases, an awful lot of waste piles up just because things fall through the cracks between most organizations. Partnering can close these cracks, reduce the waste, and create significant savings.

2. *Leveraging core competence.* Another source of impact from partnering comes from each partner being able to tap into the expertise and core competence of the other. So, for example, UPS, with its fleet of thousands of vehicles, will inevitably know much more about fleet management than Hillenbrand. For UPS, fleet management is a core competence; for Hillenbrand, fleet management is a peripheral but expensive task. With its fleet of just 400 trucks, it isn't worth the investment for Hillenbrand to build a world-class core competence in fleet management. But because UPS already has that core competence, Hillenbrand can leverage and benefit from its partner's expertise.

Leveraging of core competence in partnering isn't restricted to competence at the formal organizational level. Individuals in the partnership may also have a competence that can be leveraged. For example, Chris LaBonte of the custom molder G & F Industries, who spearheads their partnership with Bose Corporation, has a technical and manufacturing background that allows him to add personal value to Bose when shop-floor problems arise with manufacturing tools.

3. *Creating new opportunities.* The most exciting and the most creative opportunities for impact arise when the partners work together to produce something new that neither could have produced alone. When Applied Materials, who make the machines that make computer chips, partners with chip designer and manufacturer Intel on the next generation of processors, then both parties are contributing to a partnership that could profoundly affect all our lives in the next few years.

One state-of-the-art product in biotechnology is a genetically engineered treatment for hemophilia resulting from Baxter's partnership with Genetics Institute. There's an increasing number of innovative collaborations like these, in which two or more organizations combine their skills to create something new at the cutting edge. Often, because of the high capital investment involved, these innovation-focused partnerships take the form of joint ventures or strategic alliances. But whatever their formal structure or legal status, their purpose—like other partnerships—is to create impact.

Whether it's through reduction of duplication and waste, leveraging of core competence, creation of new opportunity, or a combination of all three, partnering makes its impact by improving the way in which the partnering organizations work together. As a result, partnerships enlarge the productivity pie and provide some of those all-too-rare real-world examples of synergy, where one-plus-one really does add up to something greater than two.

REDUCTION OF DUPLICATION AND WASTE

One of the most wasteful areas that lies between corporations involves logistics: the procuring, physical transportation, warehousing, and inventory of those products that move from one corporation to another. The typical vendor relationship in a business-to-business sale creates expensive waste and duplication in this area. Take an imaginary example. Supply Co. makes components that Assembler Inc. uses in its prod ucts. Supply Co. sells its components through a classic sales relationship, so that manufacturing and delivery begins when Assembler Inc. issues a purchase order following the negotiation of a sales contract between the two companies. Let's look at the steps usually involved.

Step 1. *Waste through just-in-case purchasing.*   The Purchasing group in Assembler Inc. prepares the purchase order, based on a forecast from their manufacturing function estimating how many components they need. Manufacturing is uncertain of demand, so—just to be safe—they order 10 percent more than they think they will use, knowing that they can keep the rest in inventory for the future. This just-in-case buffer stock will add to inventory cost and take up storage space, resulting in *waste* for Assembler Inc. So if Assembler Inc. has smart contract negotiators, they may eliminate their excess inventory by adding a clause that lets them send back excess or forces the supplier to hold buffer stocks. In these cases Assembler Inc. has moved their demand uncertainty on to Supply Co.'s shoulders. There's still waste, but now it's Supply Co.'s problem. All the vendor relationship has done is to decide who pays for the overproduction problem, not how it could be avoided altogether.

Step 2. *Waste through suboptimal production scheduling.*   Supply Co. sets up their production runs. Because these runs are based on a purchase order that was negotiated weeks ago, they don't reflect the true up-to-the-minute demand, resulting in runs that are either too long and produce excess inventory (*waste*) or too short so that uneconomical top-up runs may be required (*waste*). The companies have already argued this one out during the contract negotiations, so there's an agreement about such things as who pays for the additional cost of emergency runs. In other words, the parties and their lawyers have negotiated how to divide a fixed pie.

But because this isn't a partnership, nobody has said, "Wait a minute; why don't we make the pie bigger by working together to optimize production runs and then share in the savings?" In a traditional relationship that would begin to blur the boundaries between the organizations uncomfortably. Component production, traditionally, is strictly Supply Co.'s problem, and Assembler Inc. has no place interfering in something that's none of their business. In a classic vendor relationship a wasteful production run is fine, provided there's a contract to show who pays for it.

Step 3. *Waste through warehousing...*   Supply Co. sends its finished components to its warehouse, waiting to distribute them to Assembler Inc.'s warehouse at the contractually agreed times and in the agreed manner. To do this requires loading and unloading (*waste*) and checking and paperwork (*waste*), not to mention the cost of the warehouse itself and its employees (*waste*).

Step 4. *... and more warehousing.*   At the agreed-upon time, Supply Co. loads the components back on to a truck (*waste*), goes through another paperwork cycle (*waste*), and ships them to Assembler Inc.'s warehouse, where they are unloaded (*waste*), checked (*waste*), and put into inventory (*waste*). Nobody thinks to ask, "How come these components are now being unloaded all over again? Why are we entering all this inventory data twice?" Nobody asks these questions because it's a vendor relationship. The contract says that on such-and-such a day, 2300 units will be delivered, and it's the job of Assembler Inc. people to check that the contract is being fulfilled, not to ask awkward questions like, "Isn't it the dumbest thing you ever saw, for each company to have duplicate sets of warehouses and parallel [but incompatible] duplicated paperwork?"

Step 5. *Waste through inefficient transportation.*   While Supply Co. trucks drive home empty, passing Assembler Inc.'s manufacturing facility on the way (*waste*), empty Assembler Inc. trucks are driving in the opposite direction to pick up stock from their warehouse (*waste*). Anyone foolish enough to suspect that this might be a less-than-perfect procedure would be told that there's no way to coordinate it better because the contract determines the supplier's delivery times and, as they were arranged weeks ago, there's no way to match the time when Manufacturing needs components with the time that the supplier will deliver them.

We don't have to add real-life complications, such as the even longer chain of events that deals with damaged stock resulting from the six loading or unloading operations we've described in the basic transfer of products, to see that the logistics of vendor relationships are typically wasteful and rife with duplication. A rational being from another planet might find it hard to understand how such a cumbersome system ever got set up in the first place, let alone how it managed to survive for so long in a competitive business environment. And that raises a good question: How is it that these wasteful duplications are still visible all around us when, for years, companies have been working hard to save every available productivity penny? Are they blind? Don't they care?

The answer lies in the way that organizations have historically defined impact. In the now crumbling world of organizational silos, impact generally has been thought of in terms of "How much of the pie can we grab?" rather than "How big can we make the pie?" So in our example, the Purchasing function of Assembler Inc. would think of themselves as very successful, during sales negotiations, if they gained another 2 percent discount, or if they persuaded Supply Co. to accept a bigger proportion of transportation costs or to provide additional inventory without cost to the buyer. All of these concessions increase impact for the purchaser by making the components cheaper and more available. The trouble is, each improvement for the purchaser means a loss for the seller. To provide the price reduction, Supply Co. has to swallow the excess inventory or cut its margins. Even worse, the real productivity opportunities fall through the cracks between the companies.

It isn't Assembler's problem that Supply Co. has wasteful production scheduling; it doesn't matter to Supply Co. if Assembler's inventory or warehousing costs are higher than they should be. What matters is that each party get its share of the fixed pie stipulated in the supplier contract. When the parties treat the pie as fixed, then for one to get a bigger slice the other must inevitably get less. That's the classic win/lose thinking that years of vendor relationships have fostered. In contrast, partnering focuses on making the pie bigger. In a case like this, for example, the partners might

- Schedule Supply Co.'s production runs using real-time Assembler Inc. production data, so that there are fewer uneconomical runs. This would increase the pie by lowering production costs, resulting in savings to be shared by both parties.

- Develop a common tracking system so that logistics data is entered only once and can be tracked by both parties. The savings in time and effort from eliminating duplicate tracking and billing would more than pay for the cost of developing the system.

- Close down, or reduce in scale, at least one warehouse. If day-to-day volume of deliveries justifies it, possibly cut out the whole warehousing operation and make direct factory-to-factory deliveries to a schedule determined by the common logistics tracking system. Both partners would chalk up some worthwhile savings from this increase in the productivity pie.

- At a minimum, schedule deliveries so that two empty trucks from the partners aren't passing each other on the road when one truck from either partner could have both delivered and picked up. Even better, increase the pie still more by reducing the size of both delivery fleets.

Although this is a theoretical example of duplication and waste, every element of it is taken from real-life cases. Over-ordering of inventory, was, for example, a common problem for Public Service Electric and Gas, who used partnering with key suppliers as one of their strategies to cut inventory levels by more than $100 million. Shared information and joint planning of production scheduling enabled Okonite to make savings in cable costs to PSE&G, and did the same for Georgia-Pacific in their bid to keep down costs for their partner Sweetheart. McGregor Cory, as a distribution specialist, has taken over warehousing and distribution for its partners, cutting out unnecessary duplicate warehousing and reducing wasteful steps in the distribution process. As a result there's a bigger pie to share.

Stone Container supplies its partner Baxter Healthcare in North Cove, North Carolina, with corrugated packaging delivered from its facility in Charlotte, but the partners noticed that Stone's trucks were traveling home empty. Baxter has its own warehouse in Charlotte. So now when Stone delivers corrugate to Baxter, instead of returning empty, its trucks load Baxter product for delivery back to Baxter's Charlotte location. It's a small increase in the pie, but small increases are often what partnering impact is all about. Stone and Baxter have implemented over 200 projects of this kind together and, although the parties are a little reserved about the exact savings, it's clear they add up to many millions of dollars that would never have been possible under the old fixed-pie vendor relationship.

Logistics has proved a particularly fertile area in which partners can work together to reduce duplication and waste. The most famous of all partnerships, to judge by the number of words written about it, has been that between Wal-Mart and Proctor & Gamble. It has extracted most of its multimillion-dollar savings from eliminating unnecessary steps in the logistics chain by which Proctor & Gamble goods reach Wal-Mart stores. It has saved the parties several millions of dollars annually, but that doesn't make it exceptional. It has become routine for large partners to make seven-figure annual savings from streamlining and combining their logistics. An associated area that has also produced substantial bottom-line impact has been the setting up of electronic data interchange and common, or at least compatible, data processing. This commonality of systems has reduced duplication and waste by allowing partners to enter common data such as ordering, production scheduling, invoicing, billing, inventory, or transportation information once only into a database accessible to both parties. As a result the high cost of duplicate data entry can be eliminated and the parties get valuable fringe benefits, such as fewer errors from rekeyed data, together with faster access to information.

Waste from duplication is usually very visible, and its reduction makes an easy target for impact through partnering. But waste also comes in less direct forms that are just as detrimental to the partners. In particular, wasted time may prove more damaging to competitive position than wasted dollars. As we saw in the Eastman/Bechtel partnership, the ability to get on-line six months faster can make the difference between a lukewarm product and a hot one. And speaking of hot products, Whirlpool's new gas range will come to the market several months sooner as a result of a design partnership with Eaton, and will gain a competitive advantage as a result. In some fast-moving marketplaces such as the frontiers of high technology, getting there first is much more than a competitive advantage. It may be the only game in town. In terms of impact, nothing else comes close.

A chip maker like Intel, for example, could not survive—let alone dominate its market—without using partnerships to save many months of development time. For Intel, the extra time needed to work through traditional business-to-business vendor relationships would put it out of business. There's no way that Intel could design its next-generation chip and then ask potential suppliers to bid on the design of the new equipment that would be needed to make it. A traditional vendor process would add not just months but years to the time needed to bring a new generation of chips to the market. By partnering with Applied Materials, who make the machines that produce the chips, Intel can gain time from concurrent work on the design of both the chip and the sophisticated equipment needed to manufacture it.

Another way to create impact by reducing waste is to find areas in the present relationship where things just fall through the cracks between the partners. At the border between organizations there will almost always be something inefficient happening that is never put right because, at the moment, it isn't either partner's responsibility. Take a small but typical example from the partnership between hospital equipment manufacturer Hillenbrand and their transportation partner UPS.

The Hill-Rom company is part of Hillenbrand and has one of its locations in Batesville, Indiana. At this single location there are 22 different points (or doors) where UPS makes deliveries. Inevitably, when suppliers to Hill-Rom sent packages to the Batesville location, the UPS driver ended up trying to sort out which of the 22 delivery doors should receive it. So, for example, the package might be left at door 17. Somebody in Hill-Rom would receive it, look at it, and realize it wasn't theirs; probably it should go to someone at door 6, or possibly door 9. So that person would have the UPS driver pick it up on the next pass and take it to door 6, where—with luck—it would get to its intended recipient several hours late. Sometimes, without the luck, the package would circle forlornly between the 22 doors, taking several passes and a lot of effort to find its intended owner. On an average day more than 30 packages at the Batesville location were being handled more than once because of inadequate delivery instructions. It wasn't a huge amount of waste, but it reduced the efficiency of UPS deliveries and it meant that people in Hill-Rom were waiting longer to get their packages.

In a vendor relationship, who would have responsibility for reducing this waste? Not Hill-Rom; package delivery is outside their boundary, it's strictly UPS's problem as the supplier of delivery services. So UPS should put this right, you say? But in a vendor role, how can they? It isn't within their boundary as a transportation provider. They can't control how Hill-Rom's suppliers or customers address their packages—that's Hill-Rom's responsibility. Their job is to deliver as best they can to the address they have been given. In other words, nobody has responsibility for reducing this waste; it just falls between the organizational cracks. But by working together as partners, Hill-Rom and UPS contacted suppliers and persuaded them to do a better job of labeling. As a result, instead of fewer than 70 percent of the packages being delivered correctly on the first pass, the figure now is near 90 percent and climbing. Waste is reduced, UPS gets more efficient use of driver time, and Hill-Rom gets faster deliveries and uses less of its people's time in redirecting packages. Neither partner will get rich on the savings, but it's a good everyday example of how partnering can create impact by taking joint responsibility for reducing waste in a myriad of areas that would never even be explored in a vendor relationship.

Reduction of duplication and waste is the area where most partnerships begin in their quest to create impact together. As a starting point for partnering, waste reduction has many attractions. The results can be seen relatively quickly, so the partnership can make quick hits. As we've seen, this can be vitally important in the early life of the partnership when there are likely to be doubters on both sides. Another attraction is that the impact from reducing waste is usually fairly easy to measure. There is a well-documented baseline cost from the existing way of doing things; any change in how the parties operate can be costed using existing performance measures and compared with historical data. There can be little argument with results like a $50 million inventory reduction or a 25 percent saving in distribution costs. In contrast, when partnerships set out to create a totally new opportunity, such as TranCel Corporation and Baxter's joint endeavor to create a new diabetes therapy, it's harder to know whether the results could have been achieved just as cost-effectively by the partners working independently.

A final point on creating impact through the reduction of waste. In a vendor relationship, the purchasing/selling cycle itself is a major source of inefficiency and waste that can be reduced through partnering. The classic purchasing cycle of Request for Proposal, supplier evaluation and selection, contract negotiation, and purchase orders can—and usually does—take many months. We've seen how this is no longer a realistic business model for fast-moving industries. Even for more traditional markets the process is expensive and wasteful for both parties. Blue Cross/Blue Shield of Florida, for example, decided that the cost of the purchasing cycle and its sales equivalent added little value to either party. When they chose Texas Instruments as a partner, they cut unnecessary selling and purchasing cycle costs by agreeing up-front to a three-year budget—allowing them to move away from the wasteful purchase-by-purchase Request for Proposal mentality and bringing savings to both sides. Bernard Guidon, General Manager of Workstation Systems at Hewlett-Packard, observes:

Selling time itself, in terms of getting up to speed, is a waste if all you do is make a single vendor sale. When you sell added-value solutions, 80 percent of your selling time goes into really understanding the customer's business issues in the first place. It's a tremendous investment that you can only afford to do as part of a deeper relationship.

The waste generated by traditional, transactional relationships is becoming more evident to companies as they gain experience with newer and more efficient partnering relationships. From a customer perspective there's little value added from the never-ending round of selecting and negotiating with alternative vendors, then educating each new winner in the basics of the customer's business. And the process isn't attractive for the supplier either. We calculate, for example, that more than 40 percent of the profit from Huthwaite's current business relationship with a well-known telecommunications giant will go into such non-value-added areas as legal fees and contract negotiation costs. With all due respect to our intellectual property counsel, the months of expensive negotiations haven't added much in the way of value to our client, its customers, or ourselves but instead have served to slow down our work, divert the energies of both sides, limit creativity to those areas specified by the contract, and, unfortunately, remind us that we *are* on different sides—we're treated as a vendor, not a partner. The vendor role has defined a fixed border between us and has siphoned off resources that could have been used to add value. The vendor relationship itself has become a source of waste and a restriction on potential impact. Few organizations move to a partnering relationship solely to cut waste from the selling process. However, where parties have moved to partnering because of waste-reduction opportunities in a major cost area such as logistics, they usually have reaped additional benefit from real savings in both the cost of procurement and the cost of sales.

LEVERAGING CORE COMPETENCE

What do these three very disparate success stories have in common?

- Cascades paper is a relatively small paper mill in Niagara Falls, New York. It's a tough business, and margins are slim. Cascades installs a new and experimental infrared dryer. For a comparatively modest capital investment, this dryer allows them to increase daily production by 10 percent.

- The United States Postal Service decides to develop express mail tracking so that it can compete with the likes of Federal Express and UPS in terms of tracking and tracing the status of packages in its system. Tracking systems of this sort are notoriously difficult to get up and running successfully, yet USPS gets its new system into operation remarkably quickly and, by doing so, becomes a viable competitor in this premium market.

- The British Heart Foundation has 400 cost centers, each of which has bought its own office supplies. In consequence, the cost of supplies has been high—just *how* high nobody quite knows, because there's been no way to track the information or analyze costs. So they introduce a means of purchasing their office supplies that reduces costs and cuts inventory and waste, while maintaining the independence of the cost centers to order their own supplies. They also now have, at no additional cost, regular tracking and management reports to analyze their overall and local supplies expenditure.

In each of these three success stories, the common factor is that a partner helped to create the impact. But not just any partner. Each partner in these cases brought a special expertise—a core competence—that they were able to use to achieve impact. Let's look at each case to see what the core competence was and how it was leveraged.

Cascades Paper

Paper mills use a great deal of energy, so Cascades partnered with its energy supplier, National Fuel Gas, to help them take a close look at how to reduce their energy costs. Because NFG had a core competence in energy utilization, coupled with an active research and development program, they were able to provide an infrared dryer that increased production by 10 percent. Cascades' core competence wasn't in the energy field, so they would never have installed a prototype dryer by themselves. Because the partnership broke down the traditional boundaries, NFG was no longer a utility company supplying energy; it was actively participating inside the plant and looking for ways to leverage its core competence as an energy specialist. It was from this work, "walking around in the bowels of the plant," as Dan Burkhardt of NFG put it, that the idea for the infrared dryer was conceived.

The United States Postal Service

It took state-of-the-art transportation specialists like Fedex and UPS many years to develop the systems they use to track and trace the packages they carry. When the United States Postal Service wanted to introduce track-and-trace to compete in the express package market, they couldn't afford the years of development that it would take to go it alone. So they partnered with systems integrator SHL to design and source a tracking system on their behalf. Outsourcing systems of this kind is a core competence of SHL, who installed the system and now manages and operates it for the postal service. By leveraging SHL's core competence, USPS was able to get their system up much faster and at a lower cost than they could have achieved alone.

British Heart Foundation

For British Heart Foundation, having 400 independent cost centers buying office supplies created two problems. First, because each center bought independently, they didn't have the bulk buying leverage to get the best prices. Second, it just wasn't an economical proposition to keep tabs on such things as inventory levels and usage levels of office consumables at each cost center, so there was no way to monitor and control overall expenditure.

The retail chain W. H. Smith has a contract stationer operation that partners with multisite customers to supply them with everything from pencils to desks. The core competence of a contract stationer might at first sight seem to be simply the supplying of office products at good prices. But *any* supplier in the office products marketplace can do that. What made this a partnership rather than a vendor relationship was that W. H. Smith had other core competencies to offer. They also had expertise in stock control, distribution, and cost reporting. These were the core competencies that were leveraged by British Heart Foundation. W. H. Smith provided a flexible, customized product range from which the cost centers could order within an agreed-upon budget. W. H. Smith handled stock control and distribution, providing analysis and reports for management and working with them to find ways to contain their overall office-supply costs.

In each of these examples one partner has had an expertise, or core competence, that it has made accessible to the other partner and achieved impact as a result. But it was not just the core competence that created impact. In these cases and many others like them, two enabling factors have also played an important role.

The first enabler has been the partnering relationship itself. The core competence was brought into play only because of the access that resulted from the partnering relationship. Would National Fuel Gas ever have provided infrared dryers if it had been in a traditional vendor relationship as an energy supplier? Probably not. It was only through the intimacy of partnering that NFG came close enough to Cascades' business issues to see the opportunity. W. H. Smith has been able to leverage their core competencies with British Heart Foundation as partnership access has shown both parties new ways to increase impact. The intimacy of partnering, as we'll see in the next chapter, is the enabler of impact. This is particularly the case when one partner brings a core competence that the other partner must integrate into its business system. A vendor relationship is unlikely to provide the intimacy of access and information so necessary for successfully weaving a core competence into the fabric of a partner's business.

The second enabling factor that allows core competence to be leveraged comes from the way an organization defines its core competence. What is the core competence of National Fuel Gas, for example? If they were to define themselves strictly as having a traditional utility competence to supply energy efficiently, then it's not likely they would look for opportunities like the infrared dryer. Seeking out and developing such opportunities presupposes a wider definition of core competence that includes energy utilization and management. If W. H. Smith had defined themselves only as a cost-effective supplier of office products, then they would have little to offer their partners. But defining their competence in terms of stock control, distribution, cost analysis, and management information gave them additional value to offer their partners. Many organizations have found new partnering opportunities by reexamining their definition of core competence.

Fedex Logistics Services, for example, runs a "parts bank" to supply orthopedic replacement parts for surgery. These parts invariably are needed in a hurry, and Fedex frequently uses competitors to ensure that parts go out on the next flight. How did Fedex get into a business where they might not even be the carrier of the products they ship? It's a question of how they defined elements of their core competence. By defining their core competence as logistics rather than transportation, it became logical to look for opportunities to handle such things for their partners as warehousing, inventory control, and logistics software. With this definition of core competence, shipping by competing carriers makes sense.

CREATING NEW OPPORTUNITIES

Some of the most exciting partnerships are those that achieve impact by creating something new—a new product, an innovative service, or a breakthrough methodology—that utilizes the combined capabilities of each partner. These partnerships fall into two broad types. First, there are partnerships that start out from day one to create a brand-new opportunity. Second, there are partnerships that begin with the purpose of reducing waste or leveraging a core competence and then, once the partnership has established itself, go on to evolve new opportunities. It's important to make this distinction because in most cases the process of forming and operating each type of partnership is very different. If a partnership sets out from its inception to create something new, then some or all of the following conditions are likely to be present.

✔ Because the intent of the partnership is innovation, it is more likely to be initiated from each organization's Research & Development or Strategic Planning function than from either Purchasing or Sales & Marketing. So it is less likely to grow naturally out of the existing supplier/customer relationship.

✔ Because the intention is to produce something new, the partnership generally will require capital investment, which means that initially it will spend money rather than save it. As a result, the partnership will require a more elaborate justification process in each organization and top management is more likely to be closely involved.

✔ Because of the need for capital investment, formal budgetary and control structures are likely to be set up. This means that a partnership to create innovation may well be constituted as a joint venture or a formal alliance rather than the smaller-scale ad hoc arrangements that characterize partnerships designed to reduce waste or leverage competence.

✔ Because the parties commit money, the lawyers become involved. Elaborate contracts become the norm, in contrast to the other types of partnerships we've described, which depend heavily on trust and for which "contracts" often are little more than informal understandings between the parties to do whatever is in the best interests of the partnership.

For these reasons, partnerships that are set up explicitly to create new opportunities are generally not a good entry point into partnering for those whose background is in selling or purchasing and who would like to evolve partnerships out of their existing supplier-customer relationships. Fortunately, there are usually many other fruitful openings for creating impact through partnering in the areas of waste reduction and core competence that provide easier entry points. Yet many people, when they think of partnering, think primarily of partnerships designed explicitly to create new opportunities. It's true that such partnerships often contain the element of excitement that goes with new ventures, which means they're more likely to be written about in the business press. Take, for example, some of the more than a dozen partnerships to create new opportunities in the biotechnology area that just one company, Baxter, is involved with:

- Partnering with Genetics Institute to produce a genetically engineered product for treatment of hemophilia that carries no risk of human viral contamination
- Partnering with TranCel to develop a diabetes therapy by implanting a membrane that contains insulin-producing cells to provide glucose regulation
- Partnering with Weizmann Institute on a gene therapy to produce antibodies that can recognize and destroy tumors

Innovative ventures such as these push at the frontiers of new technology. They are exciting and, rightly, get media attention. But for most organizations the bread and butter of partnering—partnerships creating their initial impact and earning their keep—is still the reduction of waste and the leveraging of core competence. However, there's an interesting question that waste-reduction partnerships must address sooner or later: What do they do after the waste has been eliminated?

Partnering is a relatively new phenomenon. Most partnerships for cutting waste are still in their early stages, busy creating impact by improving efficiency and reducing duplication. But sooner or later they will run out of opportunities; the waste will be gone. This has already started to happen with some of the longer-established waste-reduction partnerships. A few of the older partnerships we contacted were reluctant to talk with us, and gave us the distinct impression they had run out of steam and gone into a low-energy maintenance mode. The productivity has been extracted and there is nothing left for these partnerships to achieve. This is a particularly likely fate for partnerships that have been set up to achieve a defined purpose. As one such partner described it: "We partnered so we could integrate our logistics and close four distribution centers. Now that's done, I guess our job is over."

Letting a partnership complete its project, and then lapse, however, may be just as shortsighted as letting a relationship with a key customer lapse in traditional vendor sales. The intimacy, access, and trust that develop in a partnering relationship may be even more valuable than the specific impact that the partnership was set up to achieve. Leveraging the partnering relationship to create new impact makes good business sense for both parties. A partnership that is satisfied with achieving a single piece of impact is wasting a valuable opportunity. The most successful partnerships are those that seek out new ways to leverage the partnering relationship itself and, in doing so, create an ever-increasing impact. The partnership between Baxter and Stone Container, for example, started out as a classic partnership to reduce waste but has since progressed to over 200 separate projects, each designed to add impact. While many of these projects have involved simple waste reduction or leveraging of core competence, others have explored new areas opened up by the close relationship that has developed between the partners. The following are some other examples of partnerships that have evolved to create new opportunities.

Meridian Travel

Meridian is a travel agency that began to partner 10 years ago by openly sharing its cost information with clients and working closely with them to reduce their overall travel expenses. CEO Cyndie Bender moved beyond this typical cost-reduction starting point for partnering and began to develop new opportunities to add more impact to her partners. These have included seminars on travel safety, an 800 service for dinner reservations, and even a courier service within 50 miles of Meridian's Cleveland headquarters that started out delivering tickets and now also delivers packages for clients.

Zymark

Zymark manufactures laboratory automation systems that improve the productivity of scientists in the pharmaceuticals industry. In today's competitive pharmaceutical business, anything that reduces product development cycles can add enormous impact. Arising from its partnership with Johnson &

Johnson, Zymark approached J & J to collaborate in developing new technology to analyze biological samples generated during new drug clinical trials. Zymark's development people conducted detailed discussions about performance, reliability, and cost, and early prototypes were run on real samples in J & J's lab. J & J now depends on the new technology to meet their ever-increasing sample turnaround challenges, and Zymark has had an opportunity to develop and refine a new product through the partnership.

American Sunroof Corporation

There are no prizes for guessing one of American Sunroof's core competencies. But they have another competence that's world-class—and it arose from a new opportunity created as a result of a partnership with Honda. The Honda partnership *did* start out with sunroofs. In fact, to further their partnership with Honda America, American Sunroof Corporation invested heavily in high-technology painting equipment to meet Honda's finish specifications for sunroofs. A change in specification meant that the new equipment would no longer be needed, so their partner Honda helped them to find new opportunities to use the equipment by sending them non-sunroof components for painting. As a result, ASC is now a world leader in automobile-component-parts painting—a business they knew little about before their partnership with Honda.

In cases like these, partnerships that started out to reduce waste or leverage a core competence have led to the creation of new opportunities. These opportunities, in turn, have often led to new products or even whole new business areas for the supplying partner. ASC didn't enter the Honda partnership with the intention of becoming a world-class component painter; similarly, when United Printing partnered with Bose, they didn't realize that the partnership would lead them into the new business area of high-resolution desktop publishing. In successful partnerships, opportunities are created that stretch a supplier's capabilities and the partnership often becomes a driving force for the development of new products. For some organizations, partnerships already play an important role in deciding the direction of research and development. In the future, the capacity of partnerships to explore and test new opportunities will play an increasingly large role in research and development strategy.

MOTOROLA–UPS: PARTNERING IMPACT AT ALL THREE LEVELS

We've seen how partnerships derive their impact from three major sources: reduction of waste, leveraging of core competence, and creation of new opportunity. These three areas are not mutually exclusive. Many of the most successful partnerships we have studied contain examples of all three sources of impact. If there's a pattern or sequence, it's this. Most partnerships begin with waste reduction, because it brings measurable and quick results. As the partners come to know each other's capabilities better, core competence becomes an increasingly important source of impact. Then, as the partnership matures, the partners discover a variety of new opportunities to add impact that may include the development of entirely new capabilities or products. An example of a partnership that shows all three types of impact is the one between Motorola and United Parcel Service.

Motorola shipped chips and finished goods from eight factories located in six Pacific Rim and Latin American countries. Their old pre-partnering distribution process was typical of that to be found in many companies, using a variety of carriers, shippers, and freight-forwarding vendors and having many steps in the distribution chain. The old system was costly and less than efficient but, even more serious for Motorola, it was too slow to respond to the changing needs of customers, who increasingly were moving to just-in-time manufacturing and reducing their inventories. Customers were demanding faster shipments but they didn't expect to pay premium rates to get them. It was clear to Motorola that they had to completely rethink their distribution process.

Motorola developed a vision of a "seven-day factory" where products would be assembled, tested, and shipped from a factory in Asia to arrive on the customer's loading dock in the United States within seven days of the order. This meant that shipping had to move products across the world in a matter of hours. Motorola decided that the best way to bring about such a radical change in their shipping needs was to partner with a distribution specialist who could work closely with them to create a new process. They tried out several possible partners and finally selected UPS. Together, the partners have been able to achieve all three types of impact:

Reduction of duplication and waste. An immediate result of the partnership was a 65 percent savings in shipping time, achieved by cutting out wasteful or duplicated steps in the shipping process. Through sharing data, the partners were able to make further savings by reducing the rekeying of shipping information and eliminating duplication in customs documentation and other paperwork. This saved costs but also helped to save time. As the partnership has matured, over 60 percent of products are shipped direct, so Motorola has been able to dismantle some of its own high-overhead distribution infrastructure, leading to further cost savings.

There have been less obvious savings as well. In some locations Motorola was critically short of factory space. By reducing the warehousing and distribution areas, they have been able to expand precious manufacturing space. The partners are continuing to integrate their information systems. As Bob Harris of Motorola says, "What we're doing is not just a movement of product but also the movement of information." There are further reductions in waste to be had in this area. So as a result of cutting duplication and waste, the partners have made the pie bigger. They have faster shipping at a lower cost to Motorola and with more revenue to UPS.

Leveraging of core competence.   UPS not only has core competence in shipping and distribution logistics, it also has competence in other areas that the partnership can leverage. For example, UPS has testing facilities that allow them to carry out shipping tests on Motorola's packaging. The partners are now leveraging this core competence to design and develop new returnable containers. In a wider sense, by getting out of the distribution business, Motorola has been able to focus better on its own core competence as a world-class manufacturer.

Creation of new opportunity.   Each partner has been able to create a new trademarked product. Motorola has used the partnership as a component of their RapidNET™ direct-delivery product marketed to Motorola's customers. UPS developed for Motorola a new product called Consolidated Clearance™, which combines the bulk shipping advantage of freight forwarding with the flexibility of individual package shipment. The partnership has created new opportunities for each partner.

The Motorola/UPS partnership illustrates many of the points we have made about impact in this chapter. It shows each of the three types of impact. It illustrates how the pie gets bigger when companies are prepared to redesign the relationship between them. Both the partners have gained as a result of this larger pie, but more importantly, their customers have gained as well. Customers now receive shipments faster, which cuts their inventory and allows them to move to JIT logistics; their costs are lower and their ability to track their shipments has been improved. Billing is simpler and, in addition, Motorola has been able to assume liability for in-transit shipments. The partnership is providing measurable impact for customers—always the ultimate test of partnering success.

GETTING TO IMPACT

As we've seen, the impact of partnering eventually reaches the consumer market and benefits all of us in terms of cheaper products, wider choices, and quicker access to those choices. That impact on the consumer is what makes partnering a lasting and irreversible force. Increasingly, partnering will be how companies will work together to create impact. But in order to achieve impact, partners must relate to each other in a new way. They must throw off the restrictions of traditional vendor relationships and replace them with new and more open ways of doing business together based on intimacy. In the next chapter we'll see exactly what's different about relationships that successfully develop intimacy. And we'll see how intimacy plays an indispensable role in achieving the kind of impact that makes everyone's pie bigger.

INTIMACY: BEYOND TRANSACTIONAL RELATIONSHIPS

Impact does not happen in a vacuum. The changes that suppliers and customers must make to achieve impact cannot be carried out in an environment that is fundamentally transactional and sale-based. Impact requires a fertile partnering environment, one that encourages mutual change and supports a long-term, in-depth approach to collaboration. Successful partnering organizations, in recognizing this, have literally reinvented the notion of supplier-customer interaction. They have learned to work together much more closely than would have been conceivable even five years ago. We call this new type of working relationship between partners *intimacy*. For suppliers, intimacy is a tremendous source of sustainable competitive advantage. Intimacy must be at the core of any supplier's partnering efforts.

INTIMACY: A BRIEF LOOK AT THE STATE OF THE ART

If someone were to design a utopia for a supplier, it might look something like this:

Instead of struggling to get to the decision maker to find out what a customer needs, the customer invites you in and puts you in charge of determining their needs, with full authority to write purchase orders on yourself. While your competitors are trying to figure out which door to go knock on, you're sitting in on critical design engineering meetings, helping to determine requirements for the future. Your competitors pick up an annual report, if they can find one, and meanwhile you've got virtually unlimited access to everything—data, people, systems, you name it. At the customer's request, you do a short stint as an employee of their company, to get to know them in detail so you can serve them better; the understanding is you'll soon move back to your company in a new role as a highly empowered broker between your organization and the customer. The customer acknowledges the long-term "lock-in" of all this, and encourages more of it by designing your company's capabilities into their systems and products. Your company has more than quadrupled its business in the last five years as a result of this customer. Now, you've figured out the magic of your relationship with this customer and are starting to take it "on the road" to your company's larger customer base.

An unlikely utopia right out of the twenty-first century? No, this is all happening—*today*—at Bose Corporation, located outside of Boston, Massachusetts, and maker of high-end audio systems. Bose is a glimpse into the future of supplier-customer relationships. But not *too far* into the future. The program they have pioneered has already been implemented at over 150 organizations, including IBM, Proctor and Gamble, Intel, AT&T, and Honeywell. They are part of an emerging "state of the art" in intimate business relationships.

A state of the art story like Bose's is an excellent entry point for thinking about intimacy. Bose and its suppliers have made a quantum leap beyond routine transactional business into something much more profitable and durable for all parties. Replicating the whole program won't be possible for many salespeople; there's a gap of willingness to change that many customers won't find easy to bridge. But Bose—and the 150 or so other companies that have made the program happen—provides a sense of direction for suppliers looking to move beyond sales calls and competitive shoot-outs.

The creator of the program (called JIT II, for "the next step after Just in Time") is Lance Dixon, Bose's Director of Purchasing and Logistics. One of the true heavy hitters in the purchasing field, Lance came across a disarmingly simple idea in the late 1980s: radical empowerment of suppliers within the customer's operating system. In theory, this means combining the roles of salesperson, purchasing agent, and planner within one person, a supplier. In practice, what it has led to is a small group of nine suppliers, called *in-plants*, who work on-site, full-time, at Bose. They are empowered to act on behalf of both supplier and customer. The "win" for Bose?

- On-site, immediate responsiveness from key suppliers
- Cost reduction through optimization of the supplier-customer interface (i.e., fewer people involved)
- Growing, accumulated expertise of top suppliers for design and production decision making
- "Designing in" preferred suppliers to new products, with specific supply standards in mind

The suppliers benefit as well. They have full access to Bose's systems, personnel, design engineering meetings, and all but the most proprietary of R&D data. This "insider" status gives them unparalleled opportunities to grow with the customer and to influence requirements for their products—a practice which is encouraged by Bose. Based on their access and knowledge, the suppliers decide what, when, and how much of a particular product or service is needed, and write orders to themselves to make it happen. Most of them get "evergreen" contracts with no end dates and no rebidding. All but indistinguishable from Bose employees, they are included in the internal Bose phone directory and provided with standard employee badges. But perhaps most important of all, *they enjoy competitive advantage as a result of the business relationship.* As Lance Dixon pointed out to us:

> There's little anyone could do to displace them at this point. They're in on the engineering meetings. They know more about our requirements than some of our own people do. We still bid new work, and they have to continue improving and driving costs down, but how could someone else possibly understand what we need as well as these guys?

The "lock-in" these suppliers have achieved, and Lance Dixon's concept of moving beyond traditional boundaries through empowered suppliers, is part of the growing story of intimacy in business relationships. However, when we first met with Lance and his suppliers, our reaction was "exciting, new, but not what a typical salesperson can make happen with a typical customer." Our hesitation was, simply, whether the principles of Bose's program could be applied to suppliers and their sales forces more generally. We supposed that the processes of the Bose program could be replicated, but that they would need to be initiated by motivated customers. We were skeptical whether there were principles that suppliers and their sales forces could use from the Bose experience. We were therefore quite taken aback to find that many of Bose's partners, or in-plants, are already bringing the concepts, with or without the whole program, to other accounts. One in-plant, Chris LaBonte of G&F Industries, told us:

> We've gone out and sold the concept. We sell partnering now. And it doesn't always mean going on-site full-time like at Bose. We've got a flexible approach; sometimes it's a day a week for one of our people. The concept is, mutual benefit and trust over time. It's a different approach. The point is, we've got growing accounts that are being driven by JIT II concepts. We no longer go in with the classic sales pitch. Instead we say, "We'd like to invite you in and we'd like to show you what we do in terms of partnering and see if you're interested."
>
> I had a CEO of a company offer me a small portion of his plastics business on a trial basis. We did it for six months using a partnered approach, and he has since offered me all of his plastic work. At Connair and Cuisinart, we had one or two jobs with each of them, but now we do partnering—and a lot more work. At some accounts, like Toys 'R' Us and Wal-Mart, we've been able to get into value-added work through partnering; our business with one account went from low six digits to seven digits. We've gone from $3 million in 1985 to now over $20 million. We're selling partnering.

Our research team spent time at Bose's headquarters exploring what these top suppliers like G&F Industries had learned about partnering that was driving their success at Bose—and elsewhere. Our first stop was Bose's transportation group, an almost comic example of the borderless organization, with several of its members having moved back and forth in employment between Bose and supplier—several times. Here, intimacy is in high gear. Four different transportation and logistics suppliers have dispensed with traditional notions of competitor versus collaborator, and have formed one seamless team. They work together in one small room and routinely exchange information—sometimes on the shared-information system and sometimes over half-height cubicles—to solve the problems of Bose's customers. As Paul Tagliamonte, manager of the group, explained the payoff to Bose:

The value of the group is it provides seamless movement of product through the distribution network. It gets us out of the usual classic problems. Traditionally, in most companies, a customer puts in an order, it gets put into a system—and then it goes into a black hole. The product leaves the dock and now another company, a shipping company, takes over and it's outside the control of your company. So now you have another company handling your customer service. It's the transportation company that is going to handle the product and hand it over to the customer. So if your customer wants to know where the product is in-transit, or if there's a delay or problem, you have no information. "Where's my product?" "Sorry, don't know. We'll call back." Now at Bose, it's a different story. If a customer calls up and says, "Problem. We have a sale event on Saturday. I know you shipped my order on time, but I just didn't leave enough time to get it by Saturday." Instead of us saying, "Well, gee whiz, I'll have to call the carrier [which one?] and see what we can do," we say, "Hold on a moment. Let me get Ron [an in-plant from Roadway Express] over here on the phone and we'll solve the problem." No one needs to tell Ron this customer is important to Bose; Ron's right here. What Ron is going to do is pull up the same screen that Bose's service people are looking at, and Ron is going to find a way to get that customer what he needs, one way or another. If you compare the usual black hole to what's happening here... Here, the customer makes one phone call to Bose, and the service rep is able to pull together all of the resources, across companies, to get the job done immediately. This is different.

The shared information systems and highly organized processes at Bose were clearly impressive. But what impressed us most was a sense of shared perspective by all of the suppliers that they truly represent the customer above all else. Here's an excerpt from the group discussion.

> LORNE JONES (TOWER GROUP INTERNATIONAL): We're quasi-customer out here. We represent the customer's needs. Because of this we can go up our own management ladders and say, "Here's a situation we're facing out at Bose." And we don't have to deal with the usual structure, your boss going to another division, up and down the chain of command. You go straight to the source. You do it, because you know and they know that you're out here as a representative of the customer.

JOHN PALLIES (AMERICAN PRESIDENT LINES): That's right. Let me tell you, whenever I go into the APL office, they always say "You guys" when talking about Bose to me. The lines do get blurred.

RON STORTZ (ROADWAY EXPRESS): It's almost like I work for both Roadway Express and Bose. Anything that's happening at Bose with regard to Roadway Express, I feel completely responsible for. Anything that happens that's good, I take responsibility for; anything that happens that's bad, I take responsibility for as well. Anything that I do affects Bose and Roadway.

JOHN PALLIES: The thing I didn't think about earlier was the need to change your perspective. Example: Shortly before I got here there was talk about a strike with one of our units. From the salesman perspective, that was just an annoyance. We have a lot of unions; they threaten to strike a lot. But from Bose's perspective the possibility of shutting down plants was very real. From my sales perspective I didn't think the strike would happen. But it had happened before, and I needed to hear that, to see it from their view. It's been a gradual process of looking at things from Bose's perspective, the customer perspective. I may not think something's important, but I have to think about what it means to Bose. I don't think most sales reps do that very well. But here, I have come to think like them. I'm becoming more and more Bose-like every day.

PAUL TAGLIAMONTE (BOSE; GROUP MANAGER): Designing your company into the customer is paramount to get this level of cooperation and growth. Usually, salespeople compete only on price. This is a different model; you harmonize your objectives with the customer. You become an integral part of the way the customer does business; it's a different perspective.

This sense of shared perspective between suppliers and customers, and the teamwork it involves, is one of the critical success factors we've observed at Bose and elsewhere, and we'll be coming back to this topic later. But we were also struck during our Bose visits by the transformation that had taken place in information sharing. On the one hand there was a shift in focus away from the normal banter of the sales process. As Dave Marble of United Printing in Warwick, Rhode Island, explained to us: "When I'm making appointments and calls now, I cut through a lot of the baloney that goes on in the up-front part of selling. Now I get right to the meat. I don't really care if you like to eat steak and eggs for breakfast, or if your favorite team won. If I'm going to be valuable to you and valuable to me, what I want to know is, what is the service that you're looking for in the marketplace? I want to know what you need, I want you to know what I've got. If I don't have information, I can't be of any value."

On the other hand, we found at Bose tremendous respect for *sharing* information, versus the usual selling focus on *getting* information. Joe Doran of Doranco, Inc., a metal component supplier, told us of meeting with Bose to share information that would shape not just his business with Bose but, in part, his company's direction:

> Information goes both ways; we don't just go ask about needs. When we've got a major capital expenditure coming up, I go to Bose and make sure it's somehow related to their needs over time. In two weeks I'll be presenting to the V.P. of manufacturing, telling him, "We're going to spend some money on capital improvements over the next two years. So tell me, what's high on your priority list that I could take back, so we can enhance our service to Bose?"

This drive toward sharing information, and specifically *information with value*, is a core skill of all of Bose's suppliers. But it's not limited to Bose; information sharing outside and beyond traditional notions of fact gathering to enable a sale seems to be a hallmark of every successful partnership we've researched.

Our sketch of the "state of the art" in intimacy, as practiced at Bose, is merely that; this story deserves its own book, and in fact, Lance Dixon has recently written one. Our purpose here isn't to provide you with a complete exposition on one company, but simply a glimpse at intimacy as it's really happening in a state-of-the-art situation. We left Bose with a pressing question. There are clearly, at Bose and elsewhere, best practices of intimacy being performed by top-flight sales forces. The question is, are there any clear principles of customer intimacy that both represent the state of the art and are also replicable by sales forces within a broad account base? The answer, we think, is yes. But it requires a very different view of "selling" as it's traditionally been understood.

A SHIFT IN PERSPECTIVE

Partnering requires a fundamental shift in perspective about selling. This shift isn't an easy one to make, but it may be the determining factor in whether a partnering relationship can be sustained or in fact sold at all. Our research suggests that most salespeople have not yet made the shift. And, as a result, many, if not most, attempts at partnering with customers do not succeed.

The story is almost always the same. The seller sees partnering as an opportunity to gain long-term guaranteed business, but doesn't see that this calls for any fundamentally different approach to selling. The customer, after months of being courted by the seller with the verbiage of partnering and collaboration, just doesn't buy it. The customer sees it as just business as usual, albeit in more flowery language. They see no reason to award any special status to the supplier, and they're certainly not going to provide lock-in in the form of sole-sourcing or special access within their organization. They're more likely to be motivated by a small discount than an eloquent exhortation to "take the next step" in the relationship.

Sadly, these customers probably are correct in their skepticism and frequent lack of interest. For when all is said and done, for many sales forces it's still about us-versus-them. Customers are still the holders of something that salespeople want, and that something is money. Salespeople are still asking for a *sale,* however cleverly they articulate it. Irritated customers told us again and again of salespeople who combined the lofty language of partnering with an objective that extended no further than a signed-and-sealed contract. New words, same old story. It's about getting the keeper of the purse to distribute its contents as generously as possible.

Much to their credit, many suppliers have taken this to heart and have made a leap forward with their customers from us-versus-them toward something more like us-and-them. We have encountered hundreds of sales professionals who have taken steps to identify some common ground as a basis for selling to customers. "My starting point," one Microsoft account executive working out of New York told us, "is what is it you, the customer, need to succeed? And what products do I have that can make sure you get that success?"

> I don't go in preaching Windows NT or Office, or anything else, until I hear what the customer's priorities are, what they're trying to achieve. It may be they have a pressing need for platform integration, but then again that may be irrelevant to them. It could be something else, like their employees are working off all sorts of different spreadsheets, word processors, etc., and that management wants to stan-

dardize desktop products. If that's the case then I'm not going to try to sell them a platform, even if that's where I thought the sale was going and even if that's where I wanted the sale to go. I'm going to sell them desktop software. I'm going to look for places where what they need and what I can offer them come together. They have to get a win for me to be successful.

Like our friend from Microsoft, many salespeople have indeed become skilled at identifying and developing common ground—the highly elusive *win-win*—with their customers. They actively look for areas where what they need—a sale—overlaps with what the customer needs. This is not to be taken lightly. Finding common ground is a highly skilled activity. Most successful sales models, including our own, are based on it. It is probably the single most important ingredient of sales effectiveness. Salespeople who can explore needs, analyze their own capabilities, and find enough overlap to do significant business have a considerable advantage over competitors. Their win-win skills allow them to dominate large accounts. Us-and-them is a huge leap forward over the old us-versus-them.

Partnering, however, requires more than us-and-them, and it's not just another leap forward. It is a fundamental *shift in perspective*. Selling's stake in the ground is still "us" and "them," even if it has shifted emphasis toward the overlap between the two. Good selling involves finding common ground between supplier and customer, but mainly for the purpose of making an immediate sale. Partnering, on the other hand, isn't about finding enough common ground to make a sale; it's about building up common ground to create a durable, collaborative relationship through which impact partnering can be achieved over a long period of time.

Organizations whose businesses require deep partnering with customers are familiar with this shift. At Applied Materials, whose top dozen or so customers account for the lion's share of revenue, building durable partnerships over time is the imperative. Invited to speak at their national sales meeting, we brought along a few researchers who met with some of their account teams; one account manager summed up her perspective as follows:

Of course we want to do business. Our customers know that. But making a sale is subtext; it can't be the focus of the collaboration.

The only valid starting point is what it is they're trying to bring to market, and how our organizations can combine capabilities to get it there. They may be thinking, "Way downstream we need to get a chip to market that has these wafer characteristics," or "We won't be in this market unless we can really push the envelope on processing speed." We can't be in there thinking about, "Let's see, is there something they need right now that we can sell?" We have to bring a long-term perspective to the table. It's not "what do you need, and how can we sell you one?" It's "Where are you going, and can we help you get there?" It probably won't have a payoff today, or tomorrow either. You have to have faith that building a core of understanding and value with the customer has its rewards, and that the rewards will come over time if you get that core solidly in place.

This high level of shared interest, of a common "core" between supplier and customer over time, is the bedrock principle of customer intimacy. The stake in the ground in partnering is not *us* or *them*. It's *we*. The focus of partnering is never *what's in it for me?* It's *what's the value we're creating together?* This is a different perspective than selling. Partnering is never sale- or transaction-based; it is business-based. It is not particularly focused on today; it is about creating value over time. Ed Ossie, Vice President of the Information Technology Group at Texas Instruments, summed it up nicely for us:

> Partnering is not another name for good selling. Selling is task-oriented. Partnering is customer-business-oriented. Partnering is about the overall scheme of things. It's about how tasks fit into the overall mission; it is not about getting the order by October.

More often than not, partnering requires focusing not on the seller-customer interaction but on the problems of the customer's customer. This is a critical shift away from the myopia of the deal toward the broader mosaic of the customer's direction and marketplace. Suppliers who interface directly between their customers and their customers' customers, such as transportation and shipping companies, often have the best grasp of this important principle. As Randa Rosenblum at Fedex explained: "Our approach is not as simple as going in and solving problems. We're not in the business of moving boxes around. We're in the business of helping our customers provide better value to their customers."

This shift in focus away from the sale transaction toward broader business value over a longer period of time is a critical element of partnering. It is this shift toward broad business value that provides the competitive advantage of partnering. The shared focus between supplier and customer on business goals and future opportunities makes the impact of partnering identifiable and possible, and in doing so provides the "lock-in"—the ever-increasing returns to insiders and the thickening barriers to outsiders—of partnering relationships.

In all strong partnerships a shared perspective is always clearly visible. Oftentimes it gets reflected in the blurring of boundaries, the increasing irrelevance of who works for the seller and who works for the customer. When suppliers and their customers have truly moved away from "us" and "them" it becomes harder and harder to identify the separate parties; they look more and more like one entity.

We saw this clearly last year when Neil and Larry flew to San Francisco, where Neil was a participating faculty member in a workshop run by McKinsey & Company, the management consultants. The workshop involves bringing teams of consultants from McKinsey together with clients for two days of intensive work on sales effectiveness. At this workshop, McKinsey consultants sat down with a group from Georgia-Pacific to hammer out strategies for GP's Southern Yellow Pine division. Larry had come along as a program observer, and commented to Neil a half-day into the program: "Who are the McKinsey people? I've not heard a single person in this room representing McKinsey." The truth was there wasn't anyone *representing* McKinsey; the entire team represented a working group for Georgia-Pacific. The statement "we need to find ways to improve our division's productivity" was just as likely to come from McKinsey as from Georgia-Pacific. It wasn't just a matter of language, either; the Georgia-Pacific group fully accepted the lack of distinction. There were no separate interests; the entire team, consisting of both parties, was working from a shared platform of common ground to solve problems as a single entity.

Blurred boundaries and shared interest beyond a sale: these are realities in strong partnering relationships. But how can suppliers move customer relationships in this direction? What, specifically, can sales forces do to shift the perspective of customer relationships from the traditional sale-focused paradigm to something broader in scope, more durable, and ultimately more locked-in?

We looked in depth at a wide variety of supplier-customer relationships to find answers to this question. Mead Packaging, we observed, got together with its customer Pillsbury and they jointly worked on the idea: *Forget that we're two separate companies; what would we do if we were just one company? What's stopping us?* The combined Mead/Pillsbury team used questions such as those as a stimulus to find the core common ground required to build a partnership. We sat in on a meeting between UPS and its customer Kodak, in which 14 people from the two organizations spent two days identifying common ground, finding "wins," and looking at the overall relationship, not sales opportunities. And we spoke with dozens of suppliers who, while not bringing whole partnering teams together for meetings, have quietly moved their customer relationships from a transaction to a business-impact focus. The question was, what were they doing that was different?

We've become convinced that the same few principles of intimacy drive almost every successful partnering relationship. The shift in perspective, toward a partnering mind-set occurs along three basic dimensions:

- Trust
- Information sharing
- The partnering team itself

Where intimacy is very high, the three dimensions exist in abundance. High levels of trust, frequent sharing of strategically important information, and a strong, organized team of people between supplier and customer are the core elements of every successful partnering relationship we've seen. The reverse is also true. Where trust is lacking, or the information shared is short-term and transaction-based, or the partnering "team" is an individual supplier and one customer who happen to like each other, the relationship rarely moves beyond the sale. More durable, locked-in customer relationships that aren't sale-based require all three of these factors. More importantly, they require shifts in thinking and action along each dimension.

BUILDING TRUST

At the very beginning of our partnering research effort, before we had a clear sense of the common driving factors behind successful partnering relationships, we did what is best described as "test marketing" of our first-cut ideas, our initial hypotheses. We put together a slide presentation with 10 or so possible critical-success factors of partnering and sent the research team around the country, slides in hand, to get feedback from leading-edge partnering organizations.

Nestled in the middle of the many complicated, and forgotten, early formulations was a slide with one word on it: *trust*. The slide was inserted by one of our researchers, Gene McCluskey. "Trust," he said, "isn't always on the surface. It's not what comes immediately to peoples' minds when you ask them about partnering. But it seems to be lurking just beneath all of the success stories we're hearing." We indulged him on this one, although it seemed awfully trite to talk about something as simple and old as trust in the complex world of partnering.

Yet that simple idea of trust turned out to be the most consistent theme, the most compelling topic, on the minds of the vast majority of people we spoke with. Over 80 percent of those we interviewed pointed to trust as the most important precondition of partnering. On a visit to Kurt Salmon Associates in Atlanta, a management consulting firm that specializes in setting up partnerships across entire supply chains, we met with vice president Randy Nord. "There *are* a lot of issues in partnering," he told us, "but trust is truly the key. Everything else has to be based on it. Without trust, there is no basis for partnering. It's the bottom line." We heard the same sentiment over and over. It is the one success factor of partnering on which almost everyone agrees.

Trust is indeed at the core of successful partnering relationships. We will go a step further and suggest, from our experience, that partnering never gets off the ground, never develops, and never takes hold without a very high level of trust between supplier and customer. But then again, trust isn't exactly a new idea, and the word predates *partnering* by at least a few millennia. One of the authors of this book, having studied history for a few years in college and ever in search of a place to put it to use, wrote in a recent white paper:

> Trust as a foundation for doing business isn't just not new. It is thousands of years old. Back in the days of Marco Polo, huge trading caravans moved back and forth between China and Europe. Somehow, separated by thousands of miles and with nothing but sailing ships to communicate, people managed to make unbelievably large loans, entrust others with their whole inventory on a rickety ship, and carry

out long-term business relationships. There were no practical means of enforcing agreements over 5000-mile distances, no legal contracts that meant anything outside of a local jurisdiction, and little chance of recovering property if your associates turned out to be swindlers. It was helpful to have some armed colleagues to back you up if the need arose, but an awful lot of business was being done on trust before English even became a modern language.

The thirteenth century may have required trustworthy associates owing to a lack of means of enforcement, but even today a lot of business—selling, not partnering—is based on simple trust. In industries such as apparel and jewelry, or for that matter high technology and finance, business is still done occasionally on a handshake and a promise. The need for trust—and for being trustworthy—isn't exactly new news to the sales profession.

On the other hand, there are striking differences between the kind of trust that salespeople typically have with customers and the kind that's evident between supplier and customer partners. If we had to sum it up, we'd say that trust in selling means being honest. "I give the customer the straight scoop, unedited and unabridged," one account representative told Dick Ruff at a training seminar.

> In the tool and dye business, you can't fool around with the customer. They may have a production run to fulfill, or a date they've committed to their customers. If we're going to ship late, or if we've got a cost overrun, or if there's a design problem, I'm on the phone with them that day to let them know what's going on and work through it. They may not be happy about it, but they know I'm giving them the facts.

In selling, trust means being straight about products, capabilities, and problems.

In partnering, though, trust isn't just about being honest and telling the truth. That's certainly a part of it. But in successful partnering relationships, trust goes much further than being candid and honest. In partnering, *trust is not about what you say; it's about who you represent.* It isn't just a question of being candid. It's a question of being as reliable as the customer's own employees in recommending the best solutions, regardless of source, and the best decisions, regardless of where they're going to lead or who's going to benefit as a result.

Unlikely as it may sound, this truly is the relationship that top suppliers have with their customers in intimate relationships. These suppliers aren't just *honest*. They are virtually *bias-free*. What they recommend to a customer is rooted always and solely in the customer's interest. They are as reliably unbiased as the customer's own buyers. This shift in perspective, so critical to partnering, is now being acknowledged and driven at senior executive levels. Bernard Guidon, head of Hewlett-Packard's $2.5-billion workstation business and a well-known figure in the high-technology field, suggested to us that:

> You need to understand very deeply where the value is to the customer. And it's absolutely true that you have to make sure they get a solution that will bring that value. That solution may involve business you don't get. You have to have the courage to recommend a competitive product if that's what the customer needs. This is how you get the level of respect for what you do, and the trust you need to win a customer's confidence forever.

We couldn't agree more. Where commitment and durability exist, they exist with customers who are sure beyond any doubt that they're getting not just *honest* advice from a *salesperson*, but *bias-free* advice from a *partner*. This is a tough transition for some sales forces to make, but it is the expectation of a growing body of customers. Fortunately, the evidence suggests that the transition is well under way.

A few examples of what this transition looks like may be seen in Fig. 4-1. What the examples in the right-hand column have in common is that they're starting fundamentally from the customer's perspective; they could just as easily come from a customer's purchasing department as from the salesperson.

Being bias-free means turning business over to a competitor when it makes sense. Chris LaBonte of G&F Industries commented to us that "You have to be clear about what your company can do, and what is better done somewhere else. To do anything that will hurt the mutual benefit with the customer is going to hurt your reputation and the partnership. Things may look appealing, but you've got to go deeper." He added:

> Bose came to us and said they've got a new project with Mazda out in Michigan using the acoustic wave technology. We said we would get involved and build a program. But we also told them it didn't make

Trust in Selling: Honest	Trust in Partnering: Bias-Free
We're competent at programming, even though system design is our core competency.	There are better programmers. We need to find you the right one.
I know you need it now, but we don't have it. We'll need to back-order it.	You need it now, so I'll get it from a competitor.
We could fulfill 80 percent of those requirements.	We can't meet all the requirements. We're going to need to partner with other suppliers to get you a complete solution.
I know you're concerned about price, but our quality's the highest.	Since price is your top concern, we'll work with you to find a way to drive costs down. Even if that means we make tradeoffs.

Figure 4-1 *Trust in selling versus trust in partnering.*

any sense for G&F to do the production molding in Sturbridge, Massachusetts, when we knew the electronic manufacturing was going to take place in Hillsdale, Michigan. We know there are good molders right in that area and it made more sense to us that Bose would work with them. We recommended to Bose that it would be more cost-effective if we made the tools, but that they get someone local in Michigan for production. From the start we had a real understanding. They said, "Okay. You guys build the tools, and we'll move them to Michigan." It was right. For G&F and Bose. Everyone had the right perspective on it.

That "right perspective" that Chris mentioned is the perspective of a bias-free supplier. It means representing the customer and their interests, exclusively, by directing business to where it can best be done. But even when turning business over to a competitor isn't required, taking a bias-free approach to customers can make a lasting impression. Eric Marcus, formerly the Chief Technology Officer at CCH, Inc., commented to us on CCH's relationship with Oracle Corporation, the fast-growing leader in database software:

> When I was with CCH, we thought we needed some major middleware software that we were planning to do with Oracle. They came in and said, "No, you don't need to do that." They started out the relationship with us by saying, "We've got a more innovative approach, and you don't have to spend as much as you think you need to." Then they put really smart people on the project to explain how it would work, and in fact we went with their suggestion. So we didn't end up with this monster project we thought we were going to have. Frankly, they'd have made more money if they'd just told us to go ahead and do what we had already planned to do. They traded off some business to get us the right solution. We'll remember that.

Whether it involves turning business over to a competitor or finding cost savings for the customer that brings you less sales revenue, taking an unbiased perspective is the cornerstone of customer intimacy. It's the basis for the trust and commitment that customers must have toward suppliers if partnering is to succeed.

But once you've brought an unbiased perspective to the customer, and developed partnering-level trust, it's absolutely essential to leverage that trust. Trust isn't a goal in and of itself, but a precondition for building value between organizations. Once you've won trust as an unbiased advisor, what do you do with it? Trust must be translated into value by the salesperson. On the one hand, trust enables salespeople to gain access to information that enables further lock-in through early access to, say, new product designs or knowledge about a change in a customer's strategy. On the other hand, trust enables salespeople to provide customers with more in-depth, important information that can help the customer's decision making. Either way, trust only makes the value of the relationship *possible*. To actualize it requires information sharing and, more specifically, a different *type* of information sharing than is usually present in selling relationships.

INFORMATION SHARING

"Knowledge itself is power," said Francis Bacon. It is the driving force of our Information Age (although, for the record, Mr. Bacon put that thought to paper about 450 years ago). Inside knowledge of a customer's needs, business direction, strategies, preferences, and orientation in the marketplace, not to mention specific details for a project you're going to compete on, is a tremendous source of competitive advantage.

It's a competitive advantage, however, that relatively few salespeople get to enjoy. From the perspective of people who are already working seamlessly with customers, the kinds of information to which most salespeople have access seem tremendously limiting. Dave Marble of United Printing, one of Bose's top suppliers, commented to us that "Most salespeople don't even know what they don't know. They don't know why they're not getting the work; they walk in the front door and have no idea what's involved in the sale." Dave is correct. In truth, though, this isn't a critique of salespeople as much as a criticism of the types and limitations of the information to which they normally have access. More often than not, selling means spending much of one's time in an information "black hole," the symptoms of which are all too familiar in the profession:

- Spending weeks or months trying to figure out who's who in an account—and perhaps applying labels of one sort or another (like "decision influencer") to various individuals (while the competition's sitting in the employee cafeteria with a senior executive, discussing the inside story of the customer's business plan)
- Running into RFPs that look suspiciously as though they were written by a specific competitor, without being able to tell who's influenced the requirements and to what extent
- Responding to exact, detailed customer requirements only to find out these weren't the "real" requirements or didn't reflect the needs or opinions of key people

The fact is that most salespeople not only lack information, but are unequipped to use information strategically within a partnering context. As a result they get further and further behind in accounts, while other suppliers have learned to build durable bridges of shared information with the customer. In a word, they get locked out; they just can't get the information they need to compete.

We've experienced the insider's side of this story with a few of our own clients. At Microsoft, for example, we had established a lot of good will over a period of a few years by bringing an innovative, coaching-based, selling-skills program to their sales force. That work earned us the right to come back to the table when Microsoft rolled out its solution provider, or partner, channel. We spent four months in a joint research effort with Microsoft, out in the field assessing sales force requirements and partnering issues. The information that moved back and forth between our two organizations was substantial and deep; we jointly interviewed dozens and dozens of sales reps, managers, teams, and corporate managers. The information came in to us, then went back out; we helped Microsoft's people make presentations to their own company on building strong partnerships within the new channel. We became co-owners of expertise, shareholders in a valuable body of knowledge.

So when our competitors came in, as they inevitably do, and offered off-the-shelf solutions to problems they weren't particularly knowledgeable about, they were, to Dave Marble's point, standing outside the door wondering what was going on. As Microsoft's project manager commented to us: "I'm reading their brochures, and there's good stuff, but in terms of partnering they don't really have the expertise to address *our* challenges." Our stronger competitors are good firms, and they offer good programs. On this project, though, they just didn't have the knowledge base to compete. They were locked out. And they were locked out largely along a dimension of information, of knowledge.

Our research suggests that most salespeople are indeed "outsiders" on the information dimension. For every one salesperson engaged in strategically important information sharing with a customer, there are probably a hundred looking in from the outside. They are neither benefiting from the value of information nor contributing information of real value to their customers. To a large extent this problem stems from selling's traditional focus on sale-based information and a focus not on *sharing* but on *getting* information.

The usual questions, such as "Where can I get their employee list?" "Who might be resistant to the sale?" "Who's the economic buyer?" and so on, are the questions of outsiders. They're good questions; someone needs to be asking them; effective salespeople have become very skilled at finding answers to those questions. But they're still the questions of an outsider, of someone looking in while a part-nering competitor is freely exchanging critical, sometimes proprietary, information with the customer. In the world of partnering, they are yesterday's news. Bringing value to the customer and achieving lock-in require not *getting* but *sharing* information—and specifically, informa-tion of value. This is not just a question of semantics. The shift from getting to sharing information is at the core of building intimacy.

With that said, we must acknowledge that often there are obstacles standing in the way of building an effective information exchange. Sometimes these obstacles are outside the influence of the supplier. One heavy equipment manufacturer we learned about during our re-search had made a huge sale the previous year to an Italian tire manu-facturer. Proud of their accomplishment, the supplier arrived at the cus-tomer's site ready to install their machine and discuss options for integrating it into the customer's total system. To their chagrin, they dis-covered that the customer had erected a giant plywood tunnel around the whole area where the machine would be installed so that the suppli-er couldn't see the rest of the plant—including the machines their equipment would have to connect with. They installed their complex piece of machinery while staring for days at giant plywood boards. As the source of this story pointed out to us somewhat dryly, this might be a good example of information *not* flowing freely between organizations.

There are those customers who, for one reason or another, will not participate in an information exchange outside the confines of traditional supplier-customer communication. The plywood tunnel story has stuck in our minds (and some others' as well, it's a popular story in partnering circles) as a metaphor for the boundary between the information suppli-ers' need to partner and the information they sometimes have access to. Salespeople often face some type of "plywood tunnel" when they're trying to get enough information to make a sale, let alone to partner.

But the wood tunnel can become self-defeating. At almost every customer site there's a supplier or two who's on the real inside track of the customer's information flow. *Somebody's* getting access. It is, in fact, very rarely outside the scope of a salesperson's influence to get the ball rolling toward better, higher-value, information sharing. More often than not the ball is in the supplier's court when it comes to mak-ing an information exchange come to life with a customer. But how do you get it started? The first principle of building an information ex-change is a very bottom-line notion of *reciprocity*.

INFORMATION SHARING PRINCIPLE #1: RECIPROCITY.   One senior manager in a Big 6 consulting firm described to us a situation that is not uncommon. He had been trying to expand business at one of his most important clients, a retail chain planning to develop a system that could convert point-of-sale data into useful information for marketing purposes. After three years of declining revenues and margins, the retailer put highest priority on a new system that would add up customer buying patterns at the point of sale and produce meaningful, timely information for product planning and development.

The consulting manager had a whole team spend a month on the proposal, and was nearly sure he had the deal. Having worked with the retailer on systems in finance, operations, and distribution, he was convinced he had an "inside track for the next major initiative." And he lost the deal. As he told us:

> We had some great contacts within MIS (management information systems) but they weren't willing to talk much about the new point-of-sale system until they'd put out to bid and received proposals from all interested vendors. We got some points of view on technology that other bidders probably didn't have, but nothing you could really take to the bank. And it worked both ways. Since we were around in the account, a few key people asked us questions before the proposal was ready that we weren't ready to supply, like pricing formulas and how much of the system we'd farm out to third parties for development. We didn't feel that supplying this kind of information was consistent with how we've worked in the past. So we played a conventional game. We told them what we thought they needed to know to make an informed decision.

The full relevance of this story wasn't clear at the time, back in the autumn of 1993. But it became clearer six months later when Larry ran into the consultant at Boston's Logan Airport and the two sat out a snowstorm catching up on business. The consulting manager brought up that account again; it had been one of his office's top opportunities in 1993, and it was lost. So they had pursued the client to find out what went wrong. As he explained:

> A few months after we lost the proposal, the client granted us a postmortem. They'd awarded the contract to a vendor who had also been in the account for a few years, but who also seemed to have a much better handle on the business issues that led to the RFP. It turned

out the issue was not really point-of-sale data for the marketing department, although that's what was stated in the RFP. The real issue was that the client anticipated consolidation of its retail stores over the next two years. When you consolidate, that is a good time to build a marketing system and tighten the link between customers and product marketing. But in terms of what they were really looking for, they wanted someone who specifically had experience developing systems in the middle of a radical restructuring. We actually had that experience, but we never knew this was an issue to them, so it never went into our proposal.

It turns out that the winning vendor was all over this point; we saw their proposal, and the entire document reeks of restructuring, not marketing. At the postmortem the client told us the other vendor hadn't made a big deal, even before the proposal, about disclosing third-party resourcing or pricing data. The pricing issue was particularly important because in the midst of a restructuring there were a lot of auditors floating around, creating great tension and pushing accounting issues to top priority. Before the RFP had ever hit the street, the vendor had given the client what they needed, and, from what I can tell, the client had shared with them a lot more information than we ever had access to. So I guess it worked both ways. Our competitor gave more data, and they got more data. What they got, in the way of data, helped them put together a winning proposal.

This account manager may not have had his finger on the pulse of the client's need, but he did get his finger on the pulse of a key issue in information sharing. It isn't about getting some piece of information to make a sale. It's about *reciprocity.* Suppliers building customer intimacy aren't waiting for the post-mortem. They're kick-starting the exchange of information with the customer and taking the initiative by contributing information of value.

Cyndie Bender, CEO of Meridian Travel in Cleveland, knows this point well. She's built a rock-solid business on the principle of giving information to her large customers. In the last 10 years, Meridian has grown from a basic travel agency to a multiservice travel company driven into new services by evolving customer needs. This growth has taken place in a fiercely competitive industry, in large part through deep information sharing between Meridian and its customers—in both directions. But the information sharing starts with a willingness on Meridian's part to put its cards on the table. As Cyndie told us:

We have an "open-book policy." We deal with people who know the industry. You can't fool them, and why would you try? There is a lot of suspicion in this industry. We had to be willing to not just talk about openness. We routinely show our clients the expense, costs and profits, on everything from flights to hotel bookings. We show clients what it is going to cost to service their needs, what Meridian's cost is, and what they will be able to do as a result. Once you open up like that, it builds communication.

Meridian's success—they haven't lost a major customer since they started the open-book policy—didn't come from asking the right question or getting the right piece of data. It came from an information exchange that, on the one hand, involves making available the core data customers need to make decisions and, on the other, launching from that discussion into a serious exchange of information about potential services and needs that Meridian could offer, like local package-delivery and safety seminars for female travelers, that would never have come up outside the context of reciprocal information sharing.

But if reciprocity means being more willing to provide more information, what is the appropriate scope of that information? There's price and costing information of the sort Meridian discloses to much advantage but which gave our Big 6 acquaintance a more difficult time. That's one type of information, where the issue is *disclosure*. There's a second type that's less related to disclosure and more related to the value brought to the relationship by the supplier through information. Here, the issue is *expertise*. In successful partnering, suppliers don't just sell products and provide a little advice when asked. They aggressively look for ways to be a resource to the customer. They bring information in the form of expertise. As Gabe Rosica, COO of Bailey Controls, suggested:

> One of the most important things is that we help the customer manage what he does and what he buys, based on what we know. We always have better inside information into where we're going and what we're going to do, and what will probably be good or bad for the customer downstream. Once there's trust in place to allow for it, we share all of that information with the customer.

By bringing both disclosure and expertise to the table, organizations such as Bailey Controls and Meridian have opened up a much wider sharing of information with their customers based on reciprocal value. This, we find, is in sharp contrast to the usual reluctance to disclose pricing data and other information like downstream product updates or perhaps small "bugs" that can go unmentioned for the time being. The usual supplier strategy that's limited to *getting* some piece of information to make a sale completely misses the point about the true driver of information sharing: value to the customer. John F. Kennedy's suggestion to "Ask not what your country can do for you. Ask what you can do for your country" probably captures the essential point. An excellent metric for partnering, indeed, is just how much further the disclosure of supplier information has proceeded beyond that of a routine supplier-customer relationship. If the answer is not at all, there are probably insufficient grounds to partner, and there is absolutely no chance of becoming an "insider" in the customer's information flow.

Assuming, though, that value has been provided to the customer and that there is reciprocal information sharing, does that information look the same as it would in a traditional vendor relationship? No. It looks very different. It has more value to both parties. And it achieves this value along two dimensions.

INFORMATION SHARING PRINCIPLE #2: BUSINESS FOCUS.   Information in selling, even when used skillfully, is primarily about a sale. It's about who, what, when, where, and how. It's an exchange that helps to make the movement of product go smoothly. It's a necessary conversation. But it isn't to be confused with an exchange of information that helps to drive overall business success. This is a key ingredient of effective information sharing in partnering. To add value, the conversation must move beyond the sale and encompass the overall business between partners, where larger needs exist and where greater value can be added.

This shift in focus was demonstrated to us at a two-day meeting of 14 people from UPS and Kodak that we had the privilege to attend as observers. UPS and their customer Kodak, after years in a traditional and self-admittedly somewhat adversarial relationship, decided they had to take the next step together toward a relationship of high value for both organizations. To get there, both organizations have committed to a broader discussion with fewer constraints. The value they're finding as partners isn't about a transaction anymore. As one of the Kodak representatives commented at the meeting:

At the beginning it was really a traditional buyer-seller type of situation. The issues on the table were "We're doing loading of the freight. Should we get a loading allowance?" Or, just maybe, "Could we do things differently in terms of claims administration?" Now we're way beyond that. It's UPS–Kodak now, and in some ways we're interchangeable. It's a different situation; it's not about buying a transportation service anymore. We started thinking through all of the possibilities that UPS had and all the needs that Kodak had, and they were not just transportation. They were logistics. They were systems. They were billing.

And UPS's perspective from the meeting:

Now our role has shifted from transportation provider to in-house consultative agent. But you have to be willing to sit at the table and roll up your sleeves and say, "Let's not just look at existing problems and solutions. Let's look at all the alternatives. We should be somebody who can help you make good decisions from an informed perspective. Let us show you what we can really do. If it works, fine. If it doesn't work, fine. But let's look at the whole picture."

This willingness to contribute across the customer's whole business, and to bring value to the table as a "consultative agent," is a key characteristic of suppliers who have been accepted as partners. The value of partnering lies largely in impact, and you can't maximize impact while limiting the discussion to delivery dates, discounts, and the other administrivia of the sales process.

Gabe Rosica of Bailey Controls sees with real clarity the competitive advantage of sharing broader, more contextual, business information with customer partners. As he suggests, the opportunities that come out of these discussions are based on being able to bring something to the table on a business, not a transactional, level:

The normal process in selling is that you have something to sell and you go to the customer and try to convince him to buy it. But where we have the trust, we find the customer coming to us and saying, "Hey, we have a need that you folks don't fill today. Would you be interested in filling it?" That wouldn't happen without this kind of relationship, because they would just go see who does this kind of work and get it. They'll see they have a need, and before they go out and look for other people to supply it, they will come to us and say, "Interested?" It's because in these relationships we know very well what they need, what the tradeoffs are, what the priorities are, how they think, even where they are going, and, overall, what they are doing. This is very important.

The competitive advantage of expanding the discussion between supplier and customer hasn't been lost on customers. Baxter International has, as a customer, taken this to its full potential. Jean Brock, their Program Manager for Value Managed Partnerships, explained to us, "Once there's mutual trust, we will share all sorts of information with a supplier. We encourage a lot of feedback. We hold supplier meeting dates where suppliers are there to brainstorm ideas and tell us what they see us doing wrong or what they need to see improved. We're looking at the total supply chain when we work with them. We get them together in groups. And not just with partners; we even bring in other large suppliers of Baxter." To become part of a "total supply chain" conversation, though, you've got to have something to say.

Becoming part of the broader mosaic of a customer's business through information sharing is at the core of effective information sharing. But there's another element to it. Information sharing cannot be solely about today's problems or needs. It requires a different time scale.

INFORMATION SHARING PRINCIPLE #3: TOMORROW, NOT TODAY.   In some of our partnering programs we bring people together across organizations for an intensive day of collaboration, problem solving, and impact creation. When clients are willing, we usually include some element—perhaps an hour or so—of experimental design that pushes toward the cutting edge, with somewhat less predictable results than tested tools and frameworks. Last year we designed a program for people starting out in partnering, one that included a new activity that we thought would be a "throwaway." The concept was simple. It asked pairs of partners to put aside business as it existed in the present and to think through market direction, as well as their capabilities and needs, as they saw them two years downstream. It then took them through a few structured exercises in which they, as partners, found areas where they could have impact together that addressed not today's problems but future challenges.

That "throwaway" hour turned out to be a powerful experience for partners. And it wasn't because of the activity itself. It was because of the partners. The activity opened up floodgates of discussion about the future, where the partners were going and how they could get there together. A few pairs walked away with entirely new game plans based on what they'd talked about. We learned something important in that program about how organizations can get the most impact out of information sharing. Solving today's problems is useful and necessary, and it's the basis of a sound business relationship. But the heaviest hit comes from bringing the *future* into the discussion, proactively addressing future potential and possibilities through information sharing.

This shift in focus toward the future hasn't been neglected by top-flight supplier organizations. Bailey Controls brings it into the center of their information sharing with customers. "In a [partnering] relationship," Gabe Rosica told us, "we give customers future glimpses into the window of where we're going. We talk to them about new technology, we talk to them about development projects, and we talk to them about planning efforts for those projects." Oftentimes, shifting the conversation into the future provides competitive advantage in and of itself. Patrick Hore, Market Research Manager of McGregor Cory, a U.K.-based contract distribution specialist, noted that:

> We are now quite enthusiastic to share with our customers our longer-term plans, and they with us. We're talking about the longer term—strategic developments; we've moved away from talking history to talking future. Maybe 12 months, maybe two years down the road. It lets us focus on what we need to do today to prepare for the future. And it gives us a clear competitive advantage within the customer base. A North American company comes to mind where we defined with them what they need into the future. As a result of this we won business from them that normally would have gone out for competitive tender.

McGregor Cory has had tremendous success building partnerships based on a forward-looking exchange of information with their customers. This forward-looking perspective on information sharing is a success factor of customer intimacy that cannot be ignored or put on the back burner. It is a source of value. You have to know where the customer is going over time in order to make the highest possible contribution. The customer has to know where you are going to get the most out of what you can offer. Supplier and customer have to find common ground not just for today, but for the future. Perhaps this is why our throwaway activity wasn't a throwaway. Just as information sharing involves a shift in perspective from the sales transaction to a wider business discussion, so too must it evolve from a focus on today's immediate needs to a broader perspective on future needs and opportunities.

Whether you do or don't achieve the competitive advantage of partnering probably will have more to do with information sharing, in terms both of access to information and the value of what you're providing and getting, than anything else. But there's a dark side to information sharing. A single point of contact between organizations, even one that includes a tag-along technical expert, cannot possibly handle the volume and types of information involved in partnering. In every instance of successful partnering we've seen, the partnering organizations have moved beyond the single-point-of-contact approach and built highly effective partnering teams.

BUILDING STRONG PARTNERING TEAMS

When information starts to flow more freely between organizations, more business gets conducted, more needs come to the surface, and more opportunities get put on the table for exploration and action. Everyone benefits from the upward growth spiral that comes about through information sharing and cooperation. That is, everyone benefits if the partnership can handle the flow of information and manage the volume of potential business. If not, opportunities get missed, needs go unsatisfied, expectations go unmet, and the partnership falls apart—as so many of them do.

The opportunities and information sharing that take place in partnering have swamped salespeople, putting enormous pressure on them to keep everything flowing. *Flowing* is the right word, because fundamentally it is a plumbing problem. We call it "the clogged pipe effect" of partnering. If you have a plumbing system that was designed to handle a few single-family homes, and you put up a new high-rise building, the system isn't going to work. You're going to get clogged pipes— or maybe worse; we'll leave the imagery to someone else. Trying to get the volume through a system never designed to handle it is a losing battle. You need wider pipes, and more of them.

Salespeople who are having success at partnering are focusing on their piece of the action and bringing in complementary resources to fill the rest of the gaps. Partnering requires a team of resources. But here we aren't talking about the familiar idea of team selling. Yet again, a shift in perspective is required to make the transition from selling to partnering. Team selling traditionally has been focused on a narrow set of questions:

- How do I put together a team to convince the customer?
- Should I bring in a sales engineer?
- How do I get the tech rep not to embarrass us?
- Are we doing enough account planning?

These questions are, appropriately for selling, focused on the sale. And that's why they're the wrong questions for partnering. In partnering the issue is getting outside the sale into a broader relationship. It requires fundamentally different thinking about putting together the team.

PUTTING TOGETHER A RESOURCE TEAM.   "For our partnering relationships," Bill Delmont, head of UPS's sales force, told us, "we bring a team that has all the resources. No matter what the opportunity is, we've got someone there who can deal with it." UPS, fighting back hard against very tough competitors in the shipping business, has had to move to the cutting edge in building durable relationships with customers. They've created a Resource Team, an interdisciplinary group that represents every function within UPS, which is brought out to cover the full range of expertise in partnering relationships. That's the high end of bringing resources to the customer; although not within the scope of most salespeople's authority, the principle is an excellent one. Salespeople represent organizations with tremendous acquired industry, market, and product expertise. They need to get this expertise to the customer in order to bring value to the relationship. The question in partnering is not "What does the team look like that can help us make the sale?" The central question in partnering is:

> Who needs to be involved so we can bring all the expertise we've got
> that the customer could potentially use as a resource?

UPS is one of a large number of organizations who've figured out that bringing a full complement of resources, based on the potential of the partnership, is the critical team success factor. McGregor Cory has, for example, built a complete sales model around "mapping" people within their own organization, on a one-for-one basis, to all of the people within a partner's organization who play a role in the relationship. As Martin Williams, their Director of Marketing and Customer Services, explained to us:

> We put together a group of individuals who have direct contact with the client organization. They're named in the document we create with the customer that establishes the relationship. These people include facilities managers, operations managers, and so forth. They're not just handling problems. When they're with the customer, just in doing their job they're selling the partnership.

Like McGregor Cory, many sales forces have begun to face up to the limitations of the lone-wolf selling model. Georgia-Pacific's Pike Hamlin commented to us on their relationship with Sweetheart Cups that:

> We have a single point-of-contact concept, one guy who they can call when they need something, so when there is a problem or an issue or something needs to be changed, this is the guy that makes that happen. But we've also got our manufacturing people at each mill meeting with Sweetheart's manufacturing people routinely. And finance people. All the way up and down the line; these parties communicate daily to weekly. The manufacturing group just met this week to talk about quality specifications. We have group meetings with people from both sides on logistics, orders, invoicing, inventory management, etc.

If the basic principle of teamwork in partnering is to bring resources directly to the customer, resources who can address the full panorama of today's issues and tomorrow's opportunities, then what exactly is the role of the salesperson? The conventional wisdom is that the salesperson becomes a coordinator, or administrator, or perhaps, more eloquently stated, the conductor of the orchestra. This is undoubtedly why most salespeople have a good bit of difficulty with the resource-team idea. They don't want to conduct the orchestra; they have neither the training for it nor the interest in doing it.

But we'd suggest that orchestra conducting isn't the right metaphor to begin with. Ron Stortz of Roadway Express suggested a more subtle analogy that probably gets closer to the truth. The salesperson in partnering relationships, he noted, is probably more like a tuba player; he or she has a specialized role. That role is to understand the customer and tend to opportunities, both existing and potential. If your sales-force model involves providing coordination of the overall relationship, then part of your time will go to administration and management. But the primary role of the salesperson, after bringing in resources, is not to manage them but to open up new opportunities where they can add value.

BRINGING IN THE CUSTOMER.   Early in our partnering research effort, we got in touch with a number of leading sales forces to find out how they were organizing their partnering teams. Typically they'd talk to us for a while, but then make a point we heard over and over. "You really need to get together with the customer," one salesperson told us of her part-nering relationship. "We're a part of it. But it's incomplete, if not down-right silly, to talk only to us. The customer's as much a part of our team as we are." That turned out to be true everywhere we looked, in terms not just of formal organization but also of outlook. The vast majority of our research ended up involving triangular meetings of Huthwaite re-searchers, sellers, and customers. And we came to an important realiza-tion. In traditional selling, the "team" comes from the selling organiza-tion. In partnering, the team comes from both organizations.

The distinction is an important one, and particularly crucial for those who are building partnering relationships with customers. There are real risks in bringing a selling perspective to a partnering relation-ship. One risk is finding a "decision maker" or other lone individual who is able to make it happen. This may be a great strategy for selling. But it's a terrible strategy for partnering. There's an issue of who, ex-actly, the "decision maker" *is* in an ongoing, evolving business relation-ship. But there's a deeper issue that represents real risk in partnering. Ed Ossie of Texas Instruments summed it up nicely, noting that "the biggest barrier to partnering is attrition and reorganization of clients. If they change, you're starting from scratch. It moves all shreds of inti-macy." In a selling relationship, the risk associated with a single buyer leaving is lost sales. In a partnership, overreliance on one person who leaves, or loses interest, or becomes an adversary, can cost you the en-tire relationship and all the investment that went into it.

Another key risk, one that is largely absent in selling, is resentment of the relationship within the customer's organization. Chris LaBonte of G&F Industries, commenting on what happens in a tight partner-ship such as JIT II, noted that:

Middle management in any organization is going to find the concept threatening. They're going to say, "Well, if they use this supplier for all of this business, they're not going to need me. So I'm going to go out and create alliances with other suppliers, and I'm going to drive it." It's human nature to say that "all the eggs shouldn't be in one basket, and I'm going to make sure they're not."

Chris's point is reflected in many of the partnerships we've studied. Where's the incentive for people within the customer's organization to buy in to a partnering relationship? There's more reason to be resentful than cooperative—unless they're part of the team itself.

Partnering requires a different view of customer involvement than salespeople traditionally have had. In selling, the best strategy is one of depth: Find a customer who can really make it happen, and work that relationship through to a successful sale. In partnering, the risks of overreliance on one or a few customers, or perhaps a buying committee, are severe. As a result, customer involvement in partnering isn't about depth. It's about breadth. Those potentially resentful middle managers need to be co-opted onto the partnering team. Customer participation should be as broad and involved as possible.

Partnering organizations—both suppliers and customers—are well aware of this need. With Okonite and PSE&G's partnership, for example, the two organizations are rotating meetings between supplier and customer site and, at each meeting, bringing more and more people into the relationship. Kenneth Doyle of PSE&G noted that

> The trust has got to be there with all the people in both organizations. If it isn't, one instance of a problem and you're out of there. One thing you need is top management commitment. But that's not all of it. Some of our people fear that Okonite will go out into the field on its own. Some people within Okonite didn't get what we were doing. So we're having monthly meetings, and we're alternating sites between Okonite and us. At each meeting we're bringing more and more people in, from both organizations. There's more buy-in from both organizations now. These meetings are helping us get better communication and more commitment.

As a partnering strategy, *breadth* is critical to managing the risks customers naturally feel as they become more dependent on and involved with a particular supplier. In partnering, the question is not about specific individuals. The question is:

Where are the customers who can bring value to this relationship, as well as customers who represent potential risk or difficulty—and how can I get all of them onto the team?

It is only when a team of people from both organizations is working together—frequently, informally, and inclusively—that partnering can take hold between supplier and customer.

SOME INTIMATE CONCLUSIONS ON CUSTOMER INTIMACY

Customer intimacy is a qualitative leap, a shift in perspective, from effective selling. Typically, selling is about finding the right person to talk to, at the right time, about the competitive advantages of a product. In partnering, the customer relationship *is* the competitive advantage. With products looking more and more the same, intimate customer relationships and the impact they enable are becoming increasingly important sources of competitive advantage, of real differentiation. For those who have been able to make the shift to intimacy, customer relationships are providing durability over time. Top sales organizations are forging relationships with customers that have sustainability outside of a particular sale or transaction. We've provided a peek into the world of customer intimacy, but in reality it's an art, and like any artistic endeavor cannot be capsulized in one chapter of one book. We'd make a couple of final suggestions, though.

First, all the evidence suggests that customer intimacy works best when it is being tracked and measured. It's a difficult concept to bring alive without hard-and-fast measures. Some partnerships have gone so far as to perform in-depth employee surveys on the partnership itself, along dimensions similar to those we've described in this chapter: communication, trust, etc. Surrounding intimacy with hard metrics is becoming common and necessary. In fact, it can help partners to isolate the drivers behind the success or the difficulty of their partnering relationship. On the other hand, intimacy can't be driven solely by metrics and documents. As we've suggested, it is driven largely by a shift in perspective on the part of suppliers and, often, sales organizations. That shift in perspective is crucial to a supplier's ability to partner with customers. We would suggest a brief "time-out" to identify where you truly stand on all of the dimensions of customer intimacy. In total we've identified six basic differences between selling and part-

SELLING		PARTNERING
Honest	→	Bias-free
Getting information	→	*Sharing* information
Transaction/sale based	→	Business based
Focused on today's problems	→	Future/potential oriented
"Lone Wolf" selling	→	Building a resource team
Depth of customer relationship	→	*Breadth* of customer relationship

Figure 4-2   *The dimensions of intimacy.*

nering in this chapter, and it's worth a moment to consider which ones are already part of your sales "ethic" and which could be moved further in a partnering direction. (See Fig. 4-2.)

Finally, we recommend not trying to convert a relationship from a traditional seller-buyer focus to one of customer intimacy all at once. It won't work. There's too much to do, and it needs to happen over time. For example, you can't decide to build trust tomorrow morning as part of a new strategy; nor can you jump from a sale-based perspective to a global vision of two organizations' combined capabilities in one meeting. It's not a gimmick you can throw at a customer; there's no point in trying to get it in place all at once. Rather, our suggestion is to pick one area where you can demonstrate increased value in the relationship, and run with it. This may involve bringing new market or industry information to the table that can really make a difference, even though it may not be particularly related to your present sales objectives. It may mean bringing new resources into the account who will add value to the customer and give them more insight into what they're trying to accomplish. Or it may be as simple as thinking through what a truly unbiased observer would recommend to the customer, and bringing this perspective into the account. Whatever it is, we would suggest that you start with one area of difference and build from there.

VISION: THE GUIDANCE SYSTEM FOR PARTNERING

NEC Business Communication Systems (East), selling "a vision of what a hospital can be," has partnered with a medical center outside Pennsylvania to bring medical care into the Information Age. Through the MedHelp system, hospital staff members get instant access to patient information on-line. All patients are assigned a single phone number that follows them around even when they switch rooms. Doctors have immediate access to an integrated database of complete information for each of their patients, at bedside. These are a few small pieces of NEC's and their customer's vision of how systems and telecommunications can bring patient-focused care to the next level.

In another industry, Foxboro, a manufacturer of process-control instruments, has created an entirely paperless facility, the Intelligent Automation Plant. The most studied manufacturing facility in the United States, it has top suppliers with open purchase orders who account for 80 percent of the business. With their suppliers, they've been able to virtually eliminate overhead and to put all investment into value-added activities.

These partnerships, and hundreds like them, didn't just happen. In successful partnering there is something more going on than simply adding value and developing strong relationships. There is something that drives the partners toward maximum impact and ensures that they achieve that impact. That thing is *vision*, a strong, shared sense of what the partnership can accomplish. It is the cornerstone, and launching point, of successful partnering efforts. "Shared vision," suggests

Manual Diaz, Hewlett-Packard's Vice President of Worldwide Sales and Marketing, "is, fundamentally, the start of any successful partnership."

Vision has gotten some bad press in recent years, for good reason. In too many organizations it has become a catch-all phrase for dreaming big dreams. That is not what vision is about in partnering. In successful partnerships, vision exists as a tangible guidance mechanism, one that provides direction to both parties and helps them accomplish large goals. When partnerships have shared vision, they tend to overcome obstacles and achieve results. When they lack vision, they tend to drift around or, sometimes, fall apart. David Montanaro of NEC explains:

> It is not only a question of agreeing that you're both on a train that's heading north. In real life it's much more like following a badly marked trail—and you're often traveling in the dark so you can't easily see where you are, let alone where your partner might be. So it's easy for one of you to be heading a bit to the west while the other veers off to the east. After a time, you're too far apart to communicate, and the whole effort starts to fall apart. I see vision not just as a big-picture agreement that sets the direction. It's also got to be a map that guides you forward and tells you if you are really still together.

In the end, vision is important because it provides an answer to the question "Why partner?" By articulating the potential value, vision provides direction to a partnership as well as justification for the expenses and risks involved in partnering. The "Why partner?" question must have an answer. There has to be something of real value that the partners are striving toward.

How do you get vision into a partnering relationship? Sometimes, through good timing or fortuitous circumstances, suppliers and customers just have a strong and compelling vision of how they can work together differently. G&F Industries and Bose, who we encountered in the last chapter, shared a compelling vision in the late 1980s of how a supplier and a customer could eliminate costs and increase overall value by empowering the supplier within the customer's operating systems. That simple vision led to the highly successful JIT II program, a partnering approach that has since been replicated at over 150 other organizations. And sometimes an organization has a truly visionary leader, one who can just reinvent a marketplace on the basis of sheer brain power. Steve Jobs of Apple in the 1970s, and Andy Grove of Intel today, are visionary leaders who need no help to bring visions of change to their customers.

But the rest of us don't experience lucky circumstances all that often, and even visionary companies don't have too many visionary leaders. It's only realistic to acknowledge that *suppliers* who are trying to develop partnering relationships need a different and better answer than "be more creative." They need a way to bring vision to their partnering efforts, one that doesn't ask them to emulate the creativity of the handful of Andy Groves out there. They need a simple structure for articulating a vision of partnership to their customers, and perhaps more importantly, for making sure that the vision becomes shared. Our research suggests that while suppliers differ tremendously in terms of how they create vision with their partners, they often follow a similar track, one that ensures both that there *is* a vision, and that it becomes a *shared* one. That track is summarized in Fig. 5-1.

1. *Assess partnering potential.*   Successful partnering organizations tend to think long and hard about whether there is sufficient partnering potential before they work on a vision or, indeed, even propose partnership at all. This is an important topic, so we'll be devoting the next chapter to the issues involved in picking the right partners. In this chapter we will focus mainly on the other three stages.

2. *Develop the partnering proposition.*   Most successful partnering suppliers recognize that there is great danger in fabricating a one-sided vision to get a partnership under way. A vision that is presented by one party never becomes shared, and it lacks the ownership and commitment necessary to make it successful. As a result, successful partnering organizations tend to avoid "vision" as the starting point; rather, they get started by articulating a simple, attractive business case from which both parties can work to develop, later on, a truly shared vision.

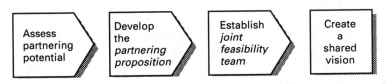

Figure 5-1   *Creating the vision.*

We call this business case the *partnering proposition,* and it's a critical part of the up-front work of building a partnership.

3. *Establish a joint feasibility team.* As an understanding of the potential value evolves out of the initial conversations around the proposition, successful organizations focus on getting together in a supplier-customer team to assess the feasibility of partnership. *They do this before the shared vision is complete.* The joint team plays a critical role in developing ownership for the partnering relationship within both organizations. We'll take a look at who needs to be on the team and why.

4. *Create the shared vision.* Once potential partners have decided that the idea of partnership is desirable, then between them they must create a shared vision that not only sets goals and objectives for the partnership, but also acts as a guidance system to steer the collaboration toward its goals.

ASSESSING THE PARTNERING POTENTIAL

Partnering, as we've seen, is a powerful and durable way for organizations to work together. Anyone who has experienced successful partnering first hand is likely to be enthusiastic about the dramatic changes in business impact and competitiveness that partnering makes possible. But this enthusiasm can be misguided if it becomes indiscriminate. Partnering isn't for everyone. It makes heavy resource demands on both organizations; it creates expectations which, if unfulfilled, can hurt future relationships. By entering into a partnership you may sometimes be cutting yourself off from attractive opportunities with your partner's competitors—particularly if partnering gives you access to proprietary data that your partner may be unwilling to share except in an exclusive relationship.

Those who have worked for some time in a partnering environment warn that it's dangerous to rush into partnering. "We don't go in to a customer and talk about partnering," says Layton Barnard of ENTEX. "The customer has to be ready to bring it up. Conditions have to be right." But what are the right conditions? What should you look for to tell you whether there's likely to be a good fit between yourself and a potential partner? How do you avoid getting in to the wrong relationship?

This is a crucial set of questions. We will return to it in the next chapter. For now, let's sound the warning that partnerships have a high casualty rate. Some estimates suggest that well over half of them fail within a year. When that happens, unsuccessful partners end up wishing they had spent more time thinking about whether conditions were right and less time rushing ahead into a partnership. It's worth stating here that without the right conditions for partnering, no amount or quality of vision is going to make up the difference. You need a good partnering situation to partner.

DEVELOPING A PARTNERING PROPOSITION

Assuming that a partnering relationship has high impact potential—that it could, for example, dramatically reduce duplication and waste, or allow a new and creative combining of partners' core strengths—how is this potential impact turned into a convincing vision? It's right here that we've seen many suppliers make serious mistakes. Fired up with enthusiasm for their own vision, suppliers rush to talk with their prospective partners about the great new opportunities that partnering could provide. Why is this a mistake? Gabe Rosica, Chief Operating Officer of Bailey Controls, provided this insight:

> It's like going out on your first date and spending the whole evening talking about marriage. You'll scare him or her off because it's just a date—it's not appropriate. But sometimes salespeople will do just that—they'll talk partnership on a first date—and sometimes they will actually make a lot of headway. But if they do, then usually there's something wrong. If you talk marriage on a first date and the person you're with responds well and wants to engage in discussion, then they are probably as crazy as you are.

Usually it's better, as Gabe suggests, not to go to a customer with a fully developed concept of partnership. Our research suggests that most successful partnering suppliers don't present their customers with grandiose ideas for collaboration; indeed, they studiously avoid presenting a unilateral vision of partnership. Effective visions are never unilateral; for partnership to work, both parties need to commit to following a shared road map. *A unilateral vision puts the author of the vision in a sales role rather than in the role of a partner.* But if the task is to engage in collaborative development rather than in selling, where do you start? How do you take an initial step in helping a potential partner to collaborate in developing an enticing vision, one that will generate excitement—and make partnering a reality?

Before you can begin to develop a shared vision, someone has to put a first stake in the ground. Somebody has to make a first attempt to answer the all-important question "Why partner?" As Hemang Davé, a Vice President at Lotus Development Corporation, put it:

> There has to be a value proposition for the customer, one that shows substantial impact on both sides. Why should two organizations change the way they do business with no compelling reason?

We call this initial articulation the *partnering proposition.* The partnering proposition gets partnership on the table for discussion by providing a first-cut view of what partnering could achieve for the two organizations. The proposition isn't a shared vision. It's a simple statement of what partnering could potentially bring to both organizations that can serve as a platform for collaborative discussion. Suppliers who've been most effective at developing partnerships have become very skilled at articulating a proposition for partnering to their customers, one that has three basic characteristics:

1. It is expressed in terms that are *brief, compelling,* and *believable.*
2. It specifies the *impact* that each party will gain as a result of partnering.
3. It specifies the *major changes* that each party must make in order to achieve that impact.

The partnering proposition, of itself, is less important than the thought process that organizations normally go through to create it. The struggle to distill partnering ideas down into simple and clear statements clarifies and sharpens thinking. It provides a model in the minds of its creators of what the partnership means. It may, indeed, remain a model that exists only in the heads of its creators and never gets written down. On the other hand, sometimes a partnering proposition becomes a prototype business case for partnering. Either way, the partnering proposition gets partnering on the table for discussion by putting an initial stake in the ground.

Brief, Compelling, and Believable

Organizations who are newer to partnering tend to develop elaborate, complicated cases for partnering, in an effort to convey every contingency and demonstrate awareness of every potential issue. Conversely, the propositions that *successful* suppliers develop for their potential partners rarely consist of more than a few sentences. Successful partnering suppliers recognize that the purpose of the proposition is to establish an initial business case for partnering that can be used to communicate both to the partner as well as internally. More importantly, they know that every element of complexity they work through on their own puts them at risk of working through details that need to be examined and evaluated *jointly* with the partner. So their initial propositions are simple and brief.

Even more importantly, good partnering propositions must convey a powerful message. Marketing gurus like Bud Hyler of Logical Marketing suggest that a powerful message must be both *compelling* and *believable*. The two don't often go together. A compelling partnering proposition might, for example, include a statement such as "Partner with us and we'll double your profitability with little effort." It's certainly compelling, but it's not likely to be believed. On the other hand, consider a statement like "If you're prepared to put in the enormous time and effort required to set up a partnership with us, there's a possibility that it will bring modest but worthwhile results." This is a very believable message, but it's hardly compelling. Compelling and believable pull against each other.

Partnering propositions need to maintain a careful balance between being compelling and being believable. A compelling proposition that isn't believable has no credibility. It will sound unrealistic. This is what typically happens when one side is overcome with excitement and missionary enthusiasm. Caught up in the compelling picture of their own vision, they don't realize how much believability they have sacrificed. As a result, their vision creates skepticism and resistance in their potential partner.

In contrast, the careful, credible, and entirely believable approach to the message can be equally ineffective if it isn't compelling enough.

We knew an engineering firm that wanted to partner with a leading high-technology company. They had set up initial discussions with some movers and shakers, at which they presented their partnership proposal. The following day we ran into one of the high-tech participants and asked him whether his company intended to go ahead. "I don't think so," he confided. "They were nice guys—and real honest about their limitations. But there wasn't any excitement in it. It sounded like a lot of effort that wouldn't yield much in the way of moving us forward as an enterprise." In other words, the partnering proposition was believable but not compelling.

Try crafting a simple proposition for a prospective partnership. You might create something like this:

> A partnership would change our role from being a component vendor to becoming the drive-train designers for Frostco's proposed new smowmobile. This would let Frostco bring the snowmobile to market several months earlier, maybe even in time for next season. It would also free up some of their internal design resources and could be done within Frostco's present budgets. We would create a drive train that would be easier for us to manufacture, which would save on our tooling costs. We would have to allocate a design team to the project, and we would expect Frostco to bear a part of that cost. However, the savings in time and resources for both of us should give us both a better product at a reduced overall cost.

You'll soon see how difficult it is to be both compelling and believable—particularly as you are unlikely at this early stage to have all the information you need to quantify the benefits. So you will be forced to make broad assertions like "reduced overall cost," "saving in time" and "improved quality." It would of course be more compelling if you could say, "at a 23 percent reduction in cost, with an 11-week gain in the time to market, and a 45 percent lower reject rate during the first three months." But the purpose of the partnering proposition is not to provide a comprehensive vision. It doesn't provide the answers; its goal is to act as a catalyst to raise important questions. It provides a stimulus for both parties to ask, "Exactly what *could* we save here?" "Would this *really* get the product to market in time for next season?" A good partnering proposition doesn't persuade people to partner, it persuades them to look more closely at whether partnering would be worthwhile.

Why is it so important to have a simple, compelling, and believable proposition? It's not as if you were intending to partner with a customer you've never met. You *know* these people. So why can't you just sit down with them and talk it out? The answer is that, much more than in a transactional sale, partnering discussions are likely to involve a range of people from both sides, many of whom you may never have met. Dennis Courtney, CIO of Dunlop Tire Corporation, describes a typical example from the early stages of their partnership with Oracle:

> We put together a 22-person cross-functional team. Oracle had to talk to our manufacturing people, warehouse people, sales and marketing people, as well as people in finance and IS. They had to satisfy everyone, to convince them that Oracle was the right partner.

In partnering relationships, a lot of people from the customer side get involved and need to see why the partnership is necessary. In addition, it's often difficult to sell partnership internally within supplier organizations. Suppliers usually see great risk in making the open-ended commitments and taking on the risks of partnership. While people from within sales and marketing may see the point, others within the supplier organization may not. We got a good taste of this in talking to an account manager at a specialty lubricant company. As he described it:

> I saw real potential to get into a new kind of relationship with [the customer]. They were high-temperature specialists and they had done very interesting R&D that extended our own. From initial discussions it seemed like there was scope for working together on some new high-temperature formulations. I saw this as being very advantageous to both parties. In the short term some of their experience would be useful, and in the long term there were a number of joint development and marketing opportunities that could be good for both of us.
>
> So I went to see my VP and I sort of sold him the idea. But then things began to unravel. When he talked it over with the labs, they had an agenda of their own and that somehow got tacked on to the basic idea. Then one of the product managers got in on the act and introduced more complications. The thing never got off the ground; it sank under its own complexity. A lesson I've learned is that you have to put a lot of effort into your internal selling, and a big piece of that effort is fighting to keep it simple.

Keeping it simple, internally, is one of the important functions of a partnering proposition. Without clear, compelling, and believable ideas—ideas that internal people can buy into—the partnering concept can fall apart before it ever gets to the customer for consideration. A strong partnering proposition, one that people can understand and that is enticing but realistic, is a necessary starting point on the road to vision.

DESCRIBING THE IMPACT

Successful partnering suppliers "make the case" for partnering by describing the potential impact that the parties can expect to gain from partnership. This might seem a little like the traditional concept of "benefits" that has been part of the language of selling since the 1920s. It isn't, and the difference is an important one. In selling, the "proposition" is about the *benefits to the customer*—how the customer gains from a product or how it meets needs that the customer has identified. The benefits used in transactional selling are all one-way. They are exclusively concerned with what the customer can gain. Partnering, as we suggested in the last chapter, involves a different perspective. The proposition is a two-way statement of potential; it's about the impact for *both* parties through collaboration.

This is much more than a play on words. Partnering vision isn't primarily about the customer; it isn't primarily about the supplier. It's about the partnership in which both organizations will invest and from which both hope to gain. A typical one-way message like "As a result of partnering with us, you will be able to reduce your inventory, contain your future costs, and have access to new developments in advance of the general market" is one-sided and tells only part of the story. It becomes a more complete, a more realistic, and a more candid proposition if it adds "And as a result of partnering with you, we will be able to schedule production more economically, reduce our own inventory costs, and have a competitive advantage from developing a better understanding of your business." As David Montanaro of NEC explains:

> A big difference between selling and partnering is that selling is only about what's in it for the customer. In a sale, you have to show things like the savings the customer will make or the improvements in efficiency and responsiveness of the customer's systems. There's not a lot about what's in it for the seller. That's assumed, but it's never dis-

cussed. You're there because you want the sale—period. No more has to be said. But in a good partnership, right from the very first exploratory contacts, both sides should be interested in what's in it for each other. It's a sign that you're in serious partnering discussions when it's just as legitimate to talk about the benefits *you* want as about benefits for the customer.

The partnering proposition must be about the potential impact for the partnership—and that means *both* parties. This can be an uncomfortable concept for people with a sales background. Years of training in one-way benefit communication have left many salespeople feeling very comfortable discussing benefits for the customer but uncertain when it comes to talking about the reciprocal benefits from partnering. In the partnering proposition, benefits for both parties must have equal weight. The partnering proposition, after all, is not about the customer or supplier; it's about the partnership.

CHANGES EACH PARTY MUST MAKE

The impact that each party stands to gain from partnering is an important part of the partnering proposition. The other part, equally important but often neglected, is an outline of what each party must pay, in terms of costs and changes, to obtain the benefits of partnering. Until the parties have worked closely together to explore feasibility, however, neither will have a clear understanding of what changes really need to be made or of the costs that those changes will entail.

This raises the question "Why talk about changes and costs at all—why not just focus on impact and benefits?" The answer is that the partnering proposition is the core of a business case for partnering—and no business case can just look at benefits without considering costs. There's another, more subtle reason, though. Partnering rests on the hypothesis that through working together differently the parties can make productivity gains. Frequently, the most immediately achievable of these gains are reductions on the cost side of the cost-benefit equation. As we've seen, a natural starting point for creating impact is through cost saving by reducing duplication and waste. By specifying the costs of the changes required to make the partnership work, the partnering proposition can present a realistic and attractive business case.

ONE PRESENTATION FITS ALL

Even if the parties are not yet ready to think as a partnership, they should be ready to take an important first step in the candid information sharing that characterizes partnering. The best test we've seen that a partnering proposition meets this condition is that it could be presented, unedited and unchanged, to people from either organization. This is an excellent way to check whether or not a partnering proposition has a genuinely bilateral message. As Rick Keene, Anixter's Executive Vice President for North America, put it:

> When you talk about partnering, you talk about the extended enterprise. You don't do *anything* based solely on your own internal needs. Suppose you put together a set of, say, 50 overheads to articulate the strategy to your Marketing Department. The same presentation should work for your client, for your supplier, for your credit department, or for sales. That's because you have a strategy articulated that's based on the market, not on internal needs. When all is said and done it must improve our supplier's position, reduce cost to market, enhance the knowledge base, or help the client's total cost to acquire and distribute goods. Anything internal that doesn't do one of these things is evil because the market isn't paying for it.

Most propositions end up, sooner or later, as a set of overhead slides that will be presented to senior executives within a supplier organization to lay out the business case for partnering. Think about a partnering situation you've got. Imagine that whatever internal presentation you have—whether it's a collection of slides or a verbal description—will, tomorrow, be shown to your intended partner. How much would you have to change? If you would need to reword points to make them more palatable, or exclude important data, then you've not produced a partnering proposition; you've produced a unilateral business case. If so, your initial thinking about the partnership may be off to a bad start. With successful partners, the business proposition—and the shared vision that eventually emerges out of it—is exactly the same for both organizations.

THE JOINT FEASIBILITY TEAM

If a partnering initiative comes from the supplier, it needs to contain something forceful enough to start the ball rolling and make the effort appear worthwhile. That's its function. A simple, compelling, and believable initial concept of how both parties stand to benefit from a partnership provides a means for starting the discussions. But make no mistake about it: A proposition created by one party is not a shared vision. In any good partnering proposition, the *content* is bilateral, because it involves the effect of partnering on each organization. But having "bilateral content" doesn't mean the vision is shared. In partnering propositions, however joint the message, only one side has developed it. It's important to recognize that a *shared* vision means that both parties have participated in its development. This is often one of the stumbling blocks for sales organizations that are new to partnering. As Luke Little, Director of the Americas Channels for Oracle, explains:

> One of the things that makes salespeople really effective in a transactional environment is an intense desire to be personally responsible for making things happen. They are lone hunter/gatherers. They think to themselves, "I'm going to make this happen all by myself. I'm completely in control and it's my neck that's on the line"—and they like that. As you get into long-term relationships, the strength of individual control becomes a weakness. You have to move toward a shared vision. If you can't do that, you can't play.

Partnering propositions, in being developed unilaterally, face three hurdles.

They lack important business information.   Partnering propositions never provide all the details. A proposition may legitimately talk about "substantial savings," "significant quality improvements," or "faster time to market." Because it's crafted by just one side, though, it's unlikely that the authors of the proposition will have enough information to quantify the full impact of partnering. Yet to make a realistic assessment of the business case for partnering, the parties need a much more tangible vision, such as "savings of not less than $3,500,000," or "a 6 percent reduction in defects," or "8 weeks sooner to market." Without this level of specificity, the vision may lay claim to an enticingly bigger pie but, as they say, it's just pie in the sky.

They lack a plan of action.   A proposition is about potential. Either party, working alone, can identify the broad potential, even if they lack the details required to turn it into a business case. But it takes both parties working together to agree on the actions they must jointly take to implement partnering and to make it a reality.

They are only propositions—and "your" propositions.   Until your partner buys into the vision and takes a stake in its ownership, there isn't the mutual commitment that will be needed for successful partnering. So "my proposition" needs to be transformed into "our vision."

To get over these hurdles and transform a one-sided proposition into a shared vision, most successful partners form a joint team—what we're calling a *joint feasibility team*—that can examine the business case and, as a result of working together, transform the proposition into something "owned" by both organizations. Rob Washburn, Hillenbrand's Vice President for Continuous Improvement, observes:

> You reach a point in partnership where you're out of the first stage, where there isn't a set of goals for the supplier, but instead there is a set of goals that are jointly developed and there is real joint responsibility for them. For example, we have a team that has about five UPS people on it and five Hillenbrand people on it, and they have the same goals. Literally, our Hillenbrand people have a goal about UPS revenue, and the UPS people have a goal on profit contribution for Hillenbrand, and they both have a goal on our customers' satisfaction.

At initial team meetings with a prospective partner, most successful suppliers do not try to sell a vision or even to sell the partnering proposition. Rather, they try to get the customer interested and excited enough to want to explore the feasibility of a partnership. But who is "the customer" in this case? It becomes critical to get the right players in the room for this initial evaluation of potential partnership.

JOINT FEASIBILITY TEAM ROLES

Who needs to be included on the joint team? For one thing, it helps for the team to have roughly equal numbers from each organization and a rough equivalence in terms of seniority and experience. From informal exploratory teams like UPS–Kodak to McGregor Cory's more formalized "zipper" approach, most exploratory teams find that ensuring that team members have counterparts with similar seniority is essential to keeping the discussions balanced and equal.

Even more important, the joint team should have certain roles represented on each side. These roles may be combined within one or two people from each organization, but they do need to be represented. The first of these roles is *hands-on expertise.* Assessing the realistic value that a partnership can achieve requires the participation of people who are close to the action and have a good understanding of what it will require to make the interface between the two organizations more productive. It's no use having a team consisting solely of big-picture visionaries if there's nobody who has an operational clue about what it will take to make the big picture happen. An effective joint team keeps a balance between high-level principles and practical implementation detail. Too often, teams consist only of high-level negotiators from each side. These teams have a poor record of success unless they quickly find a way to bring in hands-on support from those who must make it happen. Successful partnering is a mosaic painstakingly assembled from a thousand little pieces of action. Expertise and a willingness to sweat the details are essential factors for getting realistic assessment of partnering potential.

Another crucial role that needs to be present on each side is that of the *missionary*—someone who believes in the partnership and will go out to preach the faith to the corporate heathen. Unfortunately, you are unlikely to have much control over who will be on the team—at least on the customer side—so you can't always pick your missionaries in advance. But one of the purposes of the team is to make some zealous converts. By working together through the partnering possibilities and issues, most teams have little difficulty fostering their own missionaries. Speaking in more secular terms, John Pelligrino of Mead expresses much the same concept:

> As we worked together, it became clear that the partnership effort was able to produce results that were unattainable before. In retrospect, although members of the joint team grew very close and were highly enthusiastic about the partnership, we should have begun much earlier to "merchandise" this same perspective throughout our respective organizations. By not merchandising the positive changes, you limit the potential impact of the partnership. You can't just assume that the improvements will be automatically recognized by those who are not directly involved in the change process.

One of the telltale signs that a partnership has high impact potential is the willingness of people on both sides to carry the message enthusiastically through their respective corporations. Conversely, when team members are reluctant to act as missionaries it may be a sign that members recognize that the partnership lacks impact potential. There is cause for alarm if no missionaries emerge as partnership discussions progress. That's usually a danger sign of insufficient impact, and it may tell you that it's better for both parties to return to a more traditional relationship.

But perhaps the most important role for the team is to have *clout* on both sides. Partnerships face tough challenges within both organizations, and someone on the team, from each side, needs to be able to drive the effort through the myriad skeptics and challengers who typically appear once a relationship seems to be moving outside the norm. Although this is a good reason to involve senior management, it's less important to have senior management directly involved than to have general senior management buy-in and someone on the team, from each side, who can get access to senior management when they need it. Indeed, a lot of partnering teams don't have senior management representation at all. But with or without direct senior management participation, clout is crucial; we have yet to find a successful partnership that doesn't have someone on the team—from both sides—who is influential enough not to be questioned by their own organization at every turn in the road. As Andrew Mitchell, a Global Account Manager at Oracle, put it:

> To maintain the relationship and the trust level, the account management has to be senior enough to be heard and to be listened to. They have to have the clout to make sure they can control what goes on in the partnership. It's making sure that everybody understands within the organizations that we are in partnership and the partnership is based on trust, and we can't afford in any way or form to cause distrust.

Whatever other roles are or are not present on the team, having someone with internal clout—on both sides—is critical in the early stages of partnering.

Joint teams typically spend some time looking at the case for partnering and deciding whether a partnership makes good business sense. Sometimes the discussions are brief. But more often they're the beginning of an extended, important business relationship, and they take a long time. PSE&G's discussions with Okonite, a partnership we encountered in Chap. 2, for example, took many months to define. However long it takes, though, the team has one overriding purpose: to evaluate the business case for partnership and, if it's a good one, to develop a strong shared vision of what the partnering organizations can achieve together.

CREATING THE SHARED VISION

If you've developed a strong proposition for partnering, and you have a joint team with the customer that has decided that partnership would be desirable, you're ready to take the next step. You're ready to create a shared vision that will provide direction and guidance to the partnership. But what, exactly, is creating a shared vision all about? Can you apply some formula and emerge with compelling changes that will transform impact for the two organizations? Of course not. There is no simple formula. Vision requires thinking about possibilities that by definition don't yet exist. Perhaps that's why vision is so infrequently a component of business relationships. But you do need it to partner. So what do you do?

We would suggest that you don't need to have a sweeping vision of change to get started in a partnering relationship; the dramatic vision, if it ever comes, tends to emerge once partners are working together and have become more familiar with the possibilities. Successful partners usually get started with something they can get their arms around and make successful. The closest we've seen partnering organizations come to a "method" for doing this is a strategy we call the *one-company image*. The one-company image takes some thought and a little practice on the part of both partners, but in essence it's a simple and powerful idea. It is often possible to figure out where the highest impact is, and what the vision ought to be, by going through an exercise of imagining that you and your partner are no longer separate organizations. In other words, you have merged to form one company, and therefore you are free to make any changes in your working relationship that will improve the overall effectiveness of your "new venture." Frank Waterhouse, a Project Development Manager at Bechtel, uses this approach. As he explains:

If you put this partnering concept into the context where it's like starting a new company, you can really look at it and say "What are the benefits of all this" before you enter into an arrangement. You're going to spend a lot of your "overhead" [e.g., personnel costs] to develop this new "company." If you believe that your team is going to come up with innovative solutions that are going to reduce the amount of equipment or material in the project, and you think that this is really possible only through a partnering arrangement, then it might be cost-effective to partner.

John Pelligrino of Mead also brought in the idea of thinking as a single organization to help Mead's partnership with Pillsbury move forward:

Early on we tried a "one-company" exercise as a team. We asked, "What would we do differently if we were just one company?" Then we asked ourselves, "So what stops us?" It was a simple but very productive way to get a lot of ideas on the table—and it forced us to recognize some of the barriers we had to face.

When partners ask themselves what they would do differently if they were all one company—when they use the one-company image—they often come up with a list of opportunities that includes

- Elimination of duplication and waste, such as excess inventory or paperwork, that normally exist between two companies but that would never be tolerated within a single organization
- Greater sharing of information, coordination, and perhaps even opportunities to develop new products—all of which normally fall through the cracks between organizations but which would be addressed with high priority by a single organization

These changes constitute the value of partnering, and identifying them begins the process of laying out a vision of change. If you look at any of the partnerships we've described in this book—or any other partnerships, for that matter—you will find that at the core of the vision is a willingness to put aside organizational boundaries to tap into savings or new sources of productivity. As Pillsbury's Jon Christensen put it: "You must be in the mind-set that you and your partner are a bunch of people looking at a process, or a product, and the question is how you would jointly go after it if you were 'one company.' That joint mind-set is the price of admission to partnering."

What if you try an exercise like the one-company image and it results in a few good ideas but not a truly visionary notion of productivity through change? Do you push further? Our advice is no, you don't. Often it's better to have a small but workable vision than a grand scheme of change that can't be implemented. In any event, more important than defining a *sweeping* vision is defining an *achievable* vision. And there are several strategies for pushing vision along to achieve success.

THE QUICK WIN

Whether your vision is truly revolutionary or rather mundane—whether it's "Together, we can dominate this industry" or "Let's cut inventory by 3.2 percent"—it is important to combine the vision with a *quick win*. The quick win provides an immediate goal and a first successful milestone to show that the partnership is achieving results. James Adelson, Director of the Business Development Alliances Group at Lotus, explains:

> If, out of all the grand vision, you can throw down a couple of things that are really going to be a source of near-term reward, that is a way to energize a partnership. This means moving ahead toward specific steps and away from, or forward from, the general vision.

Getting a quick win is particularly important for partnerships that are emerging from troubled prior relations, as in the case of Pillsbury and their packaging supplier Mead. As Jon Christensen of Pillsbury described it:

> There were big problems in the old vendor relationship and we were on the edge of making significant capital investment to distance ourselves from Mead. So early success was important, because many of our people in Pillsbury were disillusioned and cynical about whether things would really be different. That's why it helped when Mead sent clear signals early on that things had really changed. They set up the technology fund and redesigned the process for acquiring spare parts. It was signals like these—the early wins—that made people believe that something different was finally happening.

Even when quick wins aren't possible, you can often accomplish much the same end by demonstrating the impact achieved in similar circumstances. Commenting on NEC's relationship with Little Company of Mary Hospitals and Health Care Centers, where NEC is looking for another high-impact success like the one we described at the beginning of this chapter, David Montanaro noted:

> We quickly had to make the vision real—people had to see it for themselves—so that means the team members had to go out and visit places where it was working. So the team—nursing, bioengineering, facilities people—went to visit one of our health-care customers where they have completely reengineered the hospital.
>
> When they got there the experience was so overwhelming that they will never forget it. It was like being in a resort hotel—no pages, no noises—and hard to believe this was a hospital. The nurses were cool, calm, and collected. There were terminals in the patients' rooms and no nursing stations. So team members started to think. "I don't know if we could ever do anything like this, but it would sure be nice to try. This partnership idea actually works." Then when they talked to the people at the hospital they were told, "To get here we went through hell. It was unbelievable, but today we wouldn't have it any other way. It took partnering and technology to get us here; it was tough to do, and much harder than we imagined, but we'd never go back."
>
> That way the team came away with a balanced picture of the up sides and the down sides. It's important that your test drive shows you both. That's why you test-drive the vision in the first place, to get a balanced view of what the partnership will really be like.

The quick win is a great way to move beyond the shared vision stage of a partnership. Or, as we've suggested, if a quick win isn't available you can sometimes get the same results by helping a partner to see what the results have looked like elsewhere. Either way, most successful partners get beyond shared vision and into demonstrable value very quickly.

COMBINING VISION WITH THE STEPS NEEDED TO ACHIEVE IT

Successful partners move quickly beyond the vision and into the steps required to achieve it. As Lance Dixon of Bose noted for us, it isn't enough to talk about the pot of gold; you also have to lay out the steps for getting across the rainbow. For those not familiar with the origin of Lance's image, legend has it that Irish leprechauns nefariously amassed gold, purloined from humans or rival leprechaun clans. This gold was primarily intended as ransom money, kidnapping being a time-honored Irish pastime. To prevent theft, the leprechauns buried their gold in earthenware crocks, each crock being located under a thorn bush at the end of the rainbow. All anyone had to do to locate a crock of gold was to cross to the end of the rainbow and dig it up. As the many hopeful seekers discovered, the end of the rainbow was an elusive spot and these legendary crocks of gold proved rather difficult to track down. The moral of the tale is that you can't become rich just from knowing that the gold is located in a crock at the end of the rainbow. The trick is crossing the rainbow to get to it.

Lance's image is a good one. Too many partnering teams spend their time talking only about the crock of gold. They discuss how many coins might be in it, how it might be sealed, whether it is glazed or unglazed. In other words, they focus solely on the goals of the partnership. But the reason why there are so few wealthy treasure hunters in Ireland is that none of those things matter if you can't cross the rainbow. The same is true of partnerships. As Dick McIlhattan, a Vice President at Bechtel, explains, it is not enough to have a piece of paper with a vision on it. He notes:

> In partnering you do have to spend a lot of initial time with the management of both organizations developing a vision for the relationship. But you need to move very quickly to demonstrated, quantifiable value. And you have to put a lot of work into the alliance itself; it does not happen by itself. With Eastman, a lot of management attention goes into developing the alliance and fostering the relationship. My whole effort here is to develop this alliance. It gets back to the issue that you can't say, "We have a piece of paper here that has a vision on it, so now we have an alliance."

It is important to define the vision of why the organizations are partnering, and the productivity that will come out of the partnership. As Dick McIlhattan suggests, though, partners need to move beyond that, and rather quickly. Once a joint team has a sense of the vision, it needs to lay out concrete action steps for crossing the rainbow.

SETTING TARGETS: THE GUIDED MISSILE

Though the rainbow and pot of gold are nice images, they break down when the joint team really gets to work, because teams rarely have enough information to lay out the total path across the rainbow. In a complex partnership there will be so many uncertainties and unknowns that the path can't be charted with any precision. We live in an age in which it has become almost impossible for corporate planners to lay out a definitive path for their own company, let alone lay out the joint destiny of two independently managed collaborators. A shared vision, however meticulously developed, can be outdated in a month by unexpected competitive action or by unanticipated changes in technology. The target that a shared vision is trying to hit is constantly moving.

Fortunately a different image comes to the rescue here, one that is specifically about what it takes to hit moving targets. When less effective groups get together to plan a collaboration, they often work like an old-fashioned artillery team whose job is to fire the cannon. First they locate the target. Then they sight their gun and fire it off, hoping to make a hit. Finally, they watch to see whether they have succeeded, knowing that hitting the target will get them medals. That doesn't work with the fast-moving targets of today's corporate world. Between the time it takes to sight the gun and to fire it, the target has shifted. If your vision is like a cannon, if you have a static view of where you're aiming, then your chances of hitting the target are low indeed.

A much more useful model for shared vision is to think of it as a guided missile. You begin by identifying your target: to extract the maximum productivity from the interface between your companies. Then you design a guidance system to tell you whether your vision is heading in the right direction, whether the target has moved and, if so, what midcourse corrections you need to make. In this way when you fire off the partnership missile, you may have only a rough idea of where the target will be, but you have the equivalent of a heat-seeking capability that will hunt down productivity opportunities as they emerge and lock on to them. If this sounds fanciful, consider the case of G & F Plastics, one of Bose's partners. Chris LaBonte of G & F Plastics has this description of how the "guided-missile" type of partnering vision affected him and his company:

> It wasn't altogether clear at first where this thing was going—not to me at least. But I began to think of myself as an in-plant resource who was there to seek out opportunity. And as we went along there was real synergy, because plastics were a prime commodity for Bose and there was a whole playground of opportunities. I operate by seek-

ing out ways to be part of the solution—to solve the problem, not tell them they have a problem. And that takes me into areas I hadn't ever expected. As a result, when you work as part of the team looking for opportunities and solutions, you don't play by the rules, you make the rules. You invent new ways to add value together. You see things in a different light.

For example, you see a program made out of ABS and you ask "Why?" And they say, "We were going to use it in the automotive industry, but we're not now." So you ask, "What do you need for deflection temperature?" and they tell you they need 200 degrees Fahrenheit. So you say, "Why don't you use a high-impact styrene, which has the same shrink ratio?" And they try it and you end up taking 10 or even 20 percent out of their program costs.

That's the way you seek out the opportunities, and that's how you stay in the partnering game. When you start you only have a rough idea of where it's all going to end. If you had told me on my first day here some of the things I'd find myself doing, then I don't think I'd have believed you for one moment. But, messy though it sounds, this way of thinking has reaped significant benefits for us. We've gone from $2 million to $20 million and it's become a way of life for us.

Chris LaBonte and others like him are partnering guided missiles in action, seeking the opportunity targets, locking on to them, and making moment-by-moment corrections to ensure that their actions stay on target. They prosper in a partnering environment because they have developed guidance systems that can hit moving targets while their competitors are still loading cannons and firing them off at targets that have vanished long before the shells reach their destination.

What's the lesson? The first and most important one is that the joint team must avoid the trap of designing and firing an outdated cannon. That's why it's a mistake for a partnering team to focus its vision exclusively on the goals and objectives of the partnership. The underlying assumption is that if you can define the goal or target closely enough, you can somehow tie it all down so it will still be there in the same spot by the time you've set up your cannon. That almost never works in partnering. To be successful, you *do* need to have a broad idea of goals. But you don't try to define the location of the target down to its last few inches. That's what your guidance system should do for you after the missile has been launched.

So what should a partnership guidance system look like? What are its essential components? Successful partnerships generally spend significant time up-front defining:

- *Expectations* about how the parties will work together
- *Measures* for assessing how well the partnership is earning its keep and encouraging continuous improvement

PARTNERSHIP EXPECTATIONS

A key guidance mechanism for partnership is establishing clear mutual expectations about how each party will act and what each should expect from the other. The British contract distribution specialist McGregor Cory has gone so far as to create a Partnership Document in which they set out mutual expectations with their partnered customers. This isn't a legal contract. In fact, the opening preamble specifically disclaims any legal intent:

> This document is not written nor entered into as a formal or legal agreement but is only a definite expression and record of the purpose and intention of the parties, to which they each honourably pledge themselves.

The document itself then goes on to state McGregor Cory's business policies and corporate goals. It lists the expectations that customers should have of McGregor Cory, such as "a willingness for open dialogue" and "a capacity to adapt to constant change." It sets out the partner's responsibilities, for example, "to recognize that they are a supplier to McGregor Cory within the customer chain and to be adaptable themselves where this can work to mutual advantage." In addition, the expectations document covers performance criteria and sets up agreed-upon communications channels.

Clarity of expectations, whether achieved through a written agreement or through continuing informal discussions, constitutes an important element of the guidance system. The clearer each party is about roles, responsibilities, and mutual expectations, the easier it will be for them to act quickly and consistently to steer the partnership toward constantly moving targets.

Sometimes, partnerships can miss this point by focusing not on expectations but on legal contracts. "You need to have contracts when you're talking about millions of dollars," notes NEC's David Montanaro, "but don't let the legal process define your partnership vision." In some organizations, and some partnerships, a legal contract is, simply, required. If you require a contract, so do a lot of other partnerships. But don't mistake a legal contract for the effective setting of expectations between partners. Hemang Davé of Lotus observes:

> You need a contract to record a set of agreements and a set of relationships, as a sort of checkpoint. But it isn't an end-all; it's just an intermediate step in the process. You need to focus on clear objectives, how to get a win-win, to meet each other's needs. Relationships go sour because in order to take into account every "what if," the contract ends up taking forever; a few "what if's" don't happen, and everyone becomes contract-centric, as if people don't know how to behave. So we have taken very much of a relationship-based orientation, as opposed to a contract-based orientation.

Successful partnering organizations spend ample time outside a contractual framework defining what sort of behaviors both partners should expect to see from each other—over time, as the partnership moves forward.

Partnership Measures

An essential element of any guidance system is its capability to measure deviation from the target and to take corrective action. The vision, too, needs mechanisms to measure whether it is on target. One critical function of the joint team is to specify and design some initial measures to assess whether the partnership is performing to expectations. As Jodie Glore, President of the Allen-Bradley Division of Rockwell International, explains: "You really need to sit down and agree on expectations and how you're going to measure whether or not you're successful." Successful partners spend a great deal of time defining appropriate measures to ensure that the vision becomes a reality.

An example of how measurement can guide a partnership is a confidential newsletter that Applied Materials publishes with its partner Intel. The reason it's confidential is that it contains detailed measurements of program status, key equipment performance, equipment utilization, on-time delivery performance, and service levels. Appropriately, the newsletter is called *VISION*. In each issue, Ed Brown, Applied's Vice President responsible for the Intel partnership, writes an article that ends with the words "Our success is measured by how well we serve the business success of Intel." This approach to measurement and continuous improvement is a centerpiece of the partnership's guidance system.

Almost all of the successful partnerships we studied had spent considerable time and effort setting up measurement systems to track their progress. On this one point almost every partnering organization agrees: Measures need to exist, and they need to be used. John Pelligrino of Mead suggested this to us:

> For us, measuring the effectiveness of our partnership effort with Pillsbury was particularly important, since the process began in such an atmosphere of cynicism and doubt. Establishing measurable goals not only underscored how serious we were about the partnership, but gave the team a clear definition of the victory which would be needed to satisfy the doubters. We used several diagnostic tools up-front to assess the health of the relationship as well as identify meaningful gaps. In addition to operational and quality measures such as systems performance and on-time deliveries, we assessed the partnership itself. We candidly explored such topics as communications, the relative knowledge we had about each other's processes, and how well the current relationship was working. This enabled us to measure our progress over time, assessing both hard performance criteria as well as several soft areas that might have otherwise received little attention.

In our research, we saw a wide variety of measures, ranging from Mead and Pillsbury's in-depth assessment of both hard and soft performance, to more simple productivity measures like reduced cost. Whatever your measures, defining substantive ways to "test the success" of the vision is one of the most common elements in successful partnering.

THE EVOLVING VISION

After a partnership is up and running, members of the initial team often become members of a core team that the partners will set up to oversee and guide the partnering relationship. Often this is a gradual transition such that, imperceptibly, a team that began with the task of assessing whether a vision was viable becomes the operating team whose task it is to implement the vision and to take it forward. And just as the partnership itself evolves, so does the vision. Vision isn't a one-time activity that sets up and guides a partnership in the way that the Founding Fathers set up the Constitution and the Bill of Rights to guide a fledgling republic. Like impact and intimacy, vision is part of a dynamic hunt for productivity that must evolve or atrophy. Partnering vision must be constantly reviewed and renewed.

One final word on vision. We've said that vision is both the pot of gold *and* the rainbow. Finding the gold usually means taking a creative, imaginative leap. You have to shift your view of the world away from the old view that sees organizations as having firm and fixed boundaries with enemies lurking outside the walls. This view has to be replaced with one that sees the boundaries between organizations as dynamic, fluid, and capable of being redesigned and remanaged to yield new areas of productivity. You have to see an opportunity to grow a newer and bigger pie, rather than more cunning ways to divide the pie that already exists. And to cross the rainbow you need to turn your message into a shared vision with a guidance system to keep it on-track. Above all, though, vision rests on one central concept: *impact*. Unless a vision involves real, significant, and lasting business impact, then it's no more than smoke and mirrors and poetic language.

Nor will every attractive-sounding potential partnership have the ability to create real impact. Picking the right partner is the precondition for creating the high level of potential impact that always underlies a shared vision and a successful partnership. And as we'll see in the next chapter, figuring out *who* to partner with can be very challenging—perhaps even more challenging than knowing *how* to partner.

CHOOSING
YOUR PARTNERS

"Turn all your customers into partners!" read a brochure we received at Huthwaite when we'd just started our partnering research. Apparently we could attend a public seminar where, if we weren't ready to partner by the end of the seminar with our whole customer base, we'd be entitled to attend a different seminar for free. Aside from the questionable seriousness of the brochure's proposal—we still haven't come across any "whole customer bases" that have been converted to partnering—we were glad to see some interest in the partnering field.

Behind the innocence of that brochure, though, is what arguably constitutes the most dangerous suggestion we've yet encountered on partnering. And, disturbingly, it is one we're hearing more and more as partnering gathers momentum. Increasingly we are seeing partnering pushed as a generic, all-purpose strategy for building customer relationships. The logic goes something like this: Since partnering is more profitable—a win-win—for you and your customers, it's something you should be doing with most, if not all, of them. This argument makes at least some superficial sense; if partnering is such a good way to work with customers, why not do it with everyone?

Of course, the reality is far, far different than that, as any partnering organization already knows from experience. For one thing, many, if not most, customer relationships are fine just as they are, and stand to gain little from going through the expense and difficulty of setting up a partnership. Ed Ossie, a Vice President at Texas Instruments, summed up this idea nicely: "Not every customer needs a partnership. Some just need goods and services on a timely basis. They know what they need, and it is not a partner." When a business relationship exists to get simple products or services from one organization to another, when the goal is basic delivery of a standard, everyday product, there is little point in partnering.

Partnering, after all, is a risky strategy. The fact is that it often outright fails. A study from a few years back put the failure rate at over 60 percent within the first six months of partnership. More recent research has turned up somewhat more encouraging but not radically different results. A lot of partnerships don't work out. And when they don't, they can be far more costly than if they had never been attempted in the first place. Richard Crew, President of BEST Logistics, observes:

> In partnering, there are greater risks if things go south. No harm, no foul if you're purely in a price relationship. But it's a major hit if you're partnering. In transactional relationships you have far less invested and it's easier to accept those losses. Partnering relationships really hurt if you lose them.

From a risk-management point of view, if often makes more sense to stick with a solid transactional relationship. We've even seen a few cases in which mediocre or bad partnerships have sunk an entire supplier organization; costs got out of control and revenue streams dried up as they ignored their "cash cows" and waited—and waited—for the payoff from their investment in partnering. Bad partnerships drain profits and leave suppliers weaker than if they had never engaged in partnering in the first place.

Perhaps this is why, in contrast to the popular literature, leading consulting organizations have taken a conservative and cautionary approach toward partnering. As John DeVincentis of McKinsey and Company put it:

> Partnering can be a risky strategy—especially if an organization becomes over-enthusiastic and tries to partner with too high a percentage of its customers. There are likely to be high resource and opportunity costs from excessive partnering, and a supplier relationship can often make better economic sense for both parties. Partnering is most strategically valuable if you see it as a very selective strategy. Indiscriminate partnering is very dangerous.

Our own research strongly supports these reservations about partnering. On the one hand, partnering is a powerful customer strategy that can bring competitive advantage through a more durable, committed customer base. And it can enable a supplier to bring higher impact to the marketplace, and to grow with the market, rather than simply to respond to it. But these benefits require partnering in the right circumstances and with the right customers. *Selecting the appropriate customer(s) with whom to partner is the single most important foundation of a partnering strategy.* This chapter takes a careful and methodical look at the criteria that successful supplier organizations are using to select customers for their partnering efforts.

A GOOD RELATIONSHIP: THE FOOL'S GOLD OF SELECTION CRITERIA

For many suppliers, the most enticing criterion for selecting a partner is, without doubt, a good existing relationship. "We worked out all these complex criteria for choosing partners," one general manager commented to us as we looked over a three-page list of his company's ideal customer-partner characteristics. "To be honest, though, most of the time our folks go for partnership where the relationship is already there, and where it looks like they won't hit a lot of resistance trying to get to partnership."

There *is* a foundation in common sense for selecting partners according to the strength of existing relationships. Partnering does require a tremendous amount of intimacy to succeed. Trust, information sharing, and breadth of contact across organizations are all required in abundance to make a partnership work. Traditional supplier-customer relationships, focused as they usually are on a single point of contact between a sales representative and a buyer, are often an unstable base from which to launch a partnering initiative. Gabe Rosica, Chief Operating Officer at Bailey Controls, made exactly this point to us when we interviewed him:

> If the whole basis for a partnership is the personal relationship between two people, it probably isn't on very solid ground. It needs to go a lot deeper than that on both sides. One of the hardest things we face is getting the customer to participate. Without that participation, it's hard to move forward.

As Gabe notes, it is difficult to get customer participation in a partnering conversation, and even more difficult to move the discussion forward to a real partnership. It requires a huge leap forward from the one-on-one contact of traditional selling. So choosing a prospective partner where there is already some breadth of contact makes a good deal of sense. John Pelligrino, Director of Organizational Development at Mead Packaging, provided a similar perspective for us. Brought in to facilitate the development of a partnership with Mead's customer Pillsbury, John's experience has taught him the paramount importance of having sufficient organizational closeness to get partnering relationships off the ground. As he suggested:

> Before you can partner—or even begin serious discussions about partnering—it is helpful to have access beyond the traditional purchasing function. You need access to people and to information. Without that access, that closeness to what's really going on, you can't put together a case for partnership. And even if you could build the case, you would not be able to sell it, because for many traditional purchasing functions, partnering is not their paramount concern. That's why the breadth and scope of account access is one of the criteria we use in assessing partnering potential.

For partnering to work, there must be (a) sufficient contact between organizations and (b) access to people who can make a partnership happen. In short, *intimacy* is required in partnering, and having some is a sound basis for thinking about partnering opportunities. But intimacy can also get too *much* weighting and become too significant in the partner selection process. In fact, in our research we discovered many cases where existing intimacy with a customer and the potential for partnering success did not go hand in hand.

We came across many cases of excellent, long-term customer relationships that, despite the best of efforts and tremendous goodwill, could not be converted from a traditional supplier-customer relationship to a partnership. All sorts of other factors got in the way. The following are two examples we encountered.

- One very strong business relationship we looked at involved a 14-year history of tremendous goodwill on both sides between a heavy equipment manufacturer and an automotive company. Both organizations had influential internal advocates of partnering, and intimacy was extremely high. But there was insufficient transactional volume to justify the costs of partnering; the products were high-end capital goods, and transaction volume was around three or four deals per year. No one saw a reason to migrate to a partnering relationship, and in the end both sides decided that their existing relationship was strong and sufficient for the type of business they were conducting.

- A premium wood supplier and its customer, one of the few remaining U.S.-based piano manufacturers, did have a high transaction volume, and they formed a team to explore the potential of integrating the supplier deeper into the production of finished products. But the supplier was driven solely by quality; its reputation was built on being a premier supplier of wood for high-end musical instruments. The customer, battered by pressure from imports, had a strong price focus and was interested solely in finding a way to cut costs. Talks got nowhere. In the end everyone concluded that the existing relationship was fine and, more to the point, not worth putting at risk, given their differences over quality and cost.

What was interesting to us about these and similar cases was how little correlation there was between the existing level of intimacy—in these two cases, it was very high—and the viability of partnering—in these two cases, nonexistent. Other variables, like transaction volume or cost versus quality focus ended up being more important. These cases suggested an important conclusion: *Although you must have a good relationship to partner, having a good relationship doesn't necessarily mean you can partner.*

Yet even that reasonable assumption—that you must have a good relationship to partner—turned out not to be true all the time. We encountered numerous organizations who had managed to build strong partnerships despite having poor supplier-customer relationships. UPS and Kodak, for example, after several years of struggling through a difficult relationship, got together in a hotel for a few days and said, in essence, "What we've got here isn't working. Let's see how we can turn this around with a partnership." And turn it around they did. As we saw earlier, these two organizations have taken significant steps toward building a durable and profitable long-term relationship—largely by using their troubled supplier-customer relationship as the starting point for discussion.

Mead Packaging's relationship with Pillsbury is another case of a troubled supplier-customer relationship serving as the starting point for a strong partnership. As Mead's John Pelligrino explained to us:

> Our relationship with Pillsbury was in real trouble. There was a lack of consistency in service support, and a general belief within Pillsbury that the machines we had been placing in their plants were not meeting their needs for quick changeover. They were increasingly frustrated, and we were on the verge of losing the account. They had gone out for competitive bids. There was significant mistrust on the part of both parties. The order-processing system was cumbersome and full of errors. When several of our business unit leaders met with them in 1992 in an effort to save the account, there was a real crisis atmosphere. But in retrospect, that's just what was needed. It gave us a powerful incentive to question all the existing practices and to look for radical change. It forced us to be candid. In the case of our partnership with Pillsbury, it was a bad relationship that gave us the stimulus we both needed.

The lesson from cases like these is that intimacy can be high and yet partnership potential can be very low. On the other hand intimacy can be quite low and yet a successful partnership can be built if other factors are present. So when we advise suppliers on establishing criteria for partner selection, we acknowledge the importance of having enough intimacy to get started. You have to have *something* to work with—a variety of contacts in the customer's organization, enough trust to bring up the idea of partnering at all, and so on. But we stop short of recommending that the strength of existing relationships be used as the primary criterion for selecting partners. There are other relevant criteria that much more directly and substantially influence whether a partnership can work over the long term. It is to those criteria that we now turn our attention.

STRONG CRITERIA FOR SELECTING PARTNERS

One of the questions we asked every person we interviewed was this: "What are your criteria for selecting a good partner?" In total we heard about 80 different, sometimes contradictory criteria, spanning the full range from "You have to have a shared vision of what you're trying to do" to "We only partner with customers that do more than $750k of business per year with us"—and everything in between.

Large amounts of data do provide a panorama of "what's out there," but we were left with a tough challenge. No one can work with an endless list of criteria, no matter how valid. For suppliers to select appropriate partners, they need not just valid selection criteria but a manageable *group* of criteria that provide a strong core model—a coherent and actionable framework.

It is well worth pausing for a moment to think about what constitute good criteria for any major decision, putting aside for the moment selection of a partner. In general, good decision criteria have two major attributes.

First, each individual criterion has a strong correlation with success. This means that satisfying any individual criterion should substantially affect whether the outcome is achieved. Just as importantly, failing to satisfy any individual criterion should imply probable overall failure. Good criteria are each, individually, tightly correlated with the success or failure of a decision.

Second, and just as important, good criteria as a *group* must constitute a complete yet manageable set of conditions for decision making. If there are five major criteria required to make a decision or assess a situation, and you've only identified four, you may have some fine criteria but be missing the one condition that in a specific circumstance is the most important and relevant. At the same time, 80 conditions for making a decision are unmanageable. In both cases, the individual criteria might be fine, but as a group they don't provide an overall sense of what direction to take, either because they're incomplete or because they're too unwieldy. It isn't enough to identify good *individual* conditions. You have to develop a *group* of criteria that fit together and provide a complete and manageable picture of a situation.

Our reason for mentioning these two sides of decision-making criteria is that one of the two is very easy to meet in selecting partners, but the other is more challenging. It is easy to identify preconditions for partnering; every organization that has gone through the experience of partnering has learned eight or ten "lessons" about what types of situations call for a partnering relationship. "We partner in situations where there is demonstrated management commitment for partnership on the customer's side" or "We only partner in situations where the sales volume is greater than $1 million per year" are examples we've heard of valid individual criteria. Most organizations could easily develop a lengthy checklist of conditions like these for selecting partners, if they don't already have one.

On the other hand, it is more difficult to get a big-picture sense of what types of customers and situations warrant a partnering approach—an inclusive but manageable picture of which opportunities offer the highest potential for partnering success. Here the question is not "What are the specific criteria for choosing a partner?" The question is, *what group of criteria provides an overall sense of partnership potential that people can take into the field and map against their potential partners?* That is the really important issue in partnership selection criteria.

While there is some variance from organization to organization in partnering criteria, we've found significant commonality among successful partnering organizations in choosing partners. Our research suggests that there are four basic, bottom-line conditions that determine whether a supplier-customer relationship can be successfully transformed into a partnership.

1. *Potential for impact.* Is there some real value that can come out of a partnership that couldn't be achieved in a more traditional supplier-customer relationship?

2. *Common values.* Is there sufficient commonality of values between supplier and customer to make a partnering relationship realistic and viable?

3. *Good environment for partnering.* Are the customer's buying patterns and orientation toward suppliers appropriate for a partnering relationship?

4. *Consistency with supplier's goals.* Is the relationship consistent with the supplier's own direction and market strategy?

There is a strong correlation between each of these four conditions and successful partnering. If these conditions can all be satisfied as a group, partnering usually has a good chance of succeeding. Conversely, any of these four conditions, if not met, bodes very poorly for a partnering initiative. As a group, they constitute an excellent evaluative tool for assessing potential partnerships.

POTENTIAL FOR IMPACT

The most important criterion for choosing a partner is whether or not the partnership can add value for both parties that could not be achieved from a traditional supplier relationship. This is the very first question that needs to be asked when evaluating a customer as a potential partner:

> Is there something we can achieve together as partners that we are not able to accomplish in our existing relationship as supplier and customer?

If the answer is no, there is no chance that a partnership can be successful. At some point one or the other party is going to ask, "Why am I doing this?" On the other hand when the answer is yes—when impact clearly can be achieved through partnering—there is a solid foundation for looking at partnership seriously. There is no single criterion more strongly related to partnership viability than impact. As John Keenan, Vice President of Worldwide Marketing at U.S. Data, notes:

> We are perfectly happy being a key supplier unless there's really something special to be gained from a partnership. Partnering involves incredible time, effort, and resources. It is not in our interest, or in the interest of our customers, to get into a partnership unless it opens up real opportunities for both sides that a normal supplier relationship can't offer.

Bill Budney, Vice President of Distribution Systems at PSE&G, provided a similar perspective for us in commenting on a partnership with his supplier Okonite:

> Partnering takes up big resources. With Okonite, we set up a joint team and worked on the details for six or seven months. Then both sides had to make a lot of changes—which was a big investment for both of us. There is no point in putting in all that effort unless it makes bottom-line business sense. That means the partnership has to provide extra value that we couldn't get from the old supplier relationship. It is a competitive world out there. You can only partner with a few people, so you'd better choose the right ones. Unless the partnership can add a lot of value, you shouldn't even be talking.

The challenge, of course, is that determining whether there is sufficient potential impact to justify partnership is not an easy task. It is through the give-and-take of partnering relationships that potential impact gradually develops. Just how well can you predict whether potential impact exists from your vantage point within the constraints of a traditional supplier-customer relationship? Sometimes you can just be imaginative and *find the impact* by thinking through a range of possibilities, as in these two situations:

- "To date, we've been selling them flour in bulk so they could manufacture pretzels. But if they put some machines on our site, we could bake the pretzels and package them. This would eliminate transportation costs for us and plant costs for them, and get products to market faster and fresher. They could focus on what they do best, which is product development and marketing. We could handle the manufacturing and packaging, and that's a lot more contribution than shipping bags of flour to them."

- "We've been designing training programs for the customer for four years. They have to keep staff to manage us; we have to have a dedicated account manager to manage the customer. We're stuck in an RFP-Proposal mode that's inefficient. We could become the design arm of their training group, interfacing directly with people within their organization, and they with our internal designers. If we did this, we'd eliminate overhead on both sides, integrate training design into their overall performance improvement needs, and build more responsiveness and timeliness into the product development process."

Going through this imaginative process is extremely helpful in determining if partnering is desirable with a particular customer—if you can do it. Frequently you don't know what the potential impact is until you are well into a bilateral discussion with the customer about partnering. It's something of a catch-22. You don't know if there is sufficient justification for partnership until you have enough of a partnership to explore the question. Here are a couple of helpful suggestions.

First, when trying to figure out if there is added impact to be achieved through partnering, it is essential to keep in mind the difference between *real* impact and the buzzwords of partnering. Early in our research, we talked with a number of organizations that claimed to be partnering but really were engaging in business as usual under a thin veil of buzzwords.

Some customers told us, "Yes, we partner with a lot of our suppliers. In exchange for a price break, we give them an extended contract and the title 'Preferred Partner Supplier.'" "How has the relationship changed?" we asked. "What do either of you do differently as a result of your suppliers becoming Preferred Partner Suppliers?" "Nothing," they confessed, "just that we get better prices."

This is not real partnering, and it is not a matter of semantics. There is nothing wrong with using the word *partnering* to describe a long-term contractual arrangement. But when you're thinking about where to put your resources—where you're going to share proprietary information, take on higher personnel costs, and perhaps invest in design and production—you need to be thinking about where those costs are going to achieve their highest return. Typically the highest returns don't come from situations where the word *partner* is getting thrown around loosely. They come when there is a genuine opportunity to achieve a higher level of impact through mutual change.

Contrast, for example, the usual volume-price break scheme with a strong case of mutual change for greater productivity. When Bose Corporation moved to desktop publishing in 1988, years ahead of most companies, their printing partner, United Printing, changed too, in order to keep in step with Bose's evolving needs and to build the relationship. As Dave Marble of United Printing recalled:

> Bose was one of the first companies that went to desktop publishing, which was in its infancy in those days. The printing industry just wasn't used to taking risks with low-resolution information and converting it into the kind of high-resolution information that would let us produce high-quality film to meet the standard we had to meet. So we had to decide "Do we go this way or not?"
>
> We decided that we'd better get with it or we couldn't stay productive as a partner. So we changed too. We became one of the pioneers and, as it turned out, it gave us a kind of jump on the market and on our competitors. We became experts at taking low-resolution IBM and Apple output from Bose—the kind they could design on their workstations— and using it to create final film and brochures. This wasn't just a tactical shift. Our partner changed, and we realized that we had to change too or the relationship wouldn't be as productive for either of us.

Focusing on real impact such as that achieved between United Printing and Bose, and not various buzzwords like becoming a

"Preferred Extra-Special Partner," is a good starting point for thinking about potential impact. Yet, it is still difficult to go through the imaginative process required to assess whether there is sufficient impact to partner. To get through this challenge, we usually recommend that suppliers go through the *one company image* exercise that we described in the last chapter—on their own. When suppliers envision what they might do differently with a customer if the two organizations were literally to merge, they often can come up with a starter-kit of ideas for:

- Eliminating duplication and waste, such as excess inventory or paperwork
- Greater sharing of information, coordination, and integration of systems or procedures
- Combining competencies between organizations (e.g., bring a new capability to the customer that isn't getting utilized in the existing relationship)
- Creating new value or, perhaps, developing new products

The one company image is powerful as a diagnostic, because it provides a relatively easy way to get a snapshot of whether potential impact really exists. *If we were all one company, and could make whatever changes we want, what would we do differently?* If the answer is "nothing," then there is no potential impact. If the answer is "an awful lot," there are likely to be some areas to find new impact through partnering. The beauty of using the one company image as a thought starter for choosing partners is that once you've completed the exercise you've already identified what the impact might be, and as a result you've already got some of the legwork done for developing a partnering proposition.

Whether you use the one company image as a thought starter, though, or go straight to thinking about whether there are ways that you and a potential partner could be more productive, you are asking the same fundamental question: *Is there really some potential added value—some genuine impact—in partnering, or are we barking up the wrong tree here?*

If you get to a point where you think there is potential impact through partnering, you have two related and important questions to work through. Impact is about mutual change for greater productivity, and unless both parties can change, grandiose plans for achieving impact will never get off the ground. As a supplier you're probably ready to make the necessary changes to forge a partnership. Whether the customer can or is willing to change is more uncertain. So if you've arrived at a point where you've identified some potential areas of impact, it's time to work through two questions that address the customer's change readiness.

Is the customer *able* to change? In many situations, there may indeed be *potential* impact, but it can never be actualized because the customer cannot make the necessary changes to bring it out. In the training supplier case we described earlier, for instance, none of the customer's personnel involved in the relationship are anywhere near the level of authority required to implement the organizational changes needed to partner. And, with reorganization looming on the horizon, it is extremely unlikely that the customer will be able to experiment with supplier integration for at least a year. The customer cannot partner until more senior people are brought into the partnership discussion and until their internal organizational changes have settled down. In general *a customer's ability to change is critical to evaluating whether the impact of partnering can ever be realized.* If a customer cannot make the changes required to bring out the impact, there is no point in trying to partner.

Is the customer *willing* to change? Some customers are perfectly able to make any changes they want, but they are not willing to change regardless of the potential impact achievable with a supplier. Large, older firms often pose this challenge to would-be supplier partners. For example, one systems integrator working with a telecommunications giant commented to us:

> I had a great vision of how we could take on responsibility for facilities management, application development, and system software, and develop an off-site, 24-hour help desk that would handle both system requests as well as all their other hotline needs in different areas. It was an ambitious plan, but it would have saved them millions and millions in facilities, personnel and development, and transformed their responsiveness to their own internal customers, some of whom are not satisfied with current operations.

If they wanted to do all this, they could have. But it was a threatening plan. Every change they would have had to make would have dislocated some programmer or service rep. Management would have had to cede some authority to us and admit that current operations weren't integrated or working particularly well. All the various stakeholders balked at involving us so deeply in their business. This is our experience with that type of organization. The value's just waiting to get soaked up, but they don't want to move.

The best-laid plans for impact are useless if the customer is not willing to make the changes necessary to bring the impact out. In choosing partners, you have to make a hard-nosed assessment of whether there is sufficient willingness to change to justify engaging in partnering discussions.

As a selection criterion potential impact is vitally important. David Montanaro of NEC goes so far as to suggest "If the value isn't there, neither should be the partnership. It is vitally important to start with a clear understanding of the added impact that justifies all the effort." If there is real added impact to be achieved through partnering and the customer is willing and able to make the necessary changes to bring out that impact, then partnership has a fighting chance.

COMMON VALUES

Common values are often thought of as one of those "touchy feely" subjects. So we'd be not the least bit insulted if the very title of this section raised a few eyebrows. Our research, though, strongly suggests that commonly held values between organizations are critically important enablers of successful partnering. Strong partnerships almost always involve organizations who have deeply held values in common. Partnerships between organizations who have substantial differences in what they consider important—in their values—are endless uphill struggles that usually end in failure. Identifying customers with whom you share strong values is at the core of successful partner selection, as Frank Wingate, President of Industrial Computer Corporation, suggests:

I think you have to look at the corporation that you're going to be doing business with, and look at the values of that corporation. Both the established values and the values that your antennae pick up on early in the sales cycle. If the ethics are not the same, and the business practices are not the same, it's just going to really inhibit the relationship.

In a similar light, Dick McIlhattan, a Vice President at Bechtel, commented to us:

> You have to find companies where the values of the two companies are very close. They both consider themselves to be premier companies within their businesses. They both embrace the quality process. They are both highly ethical. You can get away with some cultural differences, but not with value differences.

We've heard sentiments similar to these over and over again from successful partnering organizations. And, conversely, we've seen many cases of partnerships failing or never getting started because of differences in values. A management consulting firm we occasionally work with, for example, passed along this story to us:

> We are a consulting firm, very good at what we do [organizational restructuring]. Although we are small, we've built an international reputation in our field. We had done a number of high-profile projects for a large electronics conglomerate that had virtually no internal expertise in downsizing or restructuring. They were the ones who approached us about a possible partnership. What if we worked together, they suggested, to build up their internal consulting capacity? The plan was for us to take a long-term coaching and advisory relationship so they could end up with a world-class, internal organization change capacity. It was good for them, and we thought it would be good for us.
>
> We started with high hopes, but then the troubles began. We were driven by excellence in organizational design; they were driven solely by costs. Where we focused on implementing real empowerment throughout an organization and redesigning management structures to encourage better decision making, they were solely interested in finding out how to get an internal group up to speed on handing out pink sheets in the most painless, efficient manner. They took frameworks we'd spent years developing and mushed them together to provide some intellectual foundation for cutting their staff.
>
> We worked with them for a while, but our own people got demoral-

ized and asked to be taken off the project. We believed in fundamentally different things and, although we had everything to gain, we just
couldn't work together in a partnership. We still do project business
with them, but we're better off at arm's length. In retrospect I think
we were like oil and water. Our values were so different that the partnership was doomed from the start.

We've heard many variations on this theme. Nimble high-tech
start-ups have found their creativity crushed under the bureaucratic
weight of a giant partner who primarily values order and methodical
process. A partner who values quality above all else feels deeply dissatisfied with a collaborator who is driven only by speed and therefore
cuts corners. Tensions and mutual suspicion arise when one partner
emphasizes quick return on investment while the other believes in taking a long-term perspective. If the fundamental values of a supplier
and a customer are not in agreement, then each should think long and
hard about entering into a partnering relationship. The probability of
failure is extraordinarily high.

It is important to understand that what we're talking about here
are the deep values held by an organization, not the superficial trappings that often go under the banner of some term like "organizational
culture." It is more than possible for two organizations that on the surface seem to have very different cultures to nevertheless possess common values that will hold a collaboration together. For example, we
work closely and comfortably with McKinsey & Company. On the face
of it, the cultures of our two organizations are quite different.
Huthwaite is a small, 40-person company located on an eighteenth-
century plantation set among vineyards in rural Virginia. We dress
casually; we're easygoing. When people join us, they tend to stay with
us for many years. There's something of a family atmosphere; we have
two corporate dogs and a variety of other mammalian hangers-on.

McKinsey, on the other hand, is the *premier* consulting organization—and by our standards it's huge. Go to a McKinsey office anywhere in the world, and once you get behind the civilized and refined
reception area you'll find a pace and intensity that are the very opposite of Huthwaite. Unlike us, McKinsey has an up-or-out culture;
recruits know that most of them won't end up staying. The pressure of
the McKinsey career path taxes even the brightest and the best. The
laid-back Huthwaite culture seems to be at the opposite end of the

scale. How is it that two organizations so apparently different have worked comfortably together for over 10 years?

The answer is that, superficial cultural differences aside, we share many core values. Thirty years ago, Marvin Bower of McKinsey gave a talk at the London Business School where an impressionable 22-year-old Neil Rackham sat in the audience and listened in growing fascination. Marvin talked about the core values of consulting, about the primacy of client interests, about the obligation to be objective and candid. These were values we could believe in, and they have influenced Huthwaite greatly over the years. We have cultural and other differences, but on a level of deeply held values, we are not so far apart.

We cannot overemphasize how important it is to get beyond superficial notions of differences between organizations so that you can focus on what really matters: the underlying values that drive each organization. Sometimes the distinction can get a bit slippery, but it is a critical one. A few months ago we hosted a meeting at Huthwaite with the sales leadership team of United Parcel Service to discuss partnering. To kick off the discussion we had listed on a flipchart some factors of successful partnering; one read "compatible cultures." Bill Delmont, Vice President for Business Development at UPS, challenged us. "Don't you mean compatible *values*?" he asked. "For example, UPS works closely with Microsoft and we'd like to develop a partnering relationship with them. I'd judge that our cultures are as different as chalk and cheese, but our values are very similar."

Knowing both organizations well, we could see that he had a point. Microsoft and UPS both value excellence and responsiveness, and both reinforce those values with a litany of heroic tales of how their people have performed superhuman acts in the name of meeting a delivery deadline. Both put a very high value on dedication to the company, and both have an uncompromising competitive instinct. This is a lot to have in common between prospective partners.

The similarity of underlying values isn't immediately obvious, however. You'd have to sift through some considerable superficial differences before at last reaching the common core. The UPS headquarters in Atlanta radiates neatness and precision. Desks are tidy and uncluttered; dress is East Coast corporate formal. There is a pervasive sense of order. If you were suddenly transported from UPS to Microsoft's headquarters in Redmond, Washington, you might easily die of culture shock. One Microsoft developer's office has several hundred Post-its covering the walls and part of the ceiling. Next door, eight computer screens share space with a dismantled bicycle. The occupants have moved to a third office whose glass walls have been papered over with the slogan "Light is bad for the brain" and—consistent with this slogan—it's in semidarkness. Inside, dim figures sit on the floor among empty Diet Coke cans and a stray basketball.

As Bill Delmont suggests, these organizations are, at least superficially, like chalk and cheese. But at a deeper level they share important values about competitiveness, pride in excellence and, as we move further into the 1990s, innovation as well. We've used this example to illustrate an important criterion for choosing partners. There has to be a strong commonality of value for partnership to work. It is not a question of what people wear, how they keep their offices, or whether they are allowed to bring snacks into meetings. These are the wrong variables to look at for deciding whether values are held in common. The right variables are more in-depth notions of what each organization truly cares about—what they value deeply.

So what are the questions you should ask to determine whether you hold values in common with a potential partner? There are probably hundreds of questions that you would need to ask yourself to figure this one out completely. We offer three powerful ones that, while perhaps not inclusive of every potential value issue, will provide a core model onto which you can add additional value questions.

QUESTION 1: DO BOTH ORGANIZATIONS SHARE A "WIN-WIN" APPROACH?

This is a value issue that lies right at the heart of successful partnering. Partners cannot succeed unless they really believe in the concept of the win-win. The shift from the win-lose, adversarial battles of transactional selling to a more collaborative "Let's not just carve up the pie this time; let's make it bigger" approach does not come easily to everyone. But it is at the core of successful partnering. As John Pelligrino of Mead suggests:

> The key common value I look for—because without it a partnership just can't work—is what's often called a win-win approach. That means neither party will treat the partnership as a zero-sum game. The customer must believe, and believe genuinely, in the right of the

supplier to get a fair return. Equally, the supplier must believe as genuinely in the right of the customer to achieve value and savings from the partnership. If this isn't deeply in place on both sides, then the partnership falls back into the old antagonistic battles and it fails. Before you think of getting into partnering discussions, you need to be sure that both parties can get away from yesterday's win-lose values.

Unfortunately win-lose values still pervade many organizations. Many customers talk partnership but have in mind nothing more than a price break. Likewise many suppliers should consider whether they themselves are really bringing a win-win perspective to the table. In the name of partnering, we've seen many sales forces use yesteryear's selling tactics—manipulation, pressure to sign a contract, and so on—to close a deal. Until partnering really means *partnering*—putting aside the temptations of the deal in favor of a larger, collaborative goal—a supplier has no business pursuing a partnering relationship and, more to the point, won't succeed in doing so. The win-win approach has to be held by all parties in a partnering relationship. If it isn't, for whatever reason, then there's no point in pursuing a partnering discussion.

QUESTION 2: DO BOTH ORGANIZATIONS HAVE SIMILAR VALUES ABOUT QUALITY?

It's become quite fashionable in recent years for every business to claim *quality* as its core value. Quality is a great value, and perhaps the most important one of all. But quality is not without its tradeoffs, despite the articulate, well-reasoned literature that claims it is entirely cost-free. Most recent analysis recognizes that the costs of top-flight, high-end service and total, absolute, uncompromising quality are rather high. One study we encountered recently, for example, suggested that the final 5 percent of quality delivery accounts for 30 percent of total cost. Those numbers are subject to debate and are, in fact, being debated hotly. But there can be little doubt that the extra, final push toward perfection is an expensive undertaking that ultimately gets reflected in price. It is far less expensive to produce at a 95 percent level of perfection than at 100 percent. Many companies thrive on getting products to market that meet high, but not the highest possible, standards, and they have many satisfied customers who are happy to pay substantially less for a marginal decrease in quality or service. Let's take a look at an example to get a sense of the full possible range of quality and its tradeoffs.

There's an electronics store in Arlington, Virginia, that sells used stereos which barely work at all. A sour and bored employee wanders into the small showroom from time to time smoking a cigar, eyeing suspiciously and mostly avoiding the occasional customer who wanders in. At any given moment the store may be open or closed, depending on whether they feel like it. When they're open they may or may not have anything to sell, product replenishment not exactly being a fully automated function. "All purchases final—no refunds" is stamped on every single piece of equipment in the store. It's cash only. There are no warranties, guarantees, or even promises that the equipment will work at all. It is truly a nightmare. But if you need a stereo for fifty bucks, you can get one there. That's useful if you only have $50.

On the other hand, if you want more up-to-date, high-quality service, you go to Circuit City, where you get excellent in-store service, a great warranty, and a 30-day, no-questions-asked return policy—but you pay more for all this. You've just traded cost for quality. And it keeps going. If you're *really* willing to pay for quality, you can go to Myer-Emco, a premium stereo store in the Washington area where you get a personable sales representative who will come to your house, help you set up your system, and listen to music with you to get the placement of the speakers just right. Here, you are getting real quality. But, again, it's not free. At every step of the way you're paying a higher and higher price for better overall quality of product and service.

The quality movement has, to some extent, obfuscated the fundamental truth of the tradeoff between quality and costs (or perhaps efficiency) by treating fanatical dedication to total, unswerving perfection as the only valid goal in every situation. The reality is that there are many different ways to please a marketplace, and every supplier and every customer has their own unique orientation toward the value of quality vis-à-vis other priorities. We certainly aren't arguing against quality or the quality movement. Given customers' expectations in the 1990s, quality has to be paramount. The point, however, is that out there in industry there's a wide range of commitment to quality as a fundamental value. Everyone *talks* about quality but not everyone has the same commitment to it. The orientation of different organizations toward quality varies dramatically, from the fanatical to the nonexistent.

Thus the issue in a potential partnership is whether both supplier and customer share the same orientation toward quality. Customers pursuing lowest-cost commodity strategies won't partner successfully with suppliers who hold a best-at-every-single-thing-we-do value. Suppliers who have mastered operational excellence in producing huge volumes of identical products at low cost won't partner successfully with customers who hold highly customized delivery of service to each of *their* customers as a core value.

Determining whether your organization's values about quality are aligned with a potential partner's is extremely important. If you're a low-cost producer you'll probably disappoint a quality-driven customer. If you're a quality-driven supplier your prices and zeal will alienate a low-margin, cost-conscious customer. Suppliers and customers must have similar values about quality for partnership to work. You should not chase partnership with a customer who puts a markedly different value on quality than you do.

QUESTION 3: ARE THERE ANY VALUES UNIQUE TO THE SUPPLIER OR CUSTOMER?

Many values are commonplace and, at least nominally, are held by almost any supplier or customer to some degree. These include customer satisfaction, strong ethics, and service, among others. Cynics among us might question whether every organization out there is really living up to those noble aspirations. At a minimum, though, everyone at least claims to believe in them. They have become so familiar that thinking about them, and comparing two organizations with reference to any of them, is now almost second nature.

Not all organizational values fit this notion of "commonplace," however. Some values are unique to specific organizations, and many businesses have at least one unusual or unique value. Some companies, ourselves included, will not do business with any tobacco company, regardless of how profitable. A high-tech firm we've worked with supports environmental protection and strongly rewards business partners who do so as well. Some larger, more institutional firms are very strong on affirmative action and won't partner with organizations who've not demonstrated equally serious commitment on this front. There's an almost endless variety of possible unique or unusual values that an organization can hold dear.

Uniquely held values need to be considered even more carefully than commonly held ones like service and customer satisfaction. Almost everybody says they value service; it's rare for a supplier and customer to disagree on such a common, expected value. When it comes to *unique* values, however, their very uniqueness can create a real compatibility problem for partnering. If you as a supplier have a particularly strong corporate value about not working with tobacco companies, you may have great difficulty selling internally the idea of entering into partnership with a customer who doesn't share that value. If your customer values deeply a commitment to local community service, you may find it difficult to partner over time unless your organization can adapt to that value.

It's important to recognize and assess unique values on both sides, as early as possible in the partner selection process. There are two questions that have to be answered:

1. Do we (the supplier) have any particularly deep values that are truly unique to our organization, and if so, how would they affect the desirability of partnering with a specific customer?

2. Does the customer have a unique or unusual value, and, if so, can we adapt to their unique value?

Too often these questions get neglected. But many organizations have special, unique values that are important to them. Sometimes what they value most creates an incompatibility that must be recognized before investing in a partnering relationship.

Earlier we suggested that you do not always need a high level of intimacy to get a partnership off the ground. Here we can put that idea into a little more perspective. You can always work harder on the intimacy dimension through, say, more information sharing and a cross-organizational team. But you do need to have something in place to make intimacy possible at all, and it has to exist on Day One of a partnering relationship. *You need a common, shared sense of what is important.* Many suppliers and customers have been able to draw upon their shared values to turn around poor relations and build real partnerships. But suppliers and customers who have few or no values in common can never move a millimeter beyond a basic transactional relationship, and it is pointless even to try.

DOES THE CUSTOMER HAVE A GOOD ENVIRONMENT FOR PARTNERING?

Successful partnering requires having the right customer environment for partnering in the first place. The fact is, some customer environments make for better partnerships than others. This is not a matter of good customers versus bad customers. It's more a matter of ensuring that a customer is a viable recipient of your partnering efforts. Some won't be, regardless of potential impact, shared values, or anything else. When you're selecting a customer with whom to partner, it has to be one whose environment is conducive to a partnering relationship. Our research suggests that there are three basic issues you must consider.

1. The customer's orientation toward partnerships
2. The customer's time horizon
3. Transaction frequency

THE CUSTOMER'S ORIENTATION TOWARD PARTNERSHIPS

A few pages back we talked about the importance of having a shared sense of win-win within a partnership. Some customers truly bring that perspective to a partnership. Bill Budney, Vice President of Distribution Systems at PSE&G, commented to us, for example, that: "I'm not in the game to drive my supplier out of business. They've got to make a living, and so do we. So we've both learned to put the long-term relationship before the profit on the sale." Some customers like PSE&G have moved beyond transactional thinking and into collaborative relationships with their suppliers. On the other hand, a lot of customers have not.

Many customers' approaches to managing suppliers were developed in more adversarial times, when salespeople spent a lot of their time surreptitiously trying to obtain a corporate phone directory or to fool the secretary into transferring a sales call directly to the VP. These aren't the skills of partnering or even good selling anymore, but a lot of customers remember those times vividly and still look at suppliers as adversaries to be controlled. They see "partnering" as nothing more than an opportunity to get even more control over their suppliers and perhaps a price break or other favorable treatment. In return they provide the various trappings of partnering like a Preferred Supplier label and a long-term contract—at a rock-bottom, maybe even unprofitable price.

Randy Nord of Kurt Salmon Associates calls arrangements with these customers "bully partnerships." According to Randy, bully partnerships are those where customers use the leverage of partnership to hammer away at suppliers for the best terms they can possibly get, with little or no intention of true collaboration. Bully partners are not in it for the long term or for mutual gain. They're in it to get even more advantage out of their suppliers than they could from traditional supplier-customer relationships.

Examples of bully partnerships abound; they are probably as common as real, collaborative ones. Glen Lindemann, President of Scott Aviation, provided us with a view of one of his bully partnerships:

> One airplane manufacturer we worked with talked about partnering when it suited their need. They said "We're partnering" and all that, but they still said to "give it to us at the lowest *#%&@#&$! price." The bottom line is that they kept twisting and twisting and twisting. That's not partnering. Both sides have to agree that you are not going to use partnering as a smoke screen to beat up the supplier.

When you're dealing with a potential bully partner—one who's going to squeeze every last drop out of the partnership—you're on shaky ground and, for that matter, you're not really partnering anyway. Joe Davin, Vice President of Sales at Datex, suggested exactly this to us:

> If a customer is just looking to beat us up on price on every issue, and the value is not important to them, then it's pretty clear that every time we turn around they're just going to try to hammer us for the lowest possible price or they're going to throw everything out to bid and every supplier in the world is going to compete on it. That is just not a partnership, and it's usually pretty evident up-front. There has to be a philosophy of developing partnerships with corporations—of working in a complementary and not adversarial fashion.

The win-win is paramount in partnering, but you'll never get there if the customer's very orientation toward partnering in the first place is that it's a good technique for squeezing suppliers dry. If a customer's tendency is to go for the bully partnership, there is no point in talking about partnering at all. These customers will not provide a suitable environment for partnering; you'd be far better off developing the highest possible quality of traditional supplier-customer relationship with them—and leaving it at that.

THE CUSTOMER'S TIME HORIZON

Rick Keene, Anixter's Executive Vice President for North America, expressed with perfection a concern about partnering that we'd been hearing in many quarters since we began our research effort. "We need to get out of what is happening today and into what is happening tomorrow," Rick stated. He added:

> We need to be engaged in future conversations, we need to be able to take what we know about the market and where the technology is going. Companies are lining up with people for tomorrow; they are not lining up with people for today. You don't want to line up with somebody who isn't in it for the long haul.

Rick's concern is one that many suppliers and customers feel strongly about. In Chapter 4, we discussed the absolute necessity of bringing the future into a partnering conversation. Getting off the present and moving beyond today's transactions are key drivers of successful partnering. The future must be part of any partnering discussion, and future goals and plans must drive the purpose of the partnership itself.

A customer's time horizon—how far into the future they are working and thinking—is thus a critical factor in determining whether you are dealing with a good environment for partnering. Partnerships don't work as short-term strategies. The kinds of changes that organizations have to make to get full impact out of a partnership do not come in a day, nor do they come in a normal sales cycle. The payoffs of partnering are long term for both parties.

For these reasons, customers who represent good environments for partnering have a long time horizon—not just for the partnership, but for their own strategic direction. These customers have business plans that extend into the future and a vision of where they want to go. If you had to describe to a colleague where the customer was headed and what your potential role could be in helping them to get there, you could. Their plans are on the table, and your potential role in making them happen is identifiable.

Conversely many customers are chasing short-term goals with a cost focus, and they are unclear about where they're going. If a colleague asked you where these customers were going, your answer would likely be "Don't know." Lack of direction may not be the end of the world in a transactional relationship, but in partnering it usually is deadly. *If the customer doesn't know where they are going, how are you going to help them get there?* John Gogniat of Sun Microsystems provided some perspective on this type of customer:

> It's a showstopper if the customer does not have a clear set of goals or doesn't know where they want to go. I've actually told a customer, "Hey, you've ordered this, but what are you trying to do with it?" If a customer wants to use a partnering approach, you have to ask yourself, "How well do I understand what they're trying to do here?" You can only be a successful partner if you know where the customer's going, what the final outcome is.

This is not a minor issue. It's why suppliers who are experienced in partnering stay away from partnerships where customers are overly focused on today's issues and problems. Dick McIlhattan of Bechtel, for example, notes that "One of the real red flags for us, at the beginning of looking at an alliance, is if the company is too short-term-oriented, or is just looking at costs, there are going to be some real roadblocks to partnering." If a customer is locked into short-term, purely cost-driven thinking, it will be an uphill struggle all the way as you search around for a direction that doesn't exist. In a good partnering environment the customer thinks long-term, can articulate future goals, and has a real plan on how to get there. Even where potential impact exists and values of one sort or another are held in common, it is better to walk away from short-term, myopic thinking than hope that a customer will grow out of it.

TRANSACTION FREQUENCY

Our final suggestion for evaluating whether you have an appropriate partnering environment is to consider carefully whether the frequency of business you do with the customer is consistent with partnership. What's important here is that we are not talking about transaction *volume* but *frequency*. The two often get lumped together or confused, but the distinction is an important one. Volume is about how much business you do with a customer; frequency is about how often you do it. Many suppliers we've come across are singling out their highest-volume customers for partnership and writing off mid- or lower-volume potential partners. High-volume customers are often good places to put your partnering energy. But while there has to be enough volume to justify the investment in partnering, many successful partnerships we've studied involve relatively modest volume over time. Volume itself is not the critical issue.

On the other hand, we have found that how *often* a customer does business affects the viability of a partnership considerably. At the extreme end, we've watched organizations try to form a partnership over one solitary piece of business—usually a large one, yet still a single deal. It rarely works. Unlike volume, continuity of work—business over time—is an important element of partnering. As Bechtel's Dick McIlhattan explains:

> It is difficult to set up a long-term relationship when you only have one job. You need to have a backlog of work, not only to show results but also to start the process of improving the value added. So I question people when they come in and say, "We want to develop an alliance, and we're going to do it around one job." I'm not sure you can do that. That could be a start, a platform to start a relationship, but you need to have a number of jobs, some continuity of work to really form an alliance that adds value.

As Dick suggests, it is indeed difficult to partner around a single piece of business. To add value and to *demonstrate* that you're adding value you must have a number of opportunities in which to participate. But that's just looking at it from a supplier's perspective; there's also the important issue of the customer's perspective as it relates to transaction frequency.

Customers view suppliers differently depending on frequency of business; in low-frequency relationships, it is difficult for customers to get outside of a transactional mind-set. When business is infrequent, customers are unlikely to see the connection between different transactions and thus to acknowledge the value of the partnering relationship outside of those individual transactions. Gabe Rosica of Bailey Controls provided a perspective for us on this:

> If your whole relationship is such that somebody buys, and then they don't buy again for a long period of time, then the whole world has

changed in between, and there really isn't any basis for a partnership. It is not so much the absolute volume of a sale. It is that the volume comes on a continuous basis. If a customer has a series of isolated projects where he doesn't care whether it all comes from the same place or not, then the concept [of partnering] doesn't necessarily work. He'll say, "I am better off getting the lowest bid on each job, because there isn't much follow-on business." There are some customers who really insist on doing business this way.

Customer environments which involve the potential to do relatively continuous business over time make better candidates for partnering than those involving either single or infrequent purchases. Although most organizations already have some sort of customer segmentation model, and we hate to add to the usually befuddling collection of tiered models for grouping customers, this is one area where it's probably worth the effort. We'd suggest that, generally speaking, there are three different types of customers in terms of transaction frequency.

- *Continuous customers.*   Customers who, perhaps because of expansion and growth or an ongoing need for a particular product or service, have a consistent, relatively frequent need over time for a supplier's wares.

  Good candidates for partnering, based on transaction frequency.

- *One-off customers.*   Customers who need a specific solution to a problem, and who are going to make only one or a few purchases over the course of the relationship.

  Usually not appropriate for partnering relationships. It is better to face the fact that a single deal isn't a good venue for partnering than to try to build partnerships out of these opportunities.

- *Periodic customers.*   Customers who make periodic but infrequent purchases (e.g., quarterly), usually of more expensive products like heavy machinery or other capital goods.

  These customers can be appropriate for partnering relationships. However, large gaps of time between transactions will exert a drag on the customer's commitment and loyalty to the partnership. "Downtime" between transactions will need to be managed by the supplier.

In sum, the best environments for partnership involve customers who:

- Truly believe in the win-win concept
- Think in long enough time frames to justify a partnering relationship
- Have sufficient frequency of business to sustain a partnership and maintain commitment

Customers who see partnership as merely a way to control suppliers, have a short time horizon, or don't require continuous business over time, will present great obstacles to successful partnering.

CONSISTENT WITH SUPPLIER'S GOALS

Where you have a good partnering environment, a customer with whom you share common values, and the potential to achieve real impact, you're in good shape to explore a partnering relationship. But there is still one final criterion to consider, and it's an important one: whether the partnering opportunity is one that is truly consistent with where you are going as an organization. The question is,

Is a partnering relationship with this customer consistent with our own product and market strategy, and with our overall direction as a company?

This question may seem rather obvious, at least to executives and senior managers who spend most of their day thinking about corporate direction and who are accustomed to measuring opportunities of one sort or another against that direction. But as activity in partnering increases, it is being executed more and more at a sales force, not an executive, level. And to the sales force at large, mapping account opportunities to overall strategic goals is not a skill with a long history. Sales forces have not had to worry much about overall direction, given their traditional focus on transactional relationships. In selling, the goal is to move the product. You can sell product to the wrong customer or in the wrong industry and still make money—and even make a customer happy. You can conduct business with all sorts of buyers, from the mainstream to the fringe, from the "ideal" customer to the oddball buyer who fits no description at all. In transactional selling, suppliers can be successful moving products with or without being in sync with any overall sense of how an individual deal fits into the larger picture.

In partnering, on the other hand, customer relationships cannot be inconsistent with a supplier's direction. The effort, resources, and commitment that go into partnering mean that partnerships which are inconsistent with strategic direction can cause tremendous investment to get diverted away from the real goals of an organization. Partnerships that are not consistent with a supplier's overall strategy can and do take people, time, and energy off a supplier's chosen path and down a road that may be far astray from their intended direction. It is essential to select partners who are aligned with your organization's direction and strategy. There are three primary variables in this alignment.

Industry focus. You should pursue only those partnerships that reflect the industry direction of your own organization. If your company is shifting emphasis from technology customers to manufacturing customers, it makes more sense to pursue manufacturing partnerships than technology partnerships. If your organization is segmenting customers vertically, and believes that the growth area for your product is the casino and gaming industry, it does not make sense to put your partnering energy into pharmaceuticals. Partnerships that are not consistent with a supplier's industry direction will take resources and investment off track—potentially, for a long period of time. As a rule, partnerships should reflect the vertical or industry direction of a supplier organization.

Product direction. Partnerships are a source of customers for future business. It is critical to choose customers whose needs are consistent with the direction in which your products are headed. This means both finding partners who are aligned with future product developments and, as Pike Hamlin of Georgia-Pacific suggested to us, avoiding partnerships that might, down the road, involve unprofitable or obsolete products.

You should not partner with someone that's not a strategic direction you want to go in. If we're selling products in a certain product line that we know are not going to be there three or four years from now, or that we know have a limited profitability window, we would not want to partner with people for these products.

Partnerships often go on for years and years. So it's important to choose customers whose needs reflect not only the products you can offer today but the direction your products are likely to take over a period of time. In addition, partnerships usually offer a rich test-bed for developing and piloting new products. An increasing number of suppliers are using partnerships as product development opportunities—making it all the more important to choose partners who are consistent with your future product direction.

The customer's position in their own marketplace. Our observation from research is that many supplier organizations have settled on a theme of finding fast-track customers for partnering relationships. The logic, at least superficially, is compelling: You want to be with market leaders who will help you to grow and expand. That is often true—but not always. Yet again, it depends on a supplier's goals.

Suppliers seeking rapid growth and competitive advantage through leading-edge technology and products are, indeed, best off partnering with industry-leading customers who can help them really *push the envelope.* Partnering with this type of customer can bring collaboration around new products and new ideas as the partnership takes off in unpredictable and exciting directions.

On the other hand, suppliers seeking stable business development may be better off with mainstream customers who will present few surprises. As Texas Instruments' Ed Ossie suggested to us: "You have to ask yourself, are these the right people to be partnering with? Sometimes you don't necessarily want leading-edge partners; sometimes you want mainstream partners." A mainstream, steady partner, whose goal is less to change the world than to continue servicing it, may be more appropriate if you are looking for continuous, predictable, stable business.

These three factors—industry focus, product direction, and the customer's position in their own marketplace—are excellent considerations for selecting partners. They help ensure that the partnerships you form will be aligned with your own organization's aspirations.

CONCLUSION

In this chapter we've laid out a basic model of criteria that has four conditions for selecting good potential partners:

1. Potential for impact
2. Common values between supplier and customer
3. A good environment for partnering
4. A partnership that is consistent with the supplier's own goals

This framework is detailed enough to allow for some real decision making by field personnel, but broad enough to allow for some flexibility and customization as required by the unique needs of individual suppliers. Most likely you will need to add a few conditions, such as dollar volume minimums, to reflect your own unique organizational needs.

If we had to offer a final word of advice, it wouldn't be another criterion for selecting partners, but a suggestion that can help some organizations to put their partnering energy in the right place. Our advice is this: *Partner around your core competencies.* Partnerships are most successful when the supplier is contributing what they truly do best. At the extreme end, even the most committed supplier cannot sustain a partnership in an area where they lack real competence. As Frank Zenie, President of Zymark, commented to us: "If you're incompetent, you can be as committed as anything and the customer will pat you on the back and go do business someplace else."

Most of the time it isn't so much a question of incompetence as of relative ability in different areas. If you are world-class in software development but you dabble in support services, you should partner in software development, not support services. If your competitive strength is in high-end cartography, you should partner not with customers who need local maps for brochures but with customers who really need the high-end services at which you excel. You *can* get away with partnerships that aren't based on a core competency—and that's why we don't suggest it as a formal criterion—but the most successful partnerships usually entail each party bringing to the relationship what they truly do best. If you are presented with several opportunities, all of which meet the four basic conditions for partnering, the best opportunity is the one most closely aligned with your strongest capabilities. It's the one where you can achieve not good, but great, results for the customer—and the partnership.

CHAPTER SEVEN

PARTNERING WITH OTHER SUPPLIERS

"I'll be taking my wife on a trip to Rome, compliments of the travel industry" one of our staff mentioned to us when the research for this book had been completed. "First I got 70,000 frequent-flier miles from the research project. Then I paid my mortgage on my credit card, which gave me another air mile per dollar. I stayed at the same hotel on each trip, which gave me a week's free stay at the hotel chain and more air miles. The airline sent me free car rental certificates, which cover transportation for nine days. I ate dinner on the same card at each stop, earning me more miles and some free dinners. And I put some expenses on a phone credit card, and somehow earned some long distance time as well as more air miles. I've got a totally free trip to Europe coming up in May. Including phone calls home to Mom."

The relentless pursuit of travel freebies—it's probably affected business productivity more adversely than computer games or biweekly reengineering efforts—will be immediately familiar to many businesspeople. What is less familiar is the behind-the-scenes cooperation and shared innovation among an entire industry of suppliers that has made it possible. Lost virtues like customer loyalty are being recreated as travel industry suppliers find energy and synergy between their respective offerings. This creation of market value through cooperation with other suppliers is an exciting and important part of the partnering story. Like partnering with customers, partnering with other suppliers is transforming how organizations work together.

Intense supplier cooperation is very visible when you can observe it as a direct consumer, as with travel perks. But the shift toward cooperation between suppliers goes much, much deeper, and it is transforming entire industries. It ranges from the very simple to the truly revolutionary. At the low end, a calendar maker in Reston, Virginia (where two of the authors live) is printing new calendars that place local businesses and phone numbers in appropriate date boxes. The flower shop's phone number, for example, is preprinted in the February 12 box under the header "Don't forget the flowers!"—two days before Valentine's day. The calendar is stuffed with helpful reminders throughout the year about local business-es that can help you out in a crunch. It's a simple but elegant example of suppliers teaming up to deliver new value and win market share.

At the other extreme, supplier collaboration can truly change the world. When Microsoft and Intel combined forces around microcom-puter chips and operating systems, the collaboration between the two companies literally rewrote the map of the personal computer industry. And when, in the late 1980s, entire supply chains in apparel and food distribution combined forces around partnering models such as Quick Response (QR), they revolutionized the levels of quality and respon-siveness they could deliver to consumers. Today many retail supply chains are highly integrated, efficient, technology-driven partnerships that get the wool off the sheep and onto the coat rack with barely a missed step or a lost dollar between the five or six suppliers typically involved in the chain.

What these companies are doing is, truly, history in the making. The centuries-old notion of individual economic actors battling it out in Thomas Hobbes' solitary, poor, nasty, brutish, and short "state of nature" is collapsing under a rising tide of cooperation and collabora-tion between suppliers to get value to the marketplace. This is more than just an exciting part of the partnering story. For many organiza-tions, partnering with other suppliers is already the dominant model of delivering products and services to customers. There are at least three strong reasons for it.

1. Efficiencies and economies of scale.   Increasingly, suppliers are able to cut costs and achieve efficiencies by partnering with other sup-pliers around technology. This is particularly prominent in retail, as in J. C. Penny's integration with its suppliers of systems for inventory con-trol and product replenishment. Sometimes supplier partnering isn't about ironing out supply chains but achieving economies of scale, enabling large groups of suppliers to cut costs by pooling talent or resources. For example, The Advisory Board, a Washington, D.C.–based consulting firm, provides best practices studies to huge groups of health care and education organizations, charging a modest fee to each and in return providing broad-scope research and analysis for all members to share. Few, if any, organizations could afford the level of research that they provide—unless these organizations combine forces in a consortium.

Whether it involves "tightening up" a supply chain through technology or achieving economies of scale in R&D, one reason supplier partnering has evolved is out of a need to find greater efficiencies and achieve greater productivity. In this sense it doesn't differ substantially from the catalyst behind much supplier-customer partnering: the search for greater productivity.

2. New market value. In some industries, supplier-to-supplier partnering has really moved to the next level: achieving more value by combining forces to bring something entirely new to the marketplace. This is about *bundling core competencies* to yield a new product or solution. At the highest levels, this bundling has the potential to move whole industries, as seen in Apple, IBM, and Motorola's collaboration to create the Power PC and other products. On an everyday account level, the creation of new value through collaboration is providing partnering suppliers with a strong competitive advantage.

3. Customers' demands. Of course, the most compelling reason to make any change in business strategy is always to meet the expectations and demands of customers. And supplier collaboration is increasingly a basic expectation and requirement of customers. This is particularly true in the area of high technology, where suppliers have little choice but to bite the bullet and learn how to collaborate with their competitors as well as their natural allies. Customers are looking for suppliers who not only offer products and services but fit into the overall picture and truly *cooperate* with each other. Polly Sumner, Oracle's Vice President of Worldwide Alliances, noted for us that:

> The customer has changed what they want to buy and who they want to buy it from. They believe that there is no one single supplier anymore who can provide everything. That is gone. Consequently, they

are looking behind every recommendation to see how strong the rela-tionships are, to see if these relationships are going to hold up when they try to implement the solution.

Customers are demanding strong supplier partnerships that give them both *total solutions* and *best-of-breed* products. One of Digital's cus-tomers put it like this:

> We used to focus on getting the total package, fully aware that some of the components weren't necessarily best-in-class. Or, on occasion, we'd go for a best-in-class product, knowing full well it wouldn't fit into our existing systems without tremendous patchwork by our inter-nal groups. Today, it's different. Enough suppliers are willing to team up that we can demand, and get, total solutions consisting of individ-ual parts, all of which are best-in-class.

Customers' demands for both the best individual products and the best overall solutions have killed the old model of the total solution supplier, a model that was popular and tremendously dominant in high technology during the 1970s and 1980s. In place of that model, net-works of supplier organizations have teamed up with each other and with customers to get the best individual products organized into supe-rior total solutions. As Polly Sumner notes: "Our vision is to be a best-of-breed product company with value added by customers, partners, and ourselves, so we can deliver total solutions to customers." That's a sophisticated view of where value comes from—increasingly, at the interfaces between supplier organizations—and it can be accom-plished only by taking partnering with other suppliers very seriously.

This notion of value through collaboration with other suppliers, and not just customers, is rapidly gaining attention—particularly in high technology, where solutions are complex and where the value to be gained from collaboration is extremely high. Indeed, some high-technol-ogy organizations have built huge, impressive partnering networks to meet the needs of today's customers. Lotus Corporation, for example, has brought on board over 5000 supplier partners, and continues to expand their network through visible and highly publicized partner con-ferences. Oracle has 450 employees building their partner network and thousands of supplier partners around the world. Microsoft built their Solution Provider program and has signed up over 6000 partners in a matter of two years. Within these organizations, tremendous excitement and energy are going into the development of these partnering networks.

But amid the enthusiasm for putting together huge partner networks, particularly in high technology, we'd suggest a sober look at the partnerships themselves. There's a stark contrast between the successes achieved in putting a partner infrastructure in place and the challenges involved in making partnering actually *work* with customers and other suppliers. A number of organizations have become extremely good at signing up partners and building a network, but are facing real difficulties with day-to-day supplier *collaboration*.

We've spent much of the past two years working with clients who are developing supplier networks, and, indeed, we've come across some truly strange stories that bring to light some of the more quixotic and bizarre new challenges with which partnering suppliers are having to contend. Our favorite one comes from an account manager at a Silicon Valley firm. Thoroughly flustered by the issues of supplier-to-supplier partnering, he agreed to be mentioned here on the basis of strict anonymity. So we've taken the liberty of using a few pseudonyms to tell his tale.

> We've been working together with MegaTech in a utility company for about a year. We develop UNIX applications, which are a natural fit with MegaTech's products. Now, we hear that MegaTech's talking about Novell with the customer; if the customer goes that route, we're out. That's fair, though. We've been recommending all along that the customer move to high-speed workstations, which would probably incite a riot at MegaTech if it actually happened.
>
> It's not a total state of warfare like you might think. We share a lot of R&D both ways (and just hope it doesn't backfire on us). They own a lot of our stock, so "they" includes "us" to some extent. Also, one of our VPs sits on their board of directors, so when they have their kill-the-competitors meetings, we're part of it.
>
> In accounts, it's awfully hard to figure out if they're the good guys or the bad guys. At this utility, they brought us in to the account, and we're partnering, to the extent that we're cooperating to build a total system for the customer. But when the doors are shut, and one of us isn't there with the customer, God only knows what's going on and who's going to win or lose. And while it's working so far with this utility, at an Air Force base we brought them in and they gave business to

another partner that was rightfully ours. It can get extremely confusing. You just have to keep saying to yourself, "Let's just try to do what's right for the customer, and not try to sort through the Pandora's box of partnering issues."

We like this story because it brings to light a number of the often unspoken but well-known challenges associated with collaboration between suppliers. Bringing other suppliers to your customers involves tremendous uncertainty. With other suppliers, it's never clear who's representing what interest, and it's almost guaranteed they don't represent yours. And, as André Boisvert, Seer Technologies' Senior Vice President of Business Development, noted, partnering with other suppliers brings into play very basic issues of trust and control:

> A lot of the problem comes down to account control. You know what *you're* telling the customer. When you bring in a partner, who knows what *he's* going to say in the middle of a call. Is he going to do a bait-and-switch? He may run a competitive platform. So what are the rules? How well do you trust your partner? There are a whole series of things you have to deal with in these partnerships.

André's observation is certainly in accord with our own research into supplier-to-supplier partnering. We have yet to find a single organization that has truly figured out how to eliminate the inherent challenges and conflicts of selling together with other suppliers. In fact, the evidence suggests that partnering is not working as well on a basic collaboration level as it is on an infrastructure level. For example, we interviewed a number of customers of partnering organizations to get a picture of how well this new model is working from a customer perspective. The results were somewhat discouraging. While many customers see the logic and necessity of having multiple suppliers collaborating for their business, about 70 percent of them feel strongly that it leads to:

- Lower overall service levels
- Ambiguity over who to call when problems come up
- Problems with coordination between partnering suppliers
- Frustration at being "handed over" from one supplier to another without proper involvement in the decision process

- Poor communication about the roles and responsibilities of all players in the equation
- "Turf wars" that have nothing to do with their best interest as customers

And if customers are giving supplier-to-supplier partnering a mixed report card, salespeople are giving it an even worse tally. One study we conducted found that, in stark contrast to their organizations' efforts to build huge networks of partners, salespeople had significant reservations and issues with the strategy. One account executive told us, "I put everything I've got into developing strong customer relationships. I won't throw an unknown entity at my customers, and I won't throw a known entity who might do the wrong thing. That leaves about five partners. We've got about 150 partners in this district, and I work with the same four or five over and over. I trust them; we understand each other. If my company adds another 200 partners in this district, I'm still going to work with these four or five." Overall, we found that salespeople were working with a little over 8 percent of their available partners; the other 92 percent existed mainly on mailing lists and corporate databases.

These are certainly discouraging numbers, but they continue to be supported by our ongoing research in this area. If we had to draw a single, bottom-line conclusion, we'd suggest that the seductive dream of supplier partnering—hundreds if not thousands of partners pushing products with or without your active participation (preferably without)—differs starkly from the reality that many firms are now facing. That reality is, simply, that having achieved quantity, the issue is now one of quality. Having achieved the numbers, the issue is now one of building strong relationships.

This shift in emphasis from quantity to quality is becoming more and more apparent at partnering organizations. Jodie Glore, President of Allen-Bradley (a division of Rockwell International), had this to say:

> We started partnering back in the early eighties as a company; back then it was called "joint ventures": you get 30 percent of this, we get 40 percent of that. There were a tremendous amount of joint ventures. And for us one of the real learning stories was that of the ten or twenty that we did, we maybe have one or two left. If you look at something and say, "Let's hurry up and do this together so we can

make a quick buck," that's not a partnership; we're just getting together for a situation and then we are going to move on after that.

Making a similar point, Tom Tubergen, a Partner in Andersen Consulting's Chicago office, told us:

> We don't want to have a relationship with everybody and their brother. There's no sense having a relationship with somebody that is not going to be a *robust* relationship. One-off business is not going to do anybody any good. We struggled with that for a while, but I think we're getting past that.

Allen-Bradley and Andersen Consulting are not exactly fringe organizations. Their shift in emphasis reflects a broad trend toward getting beyond numbers and into quality partnerships.

The shift toward quality doesn't imply dismantling a hard-won partner infrastructure, however; it may not even mean reducing the number of partners at all. Microsoft, for example, brought us in to develop a program that would facilitate stronger partnerships with their solution providers on a mass level. Over 500 people in eight countries, both Microsoft personnel and solution providers, attended that program to work in depth on the fundamentals of effective collaboration; other high-technology organizations are looking at similar options. Effective collaboration with individual partners can sometimes be accomplished on a mass scale, but it requires a commitment by senior management to support partnering by bringing appropriate collaboration skills and tools to the sales force.

So the good news is that achieving quality does not necessarily require reducing quantity. But it *does* mean taking the quality issue seriously. And that requires making a shift in perspective that, if we had to sum it up simply, would look like this:

> A large partner infrastructure alone doesn't translate to success; bulk sign-up of partners does not, in the end, mean effective collaboration. And partnering cannot be driven top-down through memos or exhortations to partner from senior management. *Success in supplier-to-supplier partnering comes from effective collaboration on an account level.*

So what *are* successful organizations doing to achieve strong collaboration with other suppliers? We were very fortunate to get research access at some of our largest clients, such as Digital, the Santa Cruz Operation, Applied Materials, and Microsoft, to investigate exactly this question. We started with a simple goal: find out what the most successful companies were doing who were building strong partnerships, whether these involved "sell with partner" relationships in accounts or "sell through partner" relationships that had more of a distribution channel flavor. In the end we interviewed and observed over 200 salespeople, managers, teams, partners, customers, and executives. Our conclusion is that the most successful suppliers have put great emphasis on the following four success factors:

1. Developing strong shared goals for collaboration
2. Growing the common ground
3. Defining roles with clarity, around customers' interests
4. Achieving balance in the partnership

Getting these four aspects of supplier-to-supplier partnering right, and getting them right *over time,* is the heart of effective collaboration.

DEVELOPING STRONG SHARED GOALS FOR COLLABORATION

Establishing strong shared goals for collaborating with other suppliers is a critical skill of partnering. We call it a *skill* and not a *process,* because finding and developing a strong sense of shared, common goals is not an easy, mechanistic task. It is not simply a matter of identifying leads or finding pieces of business to pursue. Suppliers who are building effective, profitable partnerships with other suppliers are carefully working out what each partner is looking to achieve and where the overlap of interests and needs can provide unique value to the marketplace. They are truly *skilled* at building shared, common ground around each partner's goals.

And they are in the minority, to be sure. Although at executive levels it isn't uncommon for partners to have a "meeting of the minds" about goals and needs, we've found that a vast majority of salespeople, at an account level, have never had a serious, in-depth meeting with their partners to talk about who is looking to get what out of the collaboration.

For example, at Microsoft Corporation, many account executives communicated to us their strong need to get face-to-face time with their partners simply to explore—for the first time—what they and their partners were looking to accomplish, what their needs were for the partnership. They were looking to get beyond the usual *rules of engagement* that, while absolutely necessary to maintaining order in supplier partnerships, do more to set limits and establish constraints than to determine what the partners can really accomplish together. And when, in a facilitated setting we designed for them, they finally did get their chance to have a more off-line, expansive conversation about what each partner was looking for in the relationship, they found themselves in the middle of exciting new discussions focused on ways to get value to the marketplace that would satisfy their respective needs. As one Digital account representative pointed out afterward: "This is what we need to be doing with Microsoft, and with all our other partners. We have just got to get beyond last-minute strategy sessions, and start talking about what we're doing together and why."

The comment is telling. A lot of supplier collaboration *is* taking place at the last minute, and often it *is* a near-adversarial contest to see who can get the most leverage out of the partnership. That may enable some quick hits, but it is not a longer-term formula for achieving success in supplier-to-supplier partnering. A formula for success is *to find a strong shared goal, and orient the partnership and its opportunity-seeking activities around it.* That shared goal may involve industry penetration, an enhanced product capability of one sort or another, or perhaps a new angle on some unique combined value that the partners can bring to the marketplace. Whatever it is, the goal has to *exist.*

Jeff Ait, Vice President of Channel Sales at the Santa Cruz Operation, provided an interesting perspective on why the goal has to exist: "How well you establish a shared outlook determines whether a business partnership will work. If expectations about what you're trying to do are different, there will always be failure." Jeff provided a typical high-technology case to illustrate his point:

> You may be approached by a supplier who wants to partner to, say, combine an operating system with their hardware to sell more plat-

forms. They say, "I'd like a great discount." You say, "Sure, but a large discount is based on making a lot of sales." Reluctantly, the partner agrees to take a large volume of product to get the discount. The partner's thinking, "Okay, we have a strategic relationship here, we're willing to invest." You're thinking, "They're obviously willing to buy in volume, so we'll give them the discount."

So the partner takes a large volume, but can't roll out their product for nine months. They're getting more and more behind as your bills come in, and they're saying, "Wait a moment. It's hard for us to find the money." You're thinking, "Uh-oh. How are they going to pay the bill?" The partnership doesn't work, because the partners had totally different ideas about what they were doing together. One is looking for a longer-term strategic relationship, the other a high-volume sale. It has to end in failure, because the expectations are totally different.

As Jeff points out so well, it isn't always so obvious what each partner is looking to get out of the partnership. What *is* obvious is that different perceptions of the "goal" can cause enormous problems. Working through goals and expectations is critical in partnering with other suppliers. So why isn't everyone just *doing* it? For one thing, sitting down and exploring the issue "what are we really looking to get out of this?" generally isn't an activity that competes well against day-to-day opportunity chasing. Chuck Volwiler, Vice President of Marketing at Hello Direct, explains:

> People like to try to avoid the actual crafting of an agreement, because it's not fun. They want to do a deal, and they want to get going, but they don't want to sit down and go through the hassle of an agreement. And there are a lot of misunderstandings that come up when you don't go through the process of crafting a real one.

Just as important, we have found that many salespeople are unclear as to what exactly constitutes a strong goal for a partnership. In fact we spent some time with partners who felt that their working relationship was not quite ideal, and asked them to describe what the goal—the purpose—of the partnership *was*. We heard many variations on "the customer wants a new order entry processing system, and OrderTech can do it, so we're bringing them in" or "We're going to look at vertical marketing in health care." These are very different types of goals, but they have some problems in common. Specifically, we found that in weaker partnerships, goals tend to be

- Established without regard to the true potential value that could be achieved from the collaboration
- Unclear about the purpose of the partnership
- Unmeasurable and unmeasured

On the other hand, in strong partnerships, goals tend to be focused more intently on unique and strong market value, they are clear, and they are easily measurable. Developing goals of this level of quality is the basis of successful collaboration with other suppliers.

ESTABLISHING A GOAL WITH REAL MARKET VALUE

It is absolutely essential that you define a collaborative goal that has real market value. Many partnerships do not possess such a goal, and as a result they suffer and decay over time. There is simply nothing that influences the success of a supplier partnership more than having, and achieving, a goal that maximally leverages the competencies of the partners and thus brings real value to the marketplace. André Boisvert of Seer Technologies provided us with a simple and elegant perspective on this challenge:

> I always have a saying that any time you do a partnership, one plus one better be greater than two, or you're just exchanging four quarters for a dollar.

André is right on the money, so to speak. Strong partnerships do something more than partner for the sake of partnering. They do something more than chase short-term deals and respond reactively to existing customers' needs. Strong partnerships find and exploit the unique capability and potential impact of the collaboration. Bernard Guidon of Hewlett-Packard, a strong advocate of building robust relationships with other suppliers as well as with customers, noted:

> Two partners have to try to come together and provide new value or unique value to a customer, value that the customer could not have without this association of partner one and partner two. The partners have to be able to say, "We are going to have this differentiation, this competitive advantage, this unique value that no one else has."

Bernard also sounded a warning for those partners who cannot make this creative leap into unique value:

> In a lot of partnerships between two companies, very often they don't think through or don't work enough to bring value to the customer. So at the end of the partnership, the customer doesn't care, because it didn't work. Or it "worked," but it doesn't get anywhere.

Indeed, many partnerships don't get anywhere because the unique impact, the real opportunity, of partnering has never been identified and codified as a goal. "Let's do some work in health care" or "We could sell some boxes through your channel, and you could make some extra money" have less potential for large profit and sustainable value than a strong goal around combined capabilities, such as:

> You have a competency in mass storage devices. We are world-class experts in compiling scientific research data. Together we could create a solution for customers who need automated access to high volumes of scientific data, like large research institutes and universities. Let's go find them.

Here, the goal is not just $1 + 1 = 2$. It's something larger, like $1 + 1 = 3$. This particular goal came from an actual partnership which we helped facilitate, and the partners have found real customers based on this expansive goal. As André Boisvert might put it, these partners are not just trading four quarters for a dollar. This creation of value is based on a question that is different from "What can we partner on?" Here the question—and it is the right one to ask—is *"What can we do that truly involves combining capabilities between our organizations to bring new value to the marketplace and to our customers?"* We would suggest that that is exactly the right question to kick off a discussion of goals between partnering suppliers.

BUILDING A GOAL THAT HAS CLARITY OF PURPOSE AND DIRECTION

It is not enough to define a goal that has market value. The goal also must be clear and provide a sense of purpose and direction for all participants from the partnering organizations. As Bernard Guidon suggests:

You need to have a very, very clear objective of what the joint team is going to do. This requires tremendous communication; the whole team needs to feel very comfortable with the objectives.

A goal does not exist in a vacuum. Its purpose is to provide clarity of purpose and direction for all those involved in the partnership. Goals that are vague or tepid, like "Let's do joint marketing," are worse than no goals at all. Developing a strong goal is the best opportunity partners ever get to lay down the expectations, direction, and purpose of their collaboration. Chuck Volwiler of Hello Direct, an experienced hand when it comes to building partnerships among complex telecommunications firms, provided this insight on the matter:

There has to be real clarity on what you're going to do, and on what you're trying to do. In one partnership, I literally carried around a few slides that communicated all this, and I'd walk through these slides with different people [at the partner's site]. The slides said, "This is what we're doing. This is what you're doing. This is what we're bringing to the relationship. This is what you're bringing to the relationship. These are the benefits we're getting. These are the benefits you're getting. This is what we're agreeing to do. This is what you're agreeing to do." People have to feel good that there's a strong relationship, but exactly what each party is doing gets very fuzzy. You've got to be able to represent it really clearly, in a way that people can understand.

As Chuck concluded, "You've got to be able to represent it in very simple and clear terms. You have to spend the time necessary to clarify what's going on." We agree. Strong partnerships are based on specific and clear goals. Partners need to agree on what they're doing, in a way that makes sense not only to the individuals involved but to wider audiences within the two organizations. "We can penetrate the Asian market" is a less effective goal than "Within two months, we should develop a marketing plan focusing on how our combined product line can compete in specific Asian countries, based on our research into Japanese and Korean buyer behavior." When developing the shared goal, it is critical to include in it enough specificity for it to be understood and actioned by both organizations. A strong goal establishes both clarity of purpose (*why* we are doing this) and clarity of direction (*how* we are going to do it).

ESTABLISHING MEASURES TO MAKE SURE THE GOAL SUCCEEDS

Measures are a critical component of partnering, a guidance system to make sure the partnership achieves what it sets out to do. In this matter, supplier-to-supplier partnering is similar to supplier-customer partnering. But there is one important difference: The customer, or more accurately, the customer's satisfaction, is a natural and ever-present metric that forces suppliers to meet certain standards. In supplier-to-supplier partnering there is no natural metric; it has to be established. Putting in place effective measures may in fact determine the success of the partnering venture. "Just to sit down and say, `We're going to do something together,'" noted Allen-Bradley's Jodie Glore, "is kind of an exercise in talking." He added:

> You have to ask the question, "How are we going to measure if we're being successful together or not?" Partnering without very strong metrics means not accomplishing what you could be accomplishing.

And the measures have to be based on what the suppliers are seeking to accomplish: their goal. Santa Cruz Operation's CEO and Chairman, Lars Turndal, gave us some time to talk about this issue. As he described it: "You have to be sure you know what kind of partnership you're doing. Is this a partnership for selling, or for marketing, or for something else?" He added:

> Partnership fails when partners are unclear on what they're trying to do. So you have to set up real goals, and then set up measurements so you can measure against these goals. If it's sales, then what's the volume we're talking about? If it's a marketing program, then what are we going to do? And a quarter from now, how are we going to measure our success?
>
> You have to be clear in the beginning what the targets are. There has to be a clear understanding of the deliverables, so people don't come to a review and say, "I didn't know that." A lot of times people come into a partnership and say, "This is a partnership; we should be able to shake hands. Don't you trust me?" This is common, but very dangerous. I might get into a partnership with you, but then you or I send in someone else and it's very hard to communicate what you and I talked over. Most partnerships fail because of irritation,

because you get conflict without measures and planning. With measures, you can see if it's successful or not successful.

Without real metrics there is no way of knowing whether a partnership is succeeding or failing. Without metrics, supplier-to-supplier partnerships can and often do drift around until they get lost. If the goal is sales, establish a quantity. If the goal is product development, put it on a timeline and establish a quality expectation. If the goal is delivering a solution to a customer, establish with the customer a means of assessing how well service is provided by the partners over time. Whatever the goal, partners need to spend adequate time establishing measures of how well the goal is being achieved. And they need to assess the partnership against these measures on an ongoing basis.

In sum, strong goals bring out the potential in the collaboration, ensure that there is clear direction and purpose, and include specific measures so the partnership can assess how well it is accomplishing its objectives. With those three elements—value, clarity, and measure—partnerships can go a long way. But is finding a strong goal the end of the story in establishing the value of a collaboration? Probably not. Growing the common ground—making the pie bigger over time—is equally important, and it becomes more central as supplier partnerships move forward.

GROWING THE COMMON GROUND

When we work with pairs of supplier partners, we ask each supplier to get started by identifying all the goals they feel they may share with their partner. And then we ask them to identify goals they may have that are not shared with their partner, as well as goals that may be in real conflict. This isn't always an easy activity, depending on the partners and how much conflict there is between them. But the activity has a real, and important, purpose: to get everything on the table for discussion, whether this involves goals that are fully shared, in deep conflict, or somewhere in between. Starting with the full scope of both partners' goals is a great way to identify a particularly strong goal for collaboration, one that meets the three criteria of *value, clarity,* and *measure.* The activity emulates what the best partnerships are

Figure 7-1 *Goals dichotomy.*

already doing: finding common ground by working through the full panoply of possibilities.

Getting all the cards on the table is a useful way to find the strongest possible shared goal. But after partners have found a strong shared goal, then what? To stop there would certainly be an accurate reflection of what successful partners are already doing when they kick off a partnership: finding a shared goal, and putting everything else aside to get down to business. (See Fig. 7-1.) This is an excellent starting point for partnering, but it is also a very limited view of what collaboration can achieve over time. The best partnering relationships we've seen progress beyond immediate goals and ask broader questions like "Is the partnership simply generating some business, or is it truly being leveraged to the maximum benefit of each partner's interests?" This requires, however, that the partners think more broadly about what the collaboration can achieve for each of them, given what each is hoping to accomplish. *This is about growing the common ground, not just finding it.* And it looks less like the "Shared Goal/Everything Else" dichotomy seen in Fig. 7-1, and more like the *goals continuum* seen in Fig. 7-2.

What the goals continuum acknowledges is that there is a broad range of goals within a partnership; some are shared, but others fall outside the range of the existing common ground. Goals that are not shared but that a partner could potentially support, since they are not in conflict, are what we call *supportable goals.* For example, "I would like this customer to make the shift to a client-server platform" or "I want to get more penetration in financial services" are goals one supplier might have that a partner might not care less about. These are normal, everyday goals that just happen to be of interest only to one partner. In many partnerships these goals never even get on the table because they aren't goals the partners share. On the other hand a partner might easily be able to help out with various unshared goals as part of the overall collabora-

Figure 7-2 *The goals continuum.*

tion—and might well be willing to do so, if these goals get into the discussion in the first place. Finding unshared goals that are supportable by the partnership is a tremendous source of leverage through partnering.

At the far end of the goals continuum are those goals that are truly in conflict. Conflicting goals don't necessarily mean open warfare or animosity. Goals in conflict are simply goals that cannot both be pursued at the same time. For example, here are two conflicting goals we've encountered several times in our research. This goal:

> The customer has expressed strong interest in moving ahead with this sale, and really needs the solution we are offering. We can close this deal right now, and I would like to do so.

is in conflict with this one:

> The customer may be willing to move ahead, but a few more months of needs development across departments will result in a solution that better meets their long-term needs and is more profitable. I want to let events unfold for a few more months.

Of these two goals, which is the "better" one? It's hard to say. They are both valid goals, in that they both respond to what each partner considers to be the customer's best interest. But while they are both *valid*, they cannot both be pursued at the same time. One goal must be chosen over the other. In our example, the partners must choose between closing the sale or leaving it open for further account development. Goals like these always involve making a choice between different solutions, solutions that may be strongly adhered to by each partner and that therefore may be difficult to resolve. These are *conflicting goals*.

The goals continuum, as we've expressed it here, provides a more complete picture of what everyone in the partnership is truly after than the more simple and limited let's-find-a-shared-goal approach. This inclusive approach to getting partners' overall interests on the table lays the groundwork for raising two of the most important questions partnerships have to deal with:

1. How can we leverage the partnership by supporting each other over time?
2. How can we take potential areas of conflict and resolve them collaboratively?

Normally, these aren't questions that come up on the first day of a partnership. But over time they become more and more critical.

The strongest partnerships we've seen leverage the partnership to help each supplier achieve their individual goals. And where goals are in conflict, strong partnerships have the wherewithal to resolve conflicts quickly and effectively. Dealing with the whole range of partners' goals, whether they are shared or not, is a core collaboration skill and a critical success factor in growing and maintaining effective partnerships.

SUPPORTABLE GOALS

Supportable goals are, to us, the most exciting part of the partnering story. When partners support each other's goals and help to make each other more successful, the routine of deal chasing gets transformed into the excitement of building success through collaboration. And it *is* exciting. We watched a pair of partners from Microsoft and Digital take the idea of finding and working through specific unshared goals on which they might be able to support each other, and in a few minutes discover $600,000 worth of business opportunity that had been sitting there, waiting for them, in an existing account. That isn't going to happen in every partnership every day. But there *is* power in getting behind a partner's goals and helping make them happen. There is a lot of potential energy in collaboration. The challenge is to bring it out.

The starting point for bringing out the energy is making sure you understand what your partner's goals really are. Rick Soskin, President and CEO of Centron, Inc., made exactly this point to us:

You can't succeed with a supplier partner without really understanding what's important to them. We may think sales volume, for instance, is what's important to a supplier. But it may not be volume. It may be meeting some definition they have of incremental sales volume or incremental customers, or maybe it has to do with how their product gets positioned in the marketplace. Without knowing what's important to them, you can't get anywhere.

Goals differ from company to company; sometimes an "obvious" goal like sales volume isn't a partner's most important objective. Sometimes a subtle goal, like increased "mind share" in a specific type of account, may be extremely important to a partner. The starting point for finding the energy in collaboration is to get a rock-solid understanding of what motivates your partner and what their most important goals are. This understanding isn't just going to happen on its own. It requires openness in the partnering conversation about goals in general. Lars Turndal of the Santa Cruz Operation advises:

> When you discuss partnership you have to try to put yourself into the other person's position. How do they think on the other side? You have to be a little more relaxed about your own agenda and your own goals, and a little more flexible in the discussion that there are different goals on both sides. It's not about going in saying, "I will get this as a partner." You need to be more open-minded than that.

Before the energy is going to come out of a collaboration, a very solid understanding by both partners of what each of them is after needs to be developed. As Lars suggests, this can be done informally through a casual and relaxed discussion with the partnership. Or, it can involve a more structured conversation that begins with a straightforward accounting of each partner's goals, as we encourage when we facilitate supplier partnerships. The point is simply that partners cannot get behind each other's unshared but supportable goals until they know what those goals *are*.

So what does a good supportable goal look like? For one thing, a good supportable goal is one that a partnership can really make happen. An application developer we know locally in Northern Virginia told us:

> We are traditionally a developer, but we wanted to get into support services. So we talked to Microsoft and said, "Hey, can you guys help us out? We want to get into service contracting." The Microsoft rep

turned us on to a few different account situations where we're well established at this point. Microsoft has the industry penetration to make something like this a reality for us.

This was a great supportable goal for Microsoft. But if our developer friend had needed assistance in getting into the design engineering market, he would have been better off seeking support somewhere else. A good supportable goal is one that the partnership is well suited to make happen, based on expertise, resources, and capabilities.

Good supportable goals also solve a real problem or satisfy a tangible need. They are not vague offers to help out or vague requests for assistance. They make a specific impact on a partner's business opportunities or objectives. Great examples abound of partners who have been able to get beyond "What am I going to get out of this?" to help a partner solve an immediate problem or tackle a specific issue. A nice case came to us from Jim Eberlin, head of sales at Tapestry Computing, Inc., a software developer. He provided what we consider to be a classic example of supporting a partner in need, in this case Oracle Corporation:

> We were working with Oracle in a number of accounts, and they told us there was a situation at a large credit card company where the Oracle license had been sold by somebody else. There was no one to do the installation and the customer was sitting there very unhappy. Oracle called us up and asked if there was anything we could do to run on out there. So we did. We did the work without any direct compensation on that installation. We said, "Okay, this is important to Oracle," and they were in a real jam, so we went out and did the work. This was our introduction to the account, and it led to a good-size development contract not a month later.

Jim's organization, Tapestry Computing, got a fast payback for his investment in the collaboration, and that's part of what makes his story an attractive one. More to the point, however, Tapestry Computing wasn't stuck in the quagmire of quid pro quos or trading favors. They got in there and helped a partner solve a problem. If a good supportable goal is one that is well-suited to the partnership, it is also one that can solve a real problem and bring impact to a partner.

To us the beauty of supportable goals is that they can have extremely high impact on the collaboration at a relatively low cost. Just how much effort, money, or resourcing does it take to help make a partner more successful? Usually, not too much. But the payoffs to the other partner and the collaboration itself can be enormous. Helping partners to be more successful by supporting their goals is the essence of collaboration and one of the key differences between *working together* and *partnering*.

We usually recommend that partners get started with this notion of supportable goals by

1. Identifying three to four different goals from each supplier that are not already shared within the partnership
2. Putting aside any that might represent potential conflict
3. Determining which single goal from each side is most easily achievable through the partnership and has the highest potential for tangible, immediate impact
4. Agreeing on what exactly the partnership can do to make each of these two goals happen

Over time the most effective partnerships generally become more and more fluid and proficient at supporting each partner's goals, and don't need to go through a process like this. For the purpose of getting started, though, this simple method is an easy way to begin moving beyond deal chasing and into growth through collaboration.

CONFLICTING GOALS

Shared and supportable goals are the exciting and positive elements of partnering. But what about the dark side—goals in conflict? Conflicting goals are all but inevitable at some point in a partnering relationship. Conflicts can range from the usual disagreements about when to close a sale, to hostile, diametrically opposed positions on, say, suppliers' roles in an account. No one likes to deal with conflicting goals. And everyone knows that ignoring them is not the answer. As Bernard Guidon of Hewlett-Packard noted: "Sometimes people don't want to talk about the negative piece. But conflicts can get under the rug, and after a while, become so big that nothing works." It isn't smart for partnerships to ignore conflicting goals, nor is it wise to try to muscle through conflicts after they have become major problems. It is essential for partnerships to have a strategy to resolve conflicts quickly and unemotionally as they arise.

Resolving Conflicting Goals.   The most effective conflict resolution strategies have come from the work of professional negotiators, and we've adapted the general concept of negotiated conflict resolution to the specific use of helping supplier partners to resolve their conflicts. So what does negotiation theory say? Simply put, that *you'll never get to resolution of a conflict by arguing out opposing positions, unless and until one partner unhappily capitulates.* "We should close the deal now" and "We should wait a few months" aren't resolvable without someone biting the bullet and giving in—at least not at the level of what the partners are *saying.* On the other hand, there's more room to devise an effective resolution when partners get beyond their initial positions and work at the level of *underlying needs.* This can be a tough concept, and like a lot of subtle ideas it is best communicated through analogy. Our favorite analogy came to us from Gary Pillette of Microsoft, who has helped facilitate a number of their solution provider partnerships. As he put it:

> When I first met my wife in Oregon, we had a real conflict. I wanted to live by the ocean. She wanted to live in the mountains. We couldn't do both, so we had a seemingly irresolvable conflict. We agreed not to discuss it for the time being, but eventually we had to work out where we were going to live. So we thought through what the real needs were.
>
> I wanted to have a place to sail; you don't need to live on an ocean to do that. It turns out that my wife's need was to wake up in the morning and see the majesty of the mountains; you can do that without living in the mountains. Working through those needs brought us to Seattle—and me to Microsoft—because Seattle is surrounded by beautiful mountains and also has some of the best sailing in North America. So the point is, we got nowhere with positions, but when we figured out what it is we both really needed, we came to a resolution that made everyone happy. You can usually find a solution if you start from the real needs.

Gary's analogy hits on what negotiation theorists like Ury and Fisher have been saying for years. Conflicts rarely get resolved satisfactorily at the level of *positions.* They get resolved more quickly, more

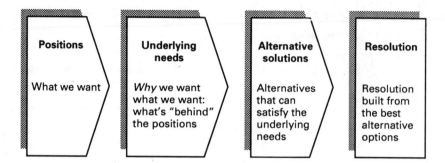

Figure 7-3 *Conflict resolution model.*

effectively, and more satisfactorily at the level of *needs*. Becoming adept with a partner at resolving conflict at a needs level is a power move for getting over differences. We've used this approach to help dozens of partners resolve tough conflicts, using a model that looks like the one in Fig. 7-3.

The idea behind this model is simple and compelling. Conflict starts over a difference in position on an issue, like "Let's close the sale today" versus "Let's wait." Before jumping to solutions or disagreement, the model encourages partners to work through what it is they're really looking for that led to those positions. These underlying needs provide a basis for devising alternative solutions that may be more amenable to both partners. And it's from these alternative solutions that a partnership can arrive at an overall resolution to the conflict. This strategy does not work in every conflict situation, but we've found that it's an extremely effective way to put conflicts to bed in most day-to-day conflicting goal situations. Let's take a look at how the model plays out in a partnering conflict.

Positions.   What each party says they want—their stated goals.

> TRIDAC CONSULTING: We want to handle all of the direct interaction with the client, T. Brown and Associates (TB&A).

> HARTT GROUP: We were brought in to the account as a partner, so we want to participate in direct customer contact with TB&A.

An unresolvable conflict at the level of positions.

Underlying Needs. What's "underneath" the partners' positions—their true needs.

TRIDAC CONSULTING: We want to maintain the strong relationship we've built with TB&A over the past three years...and we're not sure TB&A likes having multiple suppliers around.

HARTT GROUP: We need to get a better feel for TB&A's requirements before we can design our piece of the solution. And TB&A has long been a target customer of ours; we want to demonstrate our capabilities and develop credibility with them for the future.

Here, both Tridac and Hartt have moved beyond their opening salvos and identified what's underneath their positions.

Alternative Solutions. Solutions based not on the initial positions but on the underlying needs, to get a wide range of options open for consideration.

TRIDAC CONSULTING: We could help Hartt off-line to get smarter about the project and the client without threatening the customer relationship at all. We could soften TB&A's reluctance about multiple suppliers by getting Hartt some small wins. And we could easily maintain the lead in face-to-face selling, while including Hartt in a safe support role, as long as they agree not to mess around in the account while they're getting up to speed.

HARTT GROUP: We could review Tridac's documentation on TB&A to get a better understanding of the client. In the meantime, we could build credibility with the client by getting included as technical experts in joint presentations with Tridac, which would be relatively low risk to them. And we could participate in a small way in direct selling to get started, to prove to Tridac that we know what we're doing.

These alternative solutions, developed from the underlying needs, represent give and take between the partners. No one's going to get exactly what they want, so they're generating a number of alternatives they can work through together.

Resolution. An agreement for moving forward, based on the best alternative solutions.

Tridac Consulting and Hartt Group agree to:

- Share documentation and other information on TB&A, so that Hartt can "get smart" about the client.

- Have Tridac continue to take the lead in direct customer interaction, with Hartt brought in in a safe, supporting role after they're up to speed.

- Position Hartt as a leader in servicing TB&A's industry so that they can build their own credibility, and include them in technical (but not marketing) presentations

- Get Hartt a quick win, and work with TB&A to relieve concerns about multiple suppliers as the project moves forward

> *While not giving either supplier exactly what they had articulated in their opening positions, this resolution responds well to the real needs of the partnering organizations. It doesn't represent a complete victory for either partner as much as a fair resolution of a potentially difficult conflict.*

As you review the progression of events in the resolution of this conflict between Tridac and Hartt, you may be surprised by how sensibly and logically these two partners were able to take a difficult, no-compromise situation and pull out of it a reasonable, balanced resolution. For on the surface, this conflict seems to have no particularly easy resolution. Partners in high technology and distribution, for example, will be able to see how very close it is to the tough and sometimes acrimonious conflicts they face with partners all the time.

There is a very strong learning point here about dealing with conflict: *Underlying needs are a better platform for working through conflicts than stated positions.* Underlying needs provide more alternative solutions and they provide more room to maneuver. We are not suggesting that partners carry around with them a four-phase model of conflict resolution. We *are* suggesting, however, that the distinction between working from *positions* and working from *underlying needs* is an important one. "What do I want, and what do they want?" is not as effective as "What do I really need to be comfortable with this, and what do they really need?" Underlying needs are, in general, the best platform for resolving a partnering conflict.

That is, underlying needs are the best platform for resolving a conflict if the conflict can be resolved at all. What do you do when conflict with a partner is absolutely, positively beyond resolution or compromise?

Dealing with Intractable Conflict.   In the early days of partnering, suppliers chose a handful of complementary allies and natural collaborators, and sifted through their differences without great difficulty. How much conflict can there really be with allies with whom you've specifically chosen to work? Today, the situation is different. With the explosion of supplier partnering, there is a tremendous amount of activity going on between supplier organizations who are not natural allies and who may, indeed, be vicious competitors.

These organizations have to partner to survive, but they are also bringing to the partnership, and sometimes to customers, extreme conflicts that are just intractable. These are conflicts that cannot be resolved within the partnership at all. There would be no point in trying to get to the underlying need, because the underlying need might be something like, "Drive the other supplier out of the account." The best way to know if you have one of these conflicts with a partner is to see if you agree with this sentiment:

> In general, I respect them and accept their coexistence in the marketplace, but in this account, I'd really like to crush them.

If you have an intractable conflict, one that just cannot be resolved, you need a different approach than getting to the underlying needs. The strategy of last resort for truly intractable conflicts is to reorient around the customer's goals rather than the conflicting ones within the partnership. The *customer's* goals, after all, are the important ones. John Gogniat, a sales representative at Sun Microsystems, passed along to us a story much in support of this approach:

> We have a real conflict with a supplier in the network management area at a tire manufacturer. The customer currently has the other supplier's products installed. But we've come out with products that are in direct competition with those products and offer the customer some real advantages over the current way they address PCs. From a network management standpoint there are things we need to do with the other supplier to make things work, to connect their servers with our servers, and so on. The incumbent supplier doesn't particularly want to work with us and doesn't want to open up the

network to the point where we could propose our way of doing things.

This sounded like an unresolvable conflict, and we asked John how he dealt with the problem. His response:

> The only thing you can do is support the customer and say, "Here are the parts you need to integrate into your environment," and then you fully support the customer's implementation of whatever products they're using. You may get a chance to say, "By the way, here's another way to solve this problem," and you make available technical information that can help shape a decision. In situations like this, though, the only thing you can do is refocus your efforts based on the customer's goals. You can't resolve the conflict on your own.

When we counsel partners who have truly intractable conflicts, we ask them to put aside their conflicting goals and focus exclusively on what the customer needs from the partnership. That, it turns out, often leads to some practical compromises so the partners can get on with their work and make sure the customer is satisfied. In the end it's the customer's interest that matters, and it is good to keep this in mind when tough conflicts arise.

Growing the common ground is a skilled activity and it doesn't happen in a day. It's a long-term strategy of supporting partners' goals—and vice versa—to get more value out of the partnership, and working through conflicts to build more durable partnerships. So far we've been looking mostly at goals and, in general, the issue of alignment between partners around what they're seeking to accomplish. Partners, however, also have to *do* things together; it is not enough to have a goal or a plan. And this raises the important issue of defining partnering roles for the collaboration.

DEFINING PARTNERING ROLES

In our chapter on Intimacy (Chap. 4), we presented a view of supplier-customer relationships that entails a blurring of boundaries between organizations and a melding of personnel, as suppliers and customers move toward shared ground and common understanding. The strongest supplier-customer partnerships we've seen, such as those in place at Bose Corporation, involve people almost "floating" between organizations with little regard to traditional roles and responsibilities. That is a strong image and a powerful paradigm for partnering with customers. But it is a costly and damaging approach to partnering with other suppliers. In supplier-to-supplier partnering, different forces are in play, and the roles of partnering suppliers need to be defined with precise clarity. These roles also need to be oriented very carefully and specifically around customers' interests. These two themes drive role definition in successful supplier partnerships, and achieving both constitutes one of the most important skills of effective supplier collaboration.

DEFINING PARTNERING ROLES WITH CLARITY

In supplier-customer partnering, the customer communicates what they want and suppliers define their roles around the customer's needs and opportunities. There is not all that much room for miscommunication about who does what, and when there is a miscommunication, the customer usually straightens it out by getting annoyed, thereby acting as a catalyst for rethinking of role on the part of the supplier. That is a natural corrective mechanism which tends to keep suppliers closely aligned with their customers and keeps roles simple and well defined.

The same cannot be said of role definition in supplier-to-supplier partnering. Here there is potential for chaos, and great room for confusion and discord; indeed, these surface frequently in supplier partnerships. In these relationships there may be some feedback from the customer about the overall performance of the partnership—"I'm satisfied" or "I'm not pleased"—but not much is going to come in the way of customer feedback about which partner should be doing what. This is a significant difference between supplier-customer partnering and supplier-to-supplier partnering, and it is easy to omit a role or duplicate efforts as a result. We found ourselves, for example, writing the same proposal as one of our professional service partners—for the same project.

That was a little bump on the road to a successful partnership. Sometimes, however, role confusion can totally blow up the road. An insurance customer of one of our high-technology clients, when offered an opportunity to go on video for a partnering seminar, jumped at the opportunity. We sat in stunned silence in the video room as he vented his frustration on camera about the confusion and lack of coordination between his partnering suppliers:

An insurance claims processing system cannot *ever* go down. It just can't. You've got old people waiting to get checks to pay their medical bills. So last week the system crashes, and I call up one partner and say, "Get over here and fix the damn problem." He says, "You have to call the other partner's technical support desk." I call their support desk and they tell me, "That's a problem for the other partner; it's their software."

So the system was down for 18 hours while we tried to figure out how to fix it, causing millions of transactions to bottleneck, affecting our customer service and our reliability. I don't know how to say this strongly enough. *It was a nightmare.* That just cannot ever, ever happen again.

As that manager's frustration makes clear, role confusion is no minor issue in supplier partnering. It is a *critical* issue. Stefan Sjostrom of the Santa Cruz Operation goes as far as to suggest that defining roles with absolute precision is at the core of successful supplier partnering: "One of the most important success factors, and perhaps the most important of them all, is clarity of roles between the various partners. Without that as a foundation, you end up with very real and difficult problems." Confusion over roles can seriously impact the quality of service delivered to customers—and that, more than anything else, can kill a partnership, not to mention an account.

If there were a magic formula for defining who does what, we would enthusiastically provide it. Unfortunately, there isn't. It's not like staffing a project from within one organization; you can't easily assign each role to an individual person; there may be two account managers and three sales engineers involved, all of whom need to participate but who, inevitably, trip over each others' toes. And it's not just the formal organization chart that gets messy. There is often considerable overlap of desired responsibility between partners. It's unrealistic to expect or demand otherwise; when you put two closely related organizations together, you're going to have role preferences held in common.

In short, roles get hazy in supplier partnering relationships. Rick Soskin of Centron notes:

It is very unusual to have a partnership where there is a clear line between what partner A does and what partner B does. If there weren't some gray areas in there, they probably wouldn't have a real need to be partnering.

Partners with no potential areas for confusion or discord over roles probably aren't partnering; they're probably just working in the same account. If you are partnering for real, you are probably dealing with potential role confusion.

When we work with supplier partners, we ask them to take the time to think through all the different roles that need to be performed, given their particular customer situation. These roles often include, for example, account management, proposal preparation, face-to-face selling, and postimplementation follow-through. For some partnerships—those focusing on marketing programs and so forth—the roles may be completely different. But there are always identifiable roles that need to be carried out. We ask partners to identify all of the roles in their partnership based on the simple question "What is every role you need to perform to provide full coverage of responsibilities to the customer?" It's the right question because it addresses the highest risk of role confusion: neglecting a responsibility to a customer.

To achieve the kind of clarity required for establishing definitive partnering roles, we ask partners to put all of those roles across the top of a matrix that looks something like the one seen in Fig. 7-4. We then have partners work *individually* to take their best shot at identifying who's doing what, as shown in an actual case in Fig. 7-4. We have

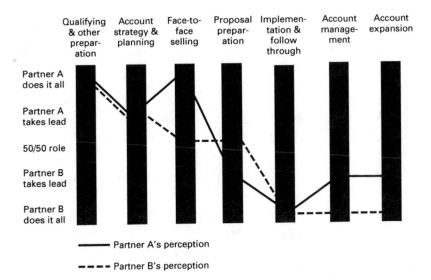

Figure 7-4 *Partnering roles matrix.*

them work separately, because when we've tried having partners do it together they quickly agree on all roles without a minute's hesitation—and fail to discuss any of them in depth. In having partners perform this activity separately, on the other hand, *we can count on two or three hands the number of partner pairs who have ever been in complete agreement on their respective roles.* There is almost always some area of disagreement or confusion. These areas represent role risk. So when partners have identified all differences of opinion or disagreement, we then give them some time to argue and iron out each role in contention. This activity, and its track record of helping partners iron out role risks, contain some important learning points. We'd suggest that role clarity emerges from a three-step process of

1. Identifying all possible roles, to guarantee full coverage of responsibilities for the customer

2. Isolating, through some process (we use the matrix), where the differences of opinion are

3. Putting agreed-upon roles aside, and spending sufficient time and energy to dissect differences of opinion and negotiate, to conclusion, on areas of disagreement

Although that's a simple approach, it has been an effective one for partners who we've counseled. When we work with partnering organizations, we go further into the actual negotiation of roles, but that's a level of detail which is unnecessary to get started and to cover the basics.

DEFINING ROLES AROUND CUSTOMERS' INTERESTS

While the framework we have just laid out is effective when it comes to ironing out basic role issues, it's a bit of an oversimplification. Deciding who gets what in an account isn't a neutral process of blandly dividing up responsibilities. Role issues, and particularly role conflict, often have less to do with task assignment than with politically charged notions of account control and ownership. Who "owns" the customer? Who is empowered to represent the partnership in customer decision making? Who gets to have dinner with the VP when he or she is in a spending kind of mood, and who has to stay back with the customer's technical support personnel and walk around with the soldering iron? In short, *who is in charge?* That question is the central catalyst behind most role conflicts. As Oracle's Polly Sumner suggests, somewhat sardonically:

> The whole thing is really hard for salespeople and partners to get. One of our system integrator partners believes they own the customer, and they perceive that anybody else in there who's making a recommendation is a tremendous threat. They're afraid of losing account control. Another integrator is in that same account, and they're certain that the account is going to buy their hardware and that they have account control. The only one who's got account control is the account themselves, and they're trying to control all of us.

Polly's humorous observation makes a serious point. As Hemang Davé, Lotus Development Corporation's Vice President of Alliances, notes:

> The control-oriented person finds it very difficult to partner because they can't control anything. One of the things that one learns after partnering for a while is that you don't control them, and they don't control you. A different philosophy has to emerge out of partnership.

This philosophy isn't coming easily to everyone. We've watched countless supplier partners argue over who has account control, who is "in charge," and who is empowered to call the shots.

On some level these probably are valid discussions, for whatever they're worth. To organizations steeped in a history of direct customer contact and close monitoring of account direction, the decentralization of power inherent in supplier-to-supplier partnering is not coming easily. To salespeople whose compensation systems are in direct conflict with their organizations' exhortations to partner, account control can be a legitimate concern, as Paul Hoffman, a Vice President at Oracle, explains:

> It comes down to the legacy of, "We've got to control it. I've got to close it. If I don't do it myself, my boss will think it happened for free, and I wasn't even involved, so therefore I'm not getting any credit for it."

For organizations who really do need to maintain ownership in accounts, such as large integrators who have multiple suppliers reporting to them, account control is a valid issue that has less to do with power struggles than with doing what they get paid by the customer to do: maintain order.

The bottom line, however, is that account control—*who's in charge*—is a distraction from the real issue in supplier-to-supplier partnering. That issue is simply:

What is best for the customer?

It sounds so simple that it's almost a cliché. That is, it's a cliché unless you have witnessed, as we have, suppliers spending a majority of their time negotiating around account control while a customer is sitting there saying, "I don't *care* who's in control. Who am I supposed to call when I have a problem?" Account control conflicts can and do lower the service levels provided to customers. Rick Soskin of Centron provided us with an excellent perspective on this. His organization, a $120 million networking hardware business, has gone through all the paces of supplier-to-supplier travails with its larger partners. Rick himself has seen account control affect not only roles within accounts, but much more broadly, the overall assignment of partners to opportunities. As he explains:

> If you try to divide up the world like FDR and the others at Yalta, you'll just divide up the world, and it won't have anything to do with the reality of how your customers want to do business. It has to be customer-by-customer. What doesn't work very well is, "We'll go after this type of account, and you go after that type of account; if they're big, we'll take them, if they're small, you take them." Some big accounts are looking for speed of service and somebody they can call up on a phone [which a smaller company may be better equipped for]. They don't want a body or the overhead that goes with a body [that larger suppliers can provide].

> If you listen to the customer, you hear the things that should tell you, "Okay, I'm going to be more important to the customer's decision process than the large company"—or vice versa. Most of our partners have a very structured approach to dividing up the customer, and that's the toughest thing we've had to deal with. I tell people, "Look, if we just listen to the customer, we'll be fine."

Distribution of account ownership and other key responsibilities is often based on marketing matrices or, more problematically, the pure muscle of negotiating strength between the partners. Is that really best for the customer? It *could* be—by coincidence, if whatever model of account control being used happens to map to the customer's needs. But it could also be way, way off.

Many partners end up winning the account-control battle at the expense of the customer. Their partners lose the battle but *should* be in charge—given the customer's needs. Account control is a valid partnering issue, but it cannot be the centerpiece of the partnership. As Bob Lozano, President of Tapestry Computing, Inc., suggests:

> You find yourself worrying about account control, and you just have to kick yourself and say, "Let's get on with it. I'm going to consciously make the decision that I'm not going to get bogged down in this. I'm going to make this work for the customer."

The centerpiece of the partnership simply *has* to be the customer's best interest.

So, when we ask partners to work through their roles, we make sure they center their role negotiation, the discussion around areas of disagreement, not on any preconceived notions of who is in charge, *wants* to be in charge, or feels they have a *right* to be in charge. We ask them to put aside, to whatever extent they are able, who sold the account or who has a better claim to the "prime" role. We ask them to focus instead on the simple but crucial question, "Granted that there's a difference of opinion over roles, what is truly best for the customer?" That is a more meaningful question than "Who's in charge?" and it turns out to be the best launching point for assigning responsibilities in a partnership.

ACHIEVING BALANCE IN THE PARTNERSHIP

Back in 1991, we met at Huthwaite with a group of sales managers from one of the largest systems integrators in the country to talk about emerging partnering issues. As we were wrapping up, the conversation went "off line" as the team began to address their reservations about their own organization's partnering strategies. One manager volunteered: "I think anyone involved in partnering has seen that if the situation is not in balance, if there's inequity in the relationship, then it's not going to work." He added:

We've been very slow to get our people ramped up on this idea. We go out with smaller companies to partner, and we have so much influence because of our size, we can basically say "Jump" and the partner says "How high?" And if they don't jump, we just call some-one else. Our people are a little arrogant about this. They need to understand that there has to be an equitable distribution of rewards for the various partners.

"Where's the problem?" we asked him. A small handful of compa-nies have the leverage, through size, customer base, or market domi-nance, to enjoy a natural upper hand in supplier relationships. Why worry about an "equitable" distribution of rewards? After all, aren't people getting out of accounts what they agree to get out of them? If they're making a profit, where's the issue? Our friend had some sober-ing words for us:

> We get other vendors to jump for us, but the first chance they get, they recommend a competitive solution. We take them off the list, and then another alliance partner does the same thing. There's no loyalty at all; they couldn't care less about us.
>
> Maybe worse. I can name off the top of my head several accounts where our "partners," I think, deliberately did us wrong. Until we start dealing with the real problem, getting our partners a fair deal, corporate's going to keep taking names off the partnering list until we have no partners left. And that means we'll get nowhere in terms of bringing complete solutions to the customer.
>
> So here you've got a situation where management is working on three thousand different angles of channel selling, except the one angle that's most important to all of our channel partners: what's in it for them? Why shouldn't they just take whatever they can get from us, and then recommend competitive solutions? This is a real problem, especially for the long term.

We have to admit that we had to think about that one for a while, and we had to hear it from several companies before it really sank in. Another group of managers, this time from Microsoft, stopped by at Huthwaite almost two years later to talk about progress with their solu-tion provider program. Chris Phinney, at the time a large account manag-er but now part of Microsoft Consulting Services, voiced sentiments sim-ilar to those we had heard from the first group: "Our solution providers have to get a real share of the rewards for this to work. We have to make sure they get a fair amount of the win. What can we do to help these solution providers to be successful? How are we helping them get something important from working with us? These are the kinds of questions we should be asking all of the solution providers we partner with."

Tim Bauer, a manager out of Phoenix and an attendee at that meeting, commented as well: "There has to be balance; it has to be a fair deal to begin with."

To us, those were important observations. As sales effectiveness consultants—and as partners with a few organizations ourselves—our angle had always been "Organizations can partner successfully only if it's a win-win." But there seem to be WIN-wins, win-WINs, and WIN-WINs. Perhaps it is more meaningful to talk about just how much "win" each partner is getting out of the collaboration. If I give you 1 percent of the reward, you may be willing to work with me—but you're not going to like it, and you may extract your retribution later. Seer Technologies' André Boisvert provided us with an insightful analogy. As André suggests, providing partners with fair deals is similar to hiring an employee:

> In partnering you've got to say to yourself, "Is my partner making enough off the deal?" It's like you coming and applying for a job. I give you the job and we negotiate it, and I'm screwing you to the last minute. You may say, "Okay," but as you're walking out the door I can tell you're not happy about it. What happens over time? The whole situation is going to fall apart. You're going to go read the 10K report, and you're going to say, "He makes *what??!!*" Without me, he couldn't be who he is, so hold on here. I got screwed!" You'll start being miserable at work. And it will start showing up in many different ways.

What we like about André's analogy is that his employee's dissatisfaction has nothing to do with how much he gets paid in an absolute sense; it could be *millions* for all we know. His dissatisfaction, rather, is focused on the imbalance of reward given his own perceived contribution of effort.

This is a tough issue for many partnering organizations. A lot of partnering suppliers are creating opportunities for other suppliers and, in fact, helping them make money. Sometimes, a *lot* of money. They're doing their part, as far as they can tell. But their partners, even after several years of working together, are no more likely to remain loyal than to do a complete bait-and-switch with a customer the moment they get into an account. As Lars Turndal of SCO suggests: "They say, 'Okay, we need you now,' but there's no loyalty. As soon as they have a chance to jump ship, they do." These partners, having sometimes spent years doing the drudge work of the partnership, while all the while getting a tiny fraction of the total prize, are willing to take the deals—they *do* need them—but they couldn't care less about the partnership when it comes time to make recommendations or to stick with a brand.

The evidence suggests that there is a strong relationship between equitable distribution of the total win and the loyalty and commitment of supplier partners. To feel loyalty and commitment to a partner, suppliers have to get not simply a win but a *fair share of the total win,* given the relative amount of effort they're putting in. In a word, partnering relationships have to be *in balance* to succeed.

ADDRESSING THE BALANCE ISSUE

Directly addressing the balance of effort and reward in a partnership—not just talking about it, but doing something about it—is a smart strategy. Balance issues are always present, and they don't just disappear or recede from view for lack of articulation. The question is not, "Is there a balance issue?" There *always* is. The question is whether suppliers are going to react to it down the road—after it emerges as a problem—or deal with it in the present, while it's neutral and easy to address.

What does a conversation about balance in a partnering relationship look like? It is a "soft" topic that is quite removed from everyday account plans and selling. It doesn't usually happen on its own. Where do you start? In our experience, the best starting point is an assessment, with a partner, of the current state of affairs in the relationship. Partners have to start with a shared sense of where the balance—or imbalance—is in the partnership. The key question is, simply, *what is each partner putting into the relationship, and what is each partner getting out of it?* To get this kind of conversation under way, we generally recommend that partners work around a basic balance-sheet model such as the one seen in Fig. 7-5. The advantage of using this type of model is that it simplifies and clarifies exactly what partners are giving to and getting from the partnership.

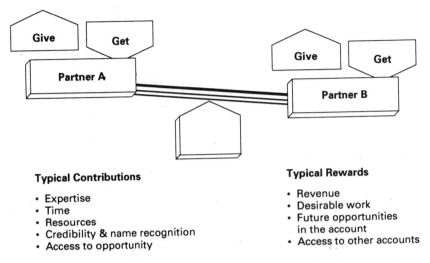

Typical Contributions

- Expertise
- Time
- Resources
- Credibility & name recognition
- Access to opportunity

Typical Rewards

- Revenue
- Desirable work
- Future opportunities
  in the account
- Access to other accounts

Figure 7-5   *Balance of contribution and reward in a partnership.*

For example, a recent partnership we helped to facilitate came up with the ideas illustrated in Fig. 7-6. This partnership displays nicely the basic idea behind the model: breaking down contribution and reward into smaller "chunks" that can be compared. It's a good model to use. But this partnership also displays what happens when people go through an activity of this kind. This partnership is not in balance. In fact, it took some very serious negotiations to straighten it out. Partner A, a Maryland training supplier, had invested tremendous resources and commitment into making the partnership work; they had received little for that effort other than vague promises to get some leads in the account. Partner A almost pulled out. And that cuts to the core issue: If you do this activity, you will likely find imbalances. What do you do about them?

REDRESSING IMBALANCES

With partnering moving out of infancy and into adolescence, there is a tremendous existing need for suppliers to have a range of approaches and techniques for evening up their relationships with other suppliers. To get started we offer a few straightforward methods, strategies that we've tested in actual partnerships and determined to be sound and simple means for redressing basic imbalances.

Partner	Contribution	Reward
A	Assistance with proposal development and overall sales effort	$80K total revenue, $45K net
	3.5 FTEs {personnel}	Potential intro to marketing group
	$35K for all-color deliverables	Getting experience in professional services training
	Implementing training globally	
B	Brought {****} into the account	$500,000 in product revenue
	Managing overall implementation	Gain experience in professional services
	Benefit of our long-standing relationiship with the customer	Developing strong contacts at executive levels

Figure 7-6 *Contribution/reward balance sheet.*

Step 1. *Look to the current opportunity to solve the problem.*   The first question in balancing a partnership is, "Is there some way we can easily adjust either the contribution or the reward of either partner, to arrive at a more equitable arrangement for this opportunity?"

The most common balance issue is over-resourcing by one supplier; partner A is committing a full-time person while partner B is happily cashing checks, owing simply to the nature of the work. Partner A can't argue that the account situation should be otherwise—it's just the way it is, based on the work involved—but partner A is increasingly displeased with the high cost of doing business in the partnership.

Before partner B makes promises of greater rewards in the future, or looks around for a new lead, is there something partner B can do today, around *this* opportunity, to adjust contributions (in this case, resources in the account) or perhaps rewards, to arrive at something more equitable? We've found that about half of all balance problems evaporate as soon as partners make some adjustments, *within the opportunity they are already working on.*

Step 2. *Look to the overall account as a larger source of balance.* Sometimes it is either impractical or impossible to tinker with an existing opportunity. The roles, rewards, and other variables have already been established and agreed to by the customer. So what can you do to achieve better balance?

The next move is to elevate the balance discussion to an account level. Are there other opportunities within the account, either existing or potential, where a partner could be getting either more business—greater rewards—or a different type of business that involves more moderate contribution of effort to get those rewards? By sticking with an existing partnering account as the focus, this step keeps the discussion "local"; it encourages fixing the balance at the source. It's about "How can we take what we've already got and make it more fair?" versus "Okay, it's not fair, we'll find you another account." It's a smart approach, because it reserves leads and opportunities in other accounts for future discussions within the partnering relationship.

Step 3. *Look to other accounts for balance.* The last step—and it *should* be the last step, because it's the final source of balancing available—is to escalate the discussion to a broad assessment of how other accounts can be brought into the fray to achieve balance. One supplier we've worked with solved a serious partnering inequity—they had made $2 million in shrink-wrapped software sales; their partner, only $40,000 in labor-intensive services in a hostile customer environment—by introducing their partner to a larger, more pleasant account where the revenue and margins were much higher. This isn't the starting point for redressing balances, but it can be an extremely effective strategy when steps 1 or 2 are impractical or impossible.

Balance in a supplier partnership isn't a "nice to have." It's a *must do.* Without balance, there can be no loyalty or commitment between partners. Without loyalty and commitment, there is no basis for collaborating. While not always the most comfortable conversation, getting the balance issue on the table early in a partnering relationship is essential. And it's essential on a continual, ongoing basis. Partnerships need to get in balance to work. They also need to *stay* in balance to work.

CONCLUSION

Partnering between suppliers is here to stay. It is increasingly the way companies just do business. It has become a routine expectation of customers. And the momentum of supplier collaboration continues to grow at an exponential pace. While it was considered exceptional in the early 1990s, earning all sorts of new-age techno-labels, today supplier partnering is not the least bit unusual or remarkable. It is already part of the mosaic of the everyday business landscape. By the year 2000 there will be few products or accounts that don't involve multiple suppliers partnering toward one objective or another.

There are fewer and fewer industries where suppliers can afford to go it alone, either in terms of costs or in terms of competitive pressure from groups of other collaborating suppliers. A few slow-track industries may escape the trend for a while. But the logic of supplier-to-supplier partnering—that combining forces to achieve productivity and impact provides a competitive edge—isn't going to pass by all that many industries without making its mark.

Where does all this leave suppliers and their sales forces? Supplier-to-supplier partnering continues to encroach upon more and more of the space of the traditional, stand-alone supplier strategy, leaving less and less room for suppliers to rely on traditional selling and marketing skills. Collaboration is the core skill of this new model of interfacing with other organizations. Those who have the skills, training, and tools to build effective, durable collaborative relationships over time with other suppliers will succeed. Those who cannot make this transition are already in trouble. In high technology, distribution, communications, and media, for example, the landscape already is littered with organizations who've been trounced by partnering competitors. How far behind can other industries really be? We don't know the answer to that question, but we suspect: not too far.

Suppliers and their sales forces cannot put aside the imperative to build collaboration skills throughout their organizations. We've worked for several years on this issue, and we've seen many organizations struggle through the transition from a selling to a collaboration environment. We've seen all the memos, exhortations to partner, theoretical models, and public relations–driven partnering events. When all is said and done, partnering is working only where the people on the front line—and that's usually salespeople—have sufficient skills and savvy to develop strong collaborative relationships with their partners. Taking those skills seriously, and ensuring that they're held broadly within partnering organizations, is going to differentiate the winners from the losers for years to come.

PUTTING IT ALL TOGETHER

Why not just skip partnering? What if you sell scrap metal, or pool cleaning products, or wood pulp, or low-end fax machines? What if you're in a market where you never even *see* a customer because your products are sold exclusively through indirect channels? What if you're a sales rep making $100,000 a year, or a company that has 30 percent gross margins? Do you really need to be concerned about partnering?

Yes, you do. For the fact is, partnering is not some flashy paradigm developed in the offices of inventive consultants. It is the way companies today, right now, are rescoping how they work with each other. It is the very source of competitive differentiation in many industries today. And increasingly it is an expectation—in some cases, a requirement—of customers. If the word *partnering* sounds a little "buzzy," you can pass by it. We used it in this book because it's a familiar word that many people are comfortable with. Whatever word you use, though, something extremely important is happening out there, as organizations find productivity and create impact by collaborating differently. And it's already affecting, or soon will affect, *every* supplier and sales force.

There is just no getting around it. If you sell commodity products on a low-cost basis, your competitors are probably already exploring how to sell nearly identical products, but with higher impact, through partnering relationships. Think back to some of our examples in this book. Take, for example, Bose's various production suppliers, who play critical roles in product development and procurement, saving Bose millions and helping them to get higher-quality products to market. Or take North American Bolt and Screw, who integrated into IBM's environment to cut cycle time from ten days to two, manage production schedules, and help design new, more standard products. Or Okonite, a cable manufacturer who, along with other partners, has helped Public Service Electric and Gas cut inventory by more than $100 million.

These are all commodity suppliers who are locking in their customers for the long haul by creating greater impact through partnering. So don't be misled by the products you sell. You may sell paper clips for a living, but there is someone out there, right now, finding a way to integrate paper clips into some larger office productivity project that's going to take away your best customers. As products come to look more alike, and prices come down, and quality becomes more and more of a "given," where else are you going to get competitive differentiation but in business relationships themselves? Kevin Brownsey, Director of Sales at W. H. Smith, the contract stationer, observed:

> Because we're in a commodity-based marketplace where a number of companies have very similar product offerings, we're having to differentiate ourselves in the eyes of our customers. You can't do that through products anymore. So the differentiation is in the services we offer, through our internal procedures, through partnering. We are very conscious about the need to tie ourselves in and lock ourselves into our customers, to become interdependent with them.

Likewise, if you sell through indirect channels, if you never see a customer, you're probably less inclined to spend time thinking about partnering. You shouldn't be. Partnering within supply chains—aligning with other suppliers through systems, operating procedures, and more in-depth relationships—is bringing higher impact and lower cost to consumers. Partnering with distributors and complementary suppliers, especially in high-technology and other cutting-edge industries, is transforming the very notion of "value" as suppliers team up to get total solutions to market. We mentioned several cases in this book of supply chain and indirect-selling partnering, but in fact there are thousands of companies finding competitive advantage through supplier collaboration. If your product doesn't provide 100 percent of the overall, total best solution—and *no* supplier provides this type of product anymore—then you need to be thinking about finding partners who will enable you to compete in today's marketplace. Because *cus-*

tomers are buying impact today, they are not simply buying products. You cannot afford to ignore this dramatic shift in customer buying behavior, whether or not you ever see a customer.

If you are a sales rep making $100,000 a year, or the manager of a business making huge margins, you might reasonably ask yourself, "Why should I want to do anything differently?" And you would be right to ask that question. It's the old "If it's not broken, don't fix it" story. The problem is, it *is* broken. As customers continue to slash their supplier bases, in some cases by over 90 percent, it's unrealistic to think you can retain your customers without finding fundamentally new ways to add value and collaborate.

Locally, for example, we know a sales executive for a printing company who made $350,000 last year selling high-end annual reports and other public relations deliverables. Two years ago, his skepticism about the whole partnering concept was extremely high, and rightly so. He had always sold on charisma and pure selling talent; his customers just plain like him. But today his customers are cutting back drastically on the number of their printing suppliers, and looking to lock in one printing vendor with whom they can "go deep" for the long term. They are not buying annual reports anymore; now they're buying:

- *Vendor-advocates,* who can integrate into their operating environments to cut costs
- *Team expertise,* to incorporate the printing and design processes into their overall business message positioning efforts
- *Seamless coordination with printers,* to get more complex, higher-quality deliverables produced faster and more responsively for shareholders and other audiences
- *Vision,* of how their media, like annual reports, can help them achieve differentiation from their competitors

These customers are no longer choosing vendors based just on products or salesmanship. They're hand-picking their few top suppliers based on value added, the strength of the collaboration, and a real vision of benefit through mutual change. You still need good selling skills, but if you're going to survive in this environment you have to have something more to offer than a standard product, everyday service, and good skills. That means that if you're making $100,000 a year, or if you have high gross margins, you may be okay for now. But in the next few years, as your customers whittle away at their supplier base—and they *will*—your survival is going to depend on whether you are bringing enough *vision, impact,* and *intimacy* to the relationship to justify selection as one of the chosen few.

PARTNERING: A SOURCE OF REAL COMPETITIVE ADVANTAGE

You cannot afford to ignore partnering. It makes too much sense. When organizations tap the largely untapped reservoir of productivity between themselves and their partners, they achieve higher impact—more value—for their customers as well as for themselves. Usually they can substantially lower costs by eliminating redundancies and waste between organizations. And with their partners, they can often combine capabilities to bring more and better value to consumers than they could possibly achieve on their own.

Put simply, partnering organizations have more to offer each other and the marketplace. And in return their transactional relationships are being transformed into sustainable, durable business over time. There is an inherent logic to partnering—the "mining" of potential productivity between organizations—that is inescapable. It is a tremendous source of competitive advantage in a world where many other sources of differentiation have dried up. Compare the potential of partnering to some of the more traditional, but largely depleted, sources of competitive advantage.

- *In many industries, products are looking more and more the same.* Global markets and cheap information and technology have brought about a convergence of products that is squeezing, and in some cases eliminating, the competitive differentiation of goods and services. Why should a customer buy your widget when they can just as easily buy someone else's, at the same price, with the same quality, even through the same distribution channel? Competing on product alone is an uphill battle that many organizations are losing. There is simply less and less opportunity for competitive differentiation based solely on product.

- *Organizations themselves are coming to look more and more similar.* After a decade of internal restructuring to squeeze out every last drop of productivity, there's little left to improve. Additional internal tinkering is producing less and less results at higher and higher cost. There's simply no more fat to cut. Many organizations have now begun to cut into the muscle. In the average large corporation, employee morale—the muscle of any company—has plummeted in the midst of the ongoing restructuring squeeze. Once organizations within an industry have reached a plateau of high internal efficiency, there are only marginal advantages to be gained from further internal tinkering. Once a source of real competitive advantage, internal efficiency is rapidly becoming yet another "given"—a component of cost that has already reached parity between competing organizations.

- *Even sales forces are looking more and more alike.* It used to be that you could invest in consultative selling skills and get some real advantage as a result. Over the past 10 or 15 years, organizations with professionalized sales forces have enjoyed tremendous competitive advantage as customers increasingly opted for customer-focused vendors in favor of their more manipulative adversaries. But today, many sales forces have institutionalized good professional selling. In some industries, such as high technology and professional services, salespeople look less like product pushers than serious, ethical, highly competent business consultants. In this kind of environment, where selling has truly emerged as a skilled profession, having a strong sales force (or, if you're a salesperson, having good selling skills) is absolutely essential to survival, but it's no longer enough of a source of competitive advantage. Today, having a strong sales force is just a ticket to the dance. A lot of competitors have tickets as well.

The fact is, today suppliers and their sales organizations are increasingly at risk if they focus exclusively on products, efficiency, or other internal sources of productivity. That's because the largest, most underutilized source of productivity doesn't lie *within* their organizations, but *between* organizations and other businesses. Smart suppliers, and smart sales forces, have always had a good instinct for finding the "energy" in a market, wherever it is. Today the energy is in partnering—in getting beyond transactions and into more durable, higher-impact business relationships.

LESSONS FROM THE FIELD: BEST PRACTICES OF PARTNERING

What is it that top-performing supplier organizations are doing to achieve long-term competitive advantage?

This is the question we raised two years ago when we began our research effort. We quickly saw that in each industry, some small group of suppliers was always coming out ahead. What was it those suppliers were doing differently? As it turned out, the answer to that question was by no means a simple one.

The truth is that there is no magic formula, no trick, and no gimmick for achieving sustainable growth and lock-in with customers. The business environment and business relationships are increasingly complex. We, for example, started with one researcher, who contacted a dozen or so top-performing companies to explore their newer approaches to business relationships. By the time our research effort had fully caught up with the magnitude of the changes taking place, a third of our company was working full-time just to visit and interview organizations on a global, cross-industry basis. Today the entire first floor of a building is dedicated to housing the transcripts, analyses, and documentation which resulted from that research. In short, there's a tremendous amount of variety and experimentation out there. And as a result there is no panacea, no catchy, all-purpose solution to today's marketplace challenges.

On the other hand, there *are* very strong common elements—best practices—that underpin what many of the top-performing organizations are doing today. We have recommended a number of those best practices throughout this book. When you sift through the complexity of what the best organizations are doing, a picture emerges of creative energy going into three primary areas:

- *Impact.*   Successful partnering organizations are putting tremendous energy into finding ways to dramatically increase the impact of working together. They are reassessing how they work with other companies, and finding that the highest impact comes from *mutual change.* When one organization—usually the supplier—changes, the impact is always limited to what one organization can do to please another. It's when *both* organizations change—when both work together to eliminate redundancy and waste, combine capabilities, and develop new value—that sustainable advantage emerges. Finding ways to change *with* customers, not *for* them, is the surest way to affect productivity and profitability for both supplier and customer. All of the cases of partnering that we've described in this book have, at the core, an element of real impact. The impact achievable through mutual change is the bottom line of successful partnering.

- *Intimacy.*   Impact cannot be achieved without a fundamentally different approach to the interaction between organizations. Top-performing companies have literally rewritten the rules of relating to other organizations to maximize the impact. These companies' approaches to interfacing with customers are barely recognizable from the vantage point of traditional selling. We provided cases in this book to help bring these approaches to light:

  - Partnering situations in which the participants don't noticeably work for any particular company because they represent the partnership exclusively

  - Partnerships where the trust and information sharing often exceeds that found within most single organizations

  - Partnering teams, made up of personnel from each partner's company, that transcend organizational boundaries to work toward the common good

World-class partnering organizations have taken the core elements of trust, information sharing, and team building and transformed themselves along each dimension to achieve real intimacy with other companies. In so doing, they've moved way beyond transactional business and into more intimate, durable relationships with their partners. Intimacy, as practiced by world-class companies, is the enabler of partnering. You cannot achieve impact—you cannot affect the bottom line in any significant way—unless there is a high degree of intimacy between partnering organizations.

- *Vision.*   Successful partnering organizations are bringing a very broad business perspective to the table. And they are using that perspective to develop a truly bilateral, shared vision with their partners. This is in sharp contrast to traditional supplier-customer relationships, in which the supplier brings an idea of how to implement its products and the customer decides whether the idea is a good one. You cannot get impact without mutual change, and you cannot accomplish mutual change without a shared, jointly developed vision. From the most visible partnerships like Wal-Mart and Proctor and Gamble to the less publicized efforts of Hello Direct and Zymark, successful partnering always involves a shared vision, a road map that puts partners on a path and helps them achieve the highest possible impact with measurable results.

Impact, intimacy, and vision. These are the critical success factors, the core elements, of almost every successful partnership we've encountered. But like all good things they are not so easy to attain. All three are critical, but they're also very elusive. Many partnerships do not achieve real impact, do not have deep intimacy, or do not work from a truly bilateral vision. One if not more of the three gets lost in the shuffle as partners try to keep up with everyday business needs. It is very easy to partner for a while without even realizing that the impact is not what it could be, that the organizations are not as close as they need to be, or that the vision has drifted and is no longer shared. And this raises a question that eventually emerges at most organizations who want to partner.

DO YOU NEED A FACILITATOR TO MAKE PARTNERING A SUCCESS?

Most successful partnerships have someone occupying a "facilitator" role. Facilitators make a lot of sense in partnering. Two organizations with differing interests and goals often need someone to help guide the partnership toward success. When partnerships hit roadblocks and detours—and they always do—it is extremely important to have someone whose responsibility it is to help redirect discussions. If partners sharply disagree on an issue, having a facilitator around can make the difference between conflict resolution and a failed partnership. Even in areas where partners do agree, it's useful to have someone around whose role it is to keep discussions moving forward.

But those are the tangible, easily understandable reasons to appoint a facilitator. More subtly, partnerships that lack facilitation rarely bring out the vision, impact, and intimacy that are potentially achievable. In other words, the partnership doesn't accomplish what it could accomplish. While the partners are busy conducting business, it's extremely useful to have someone asking questions about the partnership itself, like "Do we really have a shared understanding of what we're trying to accomplish here?", or perhaps, "Is there information we should be sharing that will help us to make the most of future opportunities?"

So finding a facilitator is a good idea. And a number of partnering organizations have found strong internal resources to fulfill this role. Mead Packaging and Pillsbury, for example, have a thriving partnership that is facilitated by John Pelligrino, an organization development manager from within Mead. John has been able to provide guidance, resolution of conflict, and direction to the partnership itself while other people have focused on more opportunity-specific issues. A number of other partnerships have found similar people to play this role. But finding a *good* facilitator can be challenging. Many facilitators are not that good. In general, we've found that the most effective facilitators have four characteristics.

1. *They have a strong task focus.*   Good facilitators are primarily interested in *getting the job done*. They don't get too sidetracked by "touchy-feely" group activities. Their less effective counterparts, in contrast, are more interested in team-building and the *processes* of partnering than in maximizing the actual business impact for which the partnership exists. Good facilitators don't waste a lot of time on processes, generic team-building exercises, and the like. They have more of an action orientation than a relationship orientation.

2. *They are business- and industry-smart.*   Good facilitators understand the technology, have some industry expertise, and above all, know what makes good business sense. In cases we observed where facilitators had failed to add value, or had even made things worse, the most common complaint was that the facilitator just didn't understand the specifics and was more concerned with group dynamics than with business and industry issues.

3. *They can operate in both a big-picture and a detailed manner.*   A common complaint we've heard about facilitators is that few of them seem equally comfortable with the overall strategic elements of the vision and the myriad tactical details needed to support it. "We hired a strategy consultant," one Microsoft solution provider told us, "and he was great when it came to things like mission statements, industry goals, or partnership aspirations. But he fell asleep in the sessions when we were talking about how to make it work, and that's when we needed the most help." Good facilitators can move back and forth between lofty discussions and the down-and-dirty detail work.

4. *They encourage a "one-company" approach.*   Good facilitators don't see themselves as mediators sitting between opposing parties. Rather, they see their role as that of a problem solver who is there to help the partnering team move forward. They tend to treat partnering teams as if they were made up of people from within a single organization.

By contrast, many of the ineffective facilitators we observed saw themselves very much in a *mediation* role. They treated partnering discussions as negotiations between antagonists, and in so doing, encouraged damaging win-lose thinking. As one victim of a traditional negotiation consultant brought in as a facilitator told us: "Every time we started to think as a team, and the boundaries between the organizations started to blur, this guy would remind us that we were representatives of our companies and should be thinking on their behalf. The only time we made real progress was when he was out sick for a week." To be effective, facilitators must help both partners to move toward a one-company approach.

What about the thorny issue of whether to bring in an outside consultant to facilitate a partnering relationship? This is an important question, since many organizations do not have internal facilitators who can reasonably meet the above criteria. Certainly, using outside resources is a strategy that many organizations have tried, and there are some outstanding success stories out there. Consultants can bring partnering expertise as well as an outsider's perspective. But they have all the usual problems associated with bringing third parties into management challenges and, in the case of partnering, potentially sensitive negotiations.

It isn't easy to decide whether to involve outsiders in a partnering initiative. On the one hand, we've seen many partnerships succeed without even a trace of third-party involvement. On the other hand, we've seen partnerships fall apart, or never even get off the ground, for lack of an informed hand who could have helped guide discussions

and keep the potential partners on track. In general we recommend that organizations try to work through partnering issues with internal resources and not bring in outsiders unless their partnership meets some of the following conditions:

- *History of mistrust or conflict.* When there is a history of mistrust or conflict, partnering organizations often benefit from a neutral presence, a third party who can steer the discussion objectively and be seen as unbiased.

- *Traditional attitudes.* Win-lose attitudes can threaten even the best-laid plans for partnership. Yet a lot of companies who want to partner do face a real challenge when it comes to adopting win-win attitudes. In these cases an outside facilitator can often help to avoid destructive win-lose discussions of how to divide the pie, and help to keep the focus instead on ways to make the pie bigger.

- *Little experience in partnering.* When either or both organizations are new to partnering, it is often helpful to have an outside source of genuine experience to help guide the partners and to give them confidence that they are moving in the right direction.

- *High stakes.* Not every partnership involves high stakes. But when one or both parties really are betting the ranch, they will need all the help they can get to come up with the best and most risk-managed solutions. When the stakes are high, it's very smart to bring in a real outside expert.

- *Multiparty partnering.* When partnering involves two organizations, it can be unclear whether a facilitator is needed or not. But when several parties in a value chain are partnering to integrate systems or share information, this level of complexity requires expert facilitation. Value chain integration of more than two parties requires outside expertise.

Bringing in outside consultants can make sense—if conditions in the partnership make it necessary, as we've described here. But whether you use external or internal resources, appointing someone to facilitate the overall relationship is one of the best means of ensuring that a partnership stays on track and achieves its maximum potential.

THE LAST WORDS

At our final meeting prior to handing this book over to the publisher, we thought long and hard about our concluding message. "What," we pondered, "is our last, done-deal, end-of-the-line, ultimate, final piece of advice or wisdom about getting partnering right that we can offer to our readers?" We figured that our research into partnering had enabled us to offer substantial expertise and insight. But we also knew that hundreds of people from companies all over the world had generously given their time, expertise, and wisdom to help make this book happen. These businesspeople struggled and experimented with partnering before it was even a word, and learned through difficult experiences how to make it work. They have thought long and hard about partnering, with their real customers and suppliers around real business opportunities. The last words on partnering, we realized, should come from them. On the pages that follow, we offer their words of wisdom.

THE LAST WORDS

Partnering is happening, and it is having a tremendous impact. Clearly, the practitioners who are making it happen should have the last word. We believe their enthusiasm and insights will influence you as much as they have affected us.

GETTING PARTNERING RIGHT

"Vendor" is no longer politically correct; today, everybody is my "partner." But the reality is, everybody *isn't* my partner. Everybody doesn't have the same things at stake, everybody doesn't have the same commitment. It reminds me of the old story about involvement and commitment. At a bacon-and-eggs breakfast, the chicken is *involved* but the pig is *committed*. In my opinion, one of the key things in a partnership is commitment, real commitment.

ERIC MARCUS, VICE PRESIDENT, CSC-VANGUARD

In the end, if you want a partnership to work, you have to concentrate on the customer, the ultimate customer requirement. At Intel, that means starting to look beyond the manufacturing OEM and the distributor to the guy that's looking for a PC. That's number one.

JOE MCGEE, PROJECT MANAGER, INTEL

UPS: In a lot of buyer-seller relationships, price drives many of the decisions, regardless of the strength or weakness of the relationship. And that was, for a long time, the relationship we had with Kodak. Today, part of the initial vision of the partnership is not to dwell on price alone. This partnership takes a much broader view of everything, based on total openness between the two organizations.

215

KODAK: From our perspective, our intent is to continue to share information—to be very open in our relationship. And if it doesn't benefit both sides, if it is not a win-win, then we have to challenge why we're doing it. There has to be a very strong benefit for both sides. We will continue to operate by that principle.

KODAK–UNITED PARCEL SERVICE ALLIANCE TEAM

BAXTER: Very early on, we made this partnership successful by structuring it so that all of our plants and all of their [Stone Container] plants had an opportunity to share and gain in the relationship. It wasn't the kind of thing where we imposed things on people— where they lost and the corporation won. We structured it so that the corporation would win but all of our plants wound up winning something also. We went out to 18 Baxter locations and 16 Stone locations that were involved, and we got the Materials Manager and the Purchasing Manager and the Plant Manager from our side, as well as the Plant Manager and the Sales Manager from Stone's local plant, involved in the relationship.

STONE CONTAINER: The Baxter engineers wanted to add considerable fiber to a container that would have cost Baxter a great deal of extra money. An average supplier who is just a vendor would have said, "Sure if you want to spend another few hundred thousand dollars a year, I'll be glad to sell it to you." We refused until we could go into the plant and study the reasons for the engineers' request for more fiber. In fact we found we could avoid that cost through different handling methods—and accomplish the same thing. So what we did was pass up almost a million dollars worth of sales that we could have had.

JIM ALBRECHT, PURCHASING MANAGER, BAXTER
JEAN BROCK, PROGRAM MANAGER, SUPPLIER RELATIONS, BAXTER
ROGER GAUEN, GENERAL MANAGER, CORPORATE SALES, STONE CONTAINER

In order for partnering to work it must center on meeting the objectives of both organizations. And those objectives must be directed towards meeting end-customers' needs. If we can build relationships that cause our partners to be successful in their business through their relationship with us, then we will benefit. You have to focus on the idea of mutual benefits.

DON BULENS, SENIOR DIRECTOR OF BUSINESS PARTNER PROGRAM,
LOTUS DEVELOPMENT CORPORATION

The key is to make sure that you line up. In other words, make sure your goals not only are the same, but all of the objectives and pieces that fit inside the goal are aligned. It isn't enough to say, "we'd like to come together and accomplish this." You have to make sure that your organizational structure and your internal systems will align, will not end up hindering you, but will in fact help you to speed the process and make it work.

JOHN VAN TOMME, VICE PRESIDENT, TRI STAR MANAGEMENT SERVICES

Lotus has chosen to put their brightest into the partnering effort, and that's because we believe that the potential value of partnering is *limitless*. It is only limited by the energy, vision, and brightness of the people involved.

HEMANG DAVÉ, VICE PRESIDENT OF ALLIANCES,
LOTUS DEVELOPMENT CORPORATION

MAKING THE PIE BIGGER

In the end, it's about bringing value to the other side of the partnership.

ROCCO POLINO, MANAGER OF SYSTEMS MARKETING, OA SYSTEMS, INC.

Let's look at what it takes to really partner. Today, you have to be realistic about expectations. We expect vendors to perform and not gouge us. We realize that vendors have to make a profit, so let's get that issue off the table from the start. After you establish that level of honesty, you get into true partnering.

KEVIN HURSEY, DIRECTOR OF CORPORATE TECHNOLOGIES,
BLUE CROSS/BLUE SHIELD OF FLORIDA

One of the real payoffs of partnering is that we don't have any surprises. In the past we had situations where we had a customer for years and things were going great, and then all of a sudden we lose the business. If you establish a true partnership you can minimize, if not eliminate, the risk of that type of surprise.

MARTIN WILLIAMS, DIRECTOR OF MARKETING AND CUSTOMER SERVICES,
MCGREGOR CORY

There are a lot of opportunities that open up once you establish a true partnership. For example, the people at Hillenbrand have the continuous improvement strategy down to an art form. They have a Director of Continuous Improvement. They live it, and they consider it one of their core competencies. We could learn some things from them in that area. On the other side, they know that one of the major trends in business in America today is to get away from traditional purchasing and transportation and manage the whole logistics effort. They see us as a means of doing that.

LARRY RUTHERFORD, NATIONAL ACCOUNTS MANAGER, UNITED PARCEL SERVICE

When it comes to the real payoff of partnering we talk a lot about how it becomes more efficient for us to work in a partnering relationship, but it's also more efficient for our customers, or clients, as well. Because they don't spend all this time evaluating who they're going to work with. That's time-consuming in terms of calendar time, it's very costly, and it creates political debates and arguments. A client's ability to bring a trusted vendor in earlier in the process to share his fundamental needs, as compared to telling someone to go off and work against a set of specifications, is an efficient process. The trusted vendor can be far more creative when he understands fundamental needs and participates in solution development.

FRANCIS ZENIE, PRESIDENT, ZYMARK CORPORATION

Partnership is different than a classic selling relationship. In a classical selling situation when you go into a negotiation one party loses, one party wins. In a partnership, both parties win. You both look at the big picture. And price is not the whole thing.

HANK DUNNENBERG, MANAGER–PREMISES SALES, SIECOR

In the past, as a sales rep for a gas utility, you just focused on delivering the product, which was the natural gas. How it was used in the plant was really of no concern to you. But now we're finding because of the market and the competition, you have to find out how the customer is using your product and how you can help them stay in business. I guess you could say partnering is working in conjunction with people to make everyone more competitive.

DAN BURKHARDT, SENIOR ENERGY CONSULTANT, NATIONAL FUEL GAS

The real thing we've seen that Oracle has done for us is they have, over the last two years, designed a program that really is a commitment to resellers. In our case they have been very instrumental in our 400 percent growth rate. We've had tremendous growth rate, and some great successes. And we largely attribute that to our partnerships.

BOB LOZANO, PRESIDENT
JIM EBERLIN, HEAD OF SALES, TAPESTRY COMPUTING, INC.

Four years ago, in 1990, we were a $5 million company. We just passed $12 million and will be at $15 million this year [1995]. In about two years we will be over $20 million. We've been growing 25 percent a year now since 1990. A lot of this growth I can attribute to our partnership with UPS. They are not only helping us with shipping, they're helping us plan and engineer our business to allow us to continue to grow.

RAY HOOPES, PRESIDENT, HERCULES HYDRAULICS

Once a partnership gets going, some interesting opportunities open up. For example, we created in-house stores in a number of our customers' manufacturing facilities. There is a very strong consensus that it has streamlined receiving and purchasing operations. Our customers have reduced the number of their employees in receiving—our employees do that. And customers don't have to manage fastener inventory, our people also do that. Now our customers are doing similar in-house stores with other suppliers. Or they ask us to manage other suppliers' inventory. We have an arrangement, for example, with another supplier where they are paying us a fee to manage their inventory from our in-house store. This helps us to defray the costs associated with managing inventory and also creates another profit center. At the same time it helps the other supplier, because they often can't mimic what we have created without incurring more costs than they would incur by giving it to us. So it's a triple win.

SAM LAUFER, VICE PRESIDENT, NORTH AMERICAN BOLT AND SCREW

Bose uses one of our competitors out of the Midwest. And the competitor was having some troubles because of the backlog of supply chain air freights. We stepped in to assist them to make sure that Bose's job got done correctly. So we worked cooperatively with a competitor. It was a sense of ownership of the problem. You can't stay out, you can't be out on the customer's site without feeling a sense of ownership. You step in and assist even a competitor, to make sure the job gets done correctly.

LORNE JONES
IN-PLANT REPRESENTATIVE AT BOSE, TOWER GROUP INTERNATIONAL

BUILDING INTIMATE RELATIONSHIPS

We intentionally try to blur the line between us and the customer. When they start to see us as an extension of their organization, we have succeeded.

CYNDIE BENDER, CEO, MERIDIAN TRAVEL, INC.

Building a relationship is essential; you have to have trust. And trust is not something that can be achieved by some schmoozing tactic; trust can only be earned.

BRECK ENGLAND, CORPORATE, SHIPLEY ASSOCIATES

In partnering, you are looking at the work processes and methodologies that your two organizations can use to become more integrated, more common. You won't have the Bechtel way of doing business, you won't have the customer's way of doing business, you'll have the team way of doing business. That requires an investment by both parties. One's own work methods are no longer employed. Rather, we have a blending and an optimization of those processes.

FRANK WATERHOUSE, MANAGER OF PROJECT DEVELOPMENT, BECHTEL

The most successful partnerships these days are where you leverage best-of-class providers and integrate them into a whole that makes sense to the ultimate user. But that does take some doing, because it requires a multipoint shared vision and it applies the concept of intimacy to a much more complex type of relationship.

MANUEL DIAZ, VICE PRESIDENT OF WORLDWIDE SALES AND MARKETING, HEWLETT-PACKARD

In high technology, there is no question that there is now a collaboration mind-set. For example, in Chicago there is a Regional Manager, Bill Conroy. Bill is one of our best Regional VPs. He actually sat down with his Consulting Manager and said, "Look, Andersen Consulting is headquartered here in Chicago. I need Andersen. They're referring all their business to other folks. Why are they doing that? Because all those guys give them business. We don't give them business. They think we're a competitor. We've got to sit down with them and ice out a patch of the territory that's going to be theirs by name. And a patch that's going to Oracle Consulting, by name. Then there is some part in the middle that we're probably just going to compete on a case-by-case basis." So he's gone and gotten the parties together, and he's gotten his consulting managers to buy into it. He's gotten Andersen to buy into it. This is good business. We really do need each other. Oracle the dominant technology provider, Andersen the dominant consulting provider. So why fight each other forever? Let's finally make some sense of this thing.

PAUL HOFFMAN, VICE PRESIDENT OF WORLDWIDE OPERATIONS,
ORACLE CORPORATION

You've got to develop a relationship with a company where you know the people, where you understand what they're doing, and where you're in more of a consultative relationship with them. Where you talk to them about their process of developing their new product, if that's what they need. We have to understand their problems. Developing this level of relationship is helpful to them and helpful to us. It's more collaborative than traditional selling.

BURLEIGH HUTCHINS, CHAIRMAN, ZYMARK CORPORATION

Partnerships are only as good as you make them. And you really have to nurture partnering relationships over time. Although companies are saying, "Yes, we're going to go forward with you over the long term," that doesn't mean our competitors are going to sit still and say, "Well, there's a corporate partnership agreement there for five years. We can't get in." Because they're going to try and break it. And they're going to try to get in there with new products. We have to work on a regular basis to maintain our position, and maintain that partnership. And the best people to do that are the salespeople, and our post-sales organizations to support the customers.

JOE DAVIN, VICE PRESIDENT OF SALES, DATEX MEDICAL INSTRUMENTATION

Partnering is a two-way street for both companies, with communication being the top priority.

DEBBIE BOWERS, IBM ACCOUNT, NORTH AMERICAN BOLT AND SCREW

The question is, how do you actually make the partnering arrangement work? In our case we have a Partnering Project Manager and a Partnering Project Engineer. They interface directly with the customer's Partnering Project Engineer. The difference from the way we typically do business is there isn't as much product review going on by the customer. One of the customer's objectives was to employ fewer resources looking over our shoulder ensuring that quality and deliverable commitments were being met. The goal is to integrate the

Bechtel team to the extent they become an extension of the customer's engineering department.

DENNIS LEAR, BUSINESS DEVELOPMENT MANAGER, BECHTEL

The amazing thing [about the Mead/Pillsbury partnership] was the success of joint accountability. In fact, we had a joke: If somebody was not in the meeting or had left the room they might get an assignment and it didn't matter if it was a Mead or a Pillsbury person.

JOHN PELLIGRINO, DIRECTOR OF ORGANIZATION DEVELOPMENT, MEAD

If you really want to get involved with partnering, you have to get the other party totally involved in your company.

BILL PITTMAN, CORPORATE VICE PRESIDENT, XEROX CORPORATION

No company can go it alone in this huge marketplace these days.

FRED MONDRAGON, MARKET SEGMENT MANAGER, SUN MICROSYSTEMS

THE "VISION" THING

We are in the midst of a transition in the computing business to tomorrow's technology. To be successful in this effort we need suppliers who will work with us as partners to overcome obstacles and lead the industry.

ED O'DONNELL, SENIOR PURCHASING MANAGER, IBM

The easiest part of working with NEC was, surprisingly, selling the concept internally. That's because NEC got it right, they came in and first of all understood our mission statement. A lot of mission statements are lofty and meaningless, and ours is not. It's very simple and we take it very seriously: We have great respect for life here and we want to improve the health care of our patients. NEC understood this right from the beginning and actioned their understanding by the way they worked with us. They didn't have many formal meetings; instead they went around and talked to the primary care givers, the nurses and the doctors. They listened. When our technical people were interested in gadgetry, they talked gadgetry, but all along they never lost sight of our mission statement.

PEGGY MAVES, MANAGER OF TELECOMMUNICATIONS,
LITTLE COMPANY OF MARY HOSPITAL AND HEALTH CARE CENTER

I absolutely believe in partnership, and it's not just about getting a distribution channel. It's about somebody understanding an industry better than you do.

André Boisvert, Senior Vice President of Business Development,
Seer Technologies

Our vision is to achieve a "seven-day" factory; that is, to input a customer's order and in seven days have the product on the customer's dock. To accomplish this we had to evaluate, challenge, and reengineer our entire process, addressing both the logistics as well as the manufacturing process. We started looking at the possibility of partnering with an integrated carrier that could provide a 72-hour cycle time from when the product was ready to leave our factory in Asia to delivery on our customer's dock in the USA. We ran a pilot with three different carriers to see which one could do the job from a quality and cost standpoint and still meet our 72-hour commitment. United Parcel Service was one of those carriers. UPS not only met our quality, cost, and cycle-time criteria, they showed an interest and willingness to work with us to develop an integrated logistics solution to meet the needs of our customers. This willingness and capability has blossomed into a full-fledged Motorola/UPS partnership, where we are working together as a team with their Worldwide Logistics Services Organization on other productivity, logistics, and value-added services initiatives.

Bob Harris, Strategic Logistics Management—World Marketing,
Motorola

In the future, let's say ten years from now, the whole supply chain process is going to be turned around and it's going to be driven by replenishing what the consumer really wants to buy. And that will start by the members of the supply chain beginning to build long-term relationships with each other that say, "I'm going to do business with you for the long term, and we're going to work together to make this whole process work more effectively and we're all going to win." That effort will be supported by a conduit that will move information almost instantaneously from the consumer purchase all the way upstream to every partner in the supply chain. And when we do that, we will move product far more smoothly from raw material source to the end user and take out at least half of the handling cost, probably reduce cycle time and inventory by 90 percent, eliminate most of the transactions, and provide a much higher level of value and more responsiveness to the consumer.

Jim Morehouse, Vice President Supply Chain Integration Practice,
A. T. Kearney, Inc.

AVOIDING THE DARK SIDE

You don't want to use this concept of partnering to get an order. On a number of occasions I have had salesmen come in and I find out that they have been working like crazy to sell this partnership idea to get a single order, when in truth it makes no sense to us or the customer. If you do it that way you damage the credibility of partnering; it becomes meaningless. Partnering is not just a way to get your foot in the door; in fact, it is a *lousy* way to get your foot in the door.

GABE ROSICA, CHIEF OPERATING OFFICER, BAILEY CONTROLS

For partnering to work means focusing on the process, not personalities. In long-term alliances, you're going to see key players come and go. Not only in your planning process but in your operations process also. If you can keep the focus on the process and keep the level of communications high, you're going to be successful. If you put the focus on personalities and a key player leaves, then you may be setting yourself up for failure.

JOE McGEE, PROJECT MANAGER, INTEL
RANDA ROSENBLUM, SENIOR MARKETING SPECIALIST, FEDERAL EXPRESS

It comes down to effective communication. You have to be very, very open with one another, with what you expect. What you can do, what you can't do. They can't overestimate their capabilities and promise something they can't deliver. And we can't expect the world. No, we have to be honest, and understand what the limitations of technology are, and what we can ask for. There has to be a lot of education and learning, and exchange of ideas and information, in order for that to happen appropriately.

BERRY KLINE, TOM RAGLIONE, AND STEVEN CONDER
BRISTOL-MYERS SQUIBB PHARMACEUTICAL GROUP

In the high-tech world, most of the people we call on don't want to see what we call "doughnut" salesmen, a guy who comes in, lays a box of doughnuts on the table, and says that he's ready to take your order. They don't have time for those guys. They need someone who can add value to them. They aren't going to spend time with you if you aren't technically adept, if you don't know your products, if you can't solve their problems.

DOUG WINTERS, ACCOUNT MANAGER– PREMISES MARKETING, SIECOR

In 1986–87, we began to take a look at our entire supplier base throughout all the Baxter divisions. We had a very large supplier base and we knew that it was important to start consolidating. As far as going into partnering, when we consolidate down to a supplier it's very important that you establish that trusting relationship, because our intention is to drive all of our business or the majority of our business to a single source. And that involves a lot of trust with the supplier and a lot of sharing. When you don't have any fallback position, when you're putting all your eggs in one basket, so to speak, you have to develop a relationship that's mutually beneficial for both parties.

JEAN BROCK, PROGRAM MANAGER, BAXTER HEALTH CARE CORPORATION

Being a partner means there is going to be some bond beyond just the product. I have observed many companies that utilize that phrase "going to be a partner with our customers," yet when it comes down to actually living up to the tenets of being a partner, like sharing of confidential information such as manufacturing capabilities, future view, capital spending, or product development efforts—it often becomes pretty shallow.

GEORGE AVDEY, BUSINESS MANAGER, CHEVRON

Sometimes people talk about partnering and they just want to squeeze the last cent out of you. It comes to a point where you say, "Well you don't want to partner, you just want to deal with us like you deal with all the other vendors, you want to negotiate the best deal." In those situations we cannot partner, because if we partner it means higher cost for us typically; we have to make executive time available, we have to have meetings, we have to participate in planning sessions. So if you are just looking for price, then we don't have a partnership, then we are just a vendor. It's not a partner thing.

KLAUS BESIER, CEO, SAP AMERICA INC.

What is it that prevents companies in general from doing business in the long run? Generally it comes down to two things, service and price. In logistics and materials movement we find that service and pricing is almost a commodity. All the large trucking companies have service performance better than 90 percent. So you could play the numbers game, pitting one carrier against the other, but over a number of years you would go through the whole population of carriers. As we thought about that, it occurred to us that you can pit one against the other and play the short-term predatory pricing game. Of course after a year your carrier isn't making money and either your service level falls or they come back for a rate increase anyway. So the approach here has been, find a quality company and stick with them. Most importantly, find ways of taking costs out by working on the problem together. That's the way you get away from the long-term price increases.

PAUL TAGLIAMONTE, TRANSPORTATION MANAGER, BOSE CORPORATION

Over the longer term, actions speak louder than words. And how people react under pressure is the acid test. My experience with partnerships is, you've just got to get right to the bottom line. You've got to ignore superfluous hype and get right down to what's important to everybody. What's their definition of a win, what's your definition of a win, and if those are synchronized, then you've got a good start for a partnership. That's important, because I don't think you can overcome a bad partnership through marketing hype and money.

BOB LAMVIK, VICE PRESIDENT SALES, THE SANTA CRUZ OPERATION

Pricing is always going to be a showstopper if you don't work out some way to deal with it. Being a partner means we never charge them the highest price we charge in the marketplace but we never charge them the lowest price either. If either party tries to push that window, it's going to cause problems. If they say, "Hey, we heard you sold somebody less than this, what's going on here?" or if we go back to them and say, "Hey, this is the list price, you've got to pay it," you are probably going to get into a difficult contest. Somehow you've got to work out the pricing so both sides can agree to it. You've got to put the pricing thing to bed, so you can work on other issues. Otherwise it is difficult to elevate beyond a transactional relationship.

M. PIKE HAMLIN, SALES STRATEGY DIRECTOR,
GEORGIA-PACIFIC CORPORATION

When I look at it from a "lessons learned" perspective, there are a couple of things that stand out. First, I would document the impact side of the relationship with the customer. I would institutionalize the impact. Lots of times it is understood but not stated. Along comes attrition, neither team has something to hang their hat on. The second thing is developing up-front what partnering means. You should claim early that you are looking for a partner, not a vendor, and get agreement up-front what this means, document it, and refer back to it.

ED OSSIE, VICE PRESIDENT INFORMATION TECHNOLOGY GROUP,
TEXAS INSTRUMENTS

CHOOSING THE RIGHT PARTNERS AND OPPORTUNITIES

It has to be somebody who you can respect in the business community. And although the partnership is based on cooperation, that doesn't mean that you cooperate on everything. You have to be comfortable in drawing the line and saying "not this one" or "not here," and they have to be comfortable doing the same thing. You each have to be comfortable saying "okay" to this.

TOM TUBERGEN, PARTNER, ARTHUR ANDERSEN

At Siecor we have identified our major Key Accounts and we have focused on beginning or continuing a journey with each of them. We look at the process as a continuum. On the one side our relationship with the customer would be an Outsider, what you would typically call a Vendor. In this type of relationship the customer looks only at the product and buys based solely on its features and benefits and first-cost price. Not much, if any, thought is given to the *value* our companies gain through the overall relationship. Our objective is, through business-solutions selling, to move the relationship toward true partnering.

LUNCE BASS, CORPORATE, SIECOR

There has to be some balance between making a strong commitment to one another and being completely locked in. For instance, for a long time we had only one supplier for an important class of products, and that supplier is in Korea. Well, Korea is a country where there's an ongoing threat of political unrest. So what would we do if something happened? Or what if the quality started slipping from them? The question is how do you guard against that, and I think the answer is being really, really careful about selecting the correct partner up front.

CHUCK VOLWILER, VICE PRESIDENT OF MARKETING, HELLO DIRECT

We operate on a three-level mode. We call them red, amber, and green, in line with the traffic lights that we have in the U.K. We categorize a green vendor as someone with whom we would have a normal buyer-supplier relationship and we would deal on the basis of price, delivery, and quality. These relationships involve the commodity items any business needs. Amber suppliers are suppliers where if there is some sort of quality failure then there's a direct impact on our customers in some way. So we look at products like telephones or fax machines, where clearly we have to have a good deal of care

about the type of relationship that we want with those suppliers, but at the end of the day we do have some choices and we can change courses and we can change colors and brands and all those sorts of things. And then at the top level we would have what we call the red category, and that is really where we've got this thing called partnering. It says we're probably not going to achieve the goals we want to achieve on our own, we need to get close to some sort of partnership which is going to last over a period of time and help us meet some specific business goals that we're looking to achieve.
STUART HICKIN, U.K. PROCUREMENT MANAGER OF SOFTWARE, BRITISH TELECOM

We really go through an extended sales cycle with partnering candidates, and that helps us weed out the ones who really are in it just for the transaction. We have a consensus organization here at Dunlop Tire Corporation, so cross-functionally we have groups of people who would all share in the relationship of the partnership. So they have a say in selecting that partner, and it really starts wearing on some potential partners when they have such an in-depth sales cycle. They have to work with more people, get to know the business better, know the players.

DENNIS COURTNEY, CIO, DUNLOP TIRE CORPORATION

PARTNERING AND THE SALES FORCE

Partnering is the preeminent sales tool of today.
RICK KEENE, EXECUTIVE VICE PRESIDENT NORTH AMERICA, ANIXTER

Our sales force at Hewlett-Packard has definitely evolved over time to be more and more a trusted adviser. Our customers are looking for our advice because we know the technology and we spend time to understand their business and to help them figure out what the best technology is to solve their problem—regardless if it's coming from HP or not. We're trusted because we really do that in a way for the customers to win, not for HP to sell. So we have structured the sales force to be this kind of strategic adviser, a partner, an eye-level type of person that really works at the business level and makes everything for the customer a win.

BERNARD GUIDON, GENERAL MANAGER OF WORKSTATION SYSTEMS,
HEWLETT-PACKARD

I see the Oracle rep being a broker of technologies, bringing teams together, that could consist of Oracle people and other application vendors and service providers—whether that be Andersen Consulting or a local integrator. It's impossible for Oracle to do it on our own.

LUKE LITTLE, DIRECTOR OF AMERICA'S CHANNELS, ORACLE CORPORATION

Our entire sales force in the last twelve months has been reorganized. We are organized around core selling teams, and those teams are led by a role that we call Account Manager. One of the leading things that an account manager is responsible for is creating partnering relationships with the customers in his or her area of responsibility.

VIJAYA VASISTA, DIRECTOR OF MARKETING, BAXTER

Partnering relationships are by definition longer, deeper, and stronger. That means the sales process will inevitably be different than it is in one-off projects. But in both cases, effective selling centers on understanding your customers' needs and addressing their problems—being, above all else, an effective listener. Knowledgeable about your industry, current with the latest developments, but above all, listening to your customer.

GEORGE FRIDDLE, BUSINESS DEVELOPMENT MANAGER, BECHTEL

In the last five years, the world of partnering has become more complex. Today there is a variety of business organizations that are key business partners for Digital. If we want our field sales force to work with our partners, I think we need to clearly articulate to the sales force what we mean by a partner, what the partner's added value is, and how best to work collaboratively with them.

VINCE DIMENNA, CHANNELS SALES MANAGER,
DIGITAL EQUIPMENT CORPORATION

If you have a partnering network and it's working, the challenge for the sales force is to communicate it as a competitive advantage.

DAVID YOKEUM, PRESIDENT, UNITED SHIPPING ASSOCIATES

Partnering with customers requires a very active role for the sales rep, and not just in trying to identify the sales opportunities. I think they have to have a better understanding of their own organization than they might otherwise need. Sometimes sales reps know what you sell but don't know what you *are*. It strikes me that when you get to partnering, salespeople have to know more about your organization than just, "Here is what we sell."

RICK SOSKIN, PRESIDENT AND CEO, CENTRON

Some reps feel once you have a strong partnering structure, perhaps you won't need the sales force anymore. My response to that is we will need the sales force more than ever, but we need them to be better and better and better. We need to improve the skills so that the salesperson becomes a better teaming person, a better matrix manager of the opportunities, and a better delegator, so that if we find an opportunity that is not good for us, then let's give it to our business partner.

JANE STAMPE, GROUP ALLIANCE MANAGER, ORACLE CORPORATION

We are a channel to market, and we will fail with any manufacturer that looks upon us as a customer. We are not a manufacturer's customer, we are an extension of their sales force. We don't consume anything. We sell it. So if a manufacturer looks upon any reseller, or us, as their customer, neither they nor the reseller will succeed. We have got to be *partners*—real live partners.

TOM ALDON, SENIOR VICE PRESIDENT OF MARKETING, ANIXTER

Right now, about 30 percent of the business we team sell, which means we do it jointly. Thirty percent of the business we find ourselves and work on, and about 30 percent of the business our partners find for us and they develop and close it without any problem. So it's roughly one-third for each. I honestly don't see how in today's environment that mix can change dramatically. I think if you reached 100 percent in any one of those categories you would be unbalanced in the way you're bringing products and services to the marketplace. You either get totally out of touch with the customer or you have sales costs so high you wouldn't be able to stay in business. A balance of direct sales and sales through partners is the key to success.

POLLY SUMNER, VICE PRESIDENT OF WORLDWIDE ALLIANCES,
ORACLE CORPORATION

INDEX

ABOUT THE AUTHORS

NEIL RACKHAM is President and CEO of Huthwaite, Inc., an international research and consulting firm based in Purcellville, Virginia. He is recognized as a pioneer in sales effectiveness, and is widely credited with bringing research and analytical rigor to the field of sales force improvement. He is the author of *SPIN Selling*, *Major Account Sales Strategy*, and *Managing Major Sales*, as well as five other books and over fifty articles. Raised in the jungles of Borneo, Neil moved to the U.K. for his education in research psychology. He came to the United States in 1976 to start the Huthwaite organization.

LAWRENCE FRIEDMAN is the Director of Client Services at Huthwaite, Inc. He designs the firm's consulting services and training programs, and provides overall leadership to research studies and "best practices" projects for clients. His expertise is in translating emerging concepts, such as partnering, into tangible client strategies and skills. Larry spent a number of years in Andersen Consulting's technology and change management practices. He did his graduate work at the University of Chicago. Larry is a frequent writer and well-known speaker on partnering in high technology.

RICHARD RUFF, Huthwaite's Executive Vice President, has responsibility for overall operations and for ensuring high-impact delivery of services to the firm's clients. His 25 years of consulting experience span academia, government, and the private sector. Dick has worked with domestic and international Fortune 500 clients on projects ranging from skills training to complex management interventions. Coauthor of *Managing Major Sales*, Dick is a sought-after public speaker on sales force strategy and management. He has a doctorate in organizational psychology from the Universitiy of Tennesse.

Refer questions to
Huthwaite, Inc.
Wheatland Manor
15164 Berlin Turnpike
Purcellville, Virginia 22132
(phone) (540) 882-3212
(fax)   (540) 882-9004